EFFECTIVE LEGAL WRITING

A STYLE BOOK FOR
LAW STUDENTS AND LAWYERS

SECOND EDITION

By

GERTRUDE BLOCK

Lecturer and Writing Specialist
University of Florida College of Law

Mineola, New York
THE FOUNDATION PRESS, INC.
1983

COPYRIGHT © 1981 THE FOUNDATION PRESS, INC.

COPYRIGHT © 1983 By THE FOUNDATION PRESS, INC.

Printed in the United States of America

Library of Congress Cataloging in Publication Data

Block, Gertrude.
  Effective legal writing.

  Includes index.
  1. Legal composition. I. Title.
KF250.B56   1983   808'.06634   83–1487

ISBN 0–88277–109–4

Block Leg.Writing Pamph. 2d Ed. FP

INTRODUCTION

This edition of *Effective Legal Writing*, like the first, is intended to help students learn to write successfully in law school and in their law careers. Even those students who, as under-graduates, were able to write effectively on non-legal subjects must shift their writing gears, for legal writing requires some skills not emphasized in college. In fact, some undergraduate disciplines require little writing of any kind; students who majored in business, for example, can use this book to gain skills either undeveloped or long neglected.

I have expanded this edition of *Effective Legal Writing* at the suggestion of some of my students, who called to my attention omissions in the first edition that they would have found useful. Added are chapters on organization (Chapter III), case analysis and argumentation (Chapter IV), and additions to the chapter on grammar and meaning (Chapter I). These additions have caused some overlap (against which I warn other writers). For example, organization is treated twice, once in Chapter III and again in Chapter V. This overlap seems justified, however, because the organization of final examinations is apt to be much less structured than that of term papers, senior theses, and articles for publication.

This book is intended to aid not only law students, but those who teach writing to law students. These instructors are sometimes adjunct professors, whose expertise is English not law. They should find particularly helpful Chapters II and III, which will orient them to the particular requirements of legal writing, and Chapter IV, which contains writing problems on legal subjects, along with sample answers. On the other hand, in some law schools, law professors teach legal writing. This book should aid them too, since law professors are best at teaching law and often have neither the time, the desire, nor the expertise to teach writing. Chapters II and III (on grammar and style) should be most useful to law professors who teach legal writing courses.

Effective Legal Writing can also be used by students and lawyers as a do-it-yourself means of learning how to write effectively. After reading Chapters I through V, they can test themselves on what they have learned by writing essay answers to the legal writing problems in Chapter VI. Sample answers follow each writing problem, so the reader can compare her own essay answer with the sample answer. Improvement will result from practice. As Epictetus correctly pointed out 2000 years ago, there is no better was to improve writing than by writing.

Persons who are neither law students nor lawyers but hope to become both can use this book to polish legal writing skills before starting law school. Such persons need have no legal training in order to use this book, since all the legal rules necessary to write answers to the essay problems are provided. Entrance to law school is usually preceded by both anticipation and trepidation. The former can be heightened and the latter diminished if the important skill of writing is improved beforehand.

The chapters in *Effective Legal Writing* need not be read in any particular order. Chapter I (Grammar and Meaning) comes first only because students seem more concerned about their inadequacy in this area than in any other. Those readers who already have a good grasp of grammatical niceties should skip Chapter I, after skimming through it to assure themselves that they do not need to study it. Law students whose primary interest is in learning how to write successful final examinations will be most interested in Chapters II, III, IV, and V. Upperclass law students and legal practitioners may find particularly useful Chapter IV, dealing with the organization of research papers and legal articles.

A word about what is not included in this book. First, the book is not intended to be a complete grammar. Only the errors that law students actually make are discussed; and I have learned what these are by reading countless papers written by law students. Today's law students are usually not as well schooled in the amenities of grammar as their predecessors twenty years ago; but of all today's college graduates, law students are probably the most literate, and they already are aware of many of the rudiments of grammar.

Nor does *Effective Legal Writing* deal with the substance of the doctrines of any field of law. Instead it attempts to fill an important need: to teach writing skills essential to law students and lawyers, but too often neglected in the law school curriculum. The techniques discussed in this book, especially case analysis and organization, are basic to all effective legal writing, including the writing of memoranda and briefs.

A word about gender. Until a woman colleague pointed it out to me, I was unaware that I was open to criticism for the use of sexist language by my exclusive use, in the first edition, of the masculine pronoun. That criticism was no doubt justified, but I plead innocent to sexism on the ground that my linguistic background causes me to view the masculine pronoun as a grammatical, not a 'sexual,' designation.

Grammatical gender has no real connection to sex; witness the German "fräulein," a neuter noun which means "young unmarried woman." And even in English, words ending in 'er,' like 'baker,' 'arbiter,' 'organizer,' and 'lawyer,' which contain Latin-derived masculine suffixes, are not usually considered 'masculine' designations. It is unfortunate that the 'man' ending (e.g., in 'chairman') and the personal pronoun 'he' (as in "If anyone so wishes, he can leave") are not viewed as unemotionally as those words and Latin-derived words with masculine 'or' endings like 'author,' 'director,' 'supervisor,' and 'administrator.'[1]

However, those not sensitive to the use of the masculine pronoun should defer to those who are, and therefore in this edition the feminine personal pronoun is used at least half the time. This alternative seems preferable to the use of the bulky and (to me) distracting 'she/he,' 'his/her,' and 's/he.'

Thanks are due to the instructors in the legal writing program at this law college, who have alerted me to the writing problems of their students and suggested adding materials in the second edition to focus upon these problems. Thanks, also, to my own students, who have made valuable suggestions about what should be included. To those students who voluntarily, despite heavy academic burdens, enroll in the writing program so as to become more effective writers, I dedicate this edition. They are, in great measure, responsible for its having been written.

Finally, thanks are due to Seymour Block, my husband, companion, and critic, and to Judith B. McLaughlin, both of whom have generously provided support and advice. These persons have contributed to the success of this second edition; I am solely responsible for its shortcomings.

GERTRUDE BLOCK

Gainesville, Florida
February, 1983

*

---

[1] Thus a recent company change of designation from 'chairmen' to 'supervisors' may have soothed ruffled feminine feelings but did nothing to eliminate the masculine denotation of the term. A relic of the former gender distinction is the continuing legal use of 'executor' and 'executrix.' That distinction, like the now old-fashioned 'author/authoress' distinction will probably eventually disappear.

FOREWORD

"First you have to get his attention," explained the farmer as he put down the two-by-four he had just pounded on the head of his mule. Mule-like, the mule was resisting the farmer's training efforts.

Writing is like that. It is gentler, of course, than batting about with a two-by-four; but the need to get attention is just as great. How then get attention from readers, often mule-like readers, whom we would persuade of this or that? Answer: Write well! [Footnote: A couple of years ago when I wrote the Foreword to the first edition of this book I said:

> "It is scary to write about writing. Scarier to write about another's writing. Scariest to write about another's writing about writing. Do I dare? What if I should commit the common comma error? Suppose I cannot find the correct word to end a sentence with! Is there a risk that I shall split an "expletive?" For the last horror stated I am indebted to an erstwhile student who expressed it just that way. (Was he pulling my leg?) I grow self-conscious; looking back I see no verbs in my second and third sentences. Fie! I am a senior scholar entitled to take some liberties with the language, just as a four-star general is permitted to design his own uniform. Furthermore, the author of this book has overcome such fears; perhaps she will overlook my errors."

I approach this opportunity with the same mixed feelings of humility and arrogance that I experienced then.]

We come quickly now to the importance of Gertrude Block's book, *Effective Legal Writing: A Style Book for Law Students and Lawyers* (2d Ed. 1983). The title suggests the book's emphasis, *legal writing*, but it is unduly restrictive, because members of many other professions outside the law will find much of interest in this book. The book is designed to help one, really almost anyone, write better, through study and practice, either alone or with accompanying instruction. And to write better is to get more attention for our thoughts.

The book begins with very basic stuff, grammar and word meaning. *De trop*, as the French might say? Not at all. More than thirty years in the practice, teaching, writing and administrative facets of the legal profession have, sad to say, shown me the need for such basic training in law school and even beyond. It is a wish only, not reality, that students enter law school well equipped to use the English language. (Did I sneak in a *French* phrase just above? All right! I'll readily excuse the reader for not recognizing that—but note that its meaning really is discernible from the rest of the paragraph, even to those who have "small Latin and less Greek.")

There are, of course, many books on grammar and lots of dictionaries. The value of Author Block's book in these areas may be its restrictive emphasis; here the spotlight is on problems that are more often encountered by lawyers than by others. I find exciting, for example, the author's treatment of style and the related manipulative use of language which begins with Chapter Two, appropriately entitled "Legal Style."

Accuracy, brevity and clarity (the A B C's) we are told quite accurately, briefly, and clearly, are the *desiderata* of legal writing —probably most other writing as well. There are some—not the author—who no doubt believe legal writing must therefore be sterile and pedestrian, quite devoid of the seminal phrase or the equestrian fillip. Not so! Perhaps it is dangerous to spice up a deed or a mortgage agreement, but in other instances the legal author may have more elbow-room as long as the writer obeys the command of A, B, and C. "Ear" is to writing as "nose" is to wine.

At the beginning of Chapter Two Author Block tells us that style is a personal thing, properly a combination of the writer's subject matter and his own personality and that stylistic efforts can be appraised only in context.

I learned at an early age that Henry James was a novelist who wrote like a psychologist and his brother, Will, was a psychologist who wrote like a novelist. This prompted in me many years ago a Walter Mitty-like desire, never fulfilled, to be known as a tax lawyer who wrote like a psychological novelist. But we are *talking* about style, about making the best use we can of the marvelous language that is ours. Author Block's second edition shouts that message. It also includes two new chapters, one on case analysis and one on organization, which should be helpful to law students and legal practitioners. The resulting product should be acclaimed.

RICHARD B. STEPHENS *
Professor of Law Emeritus
University of Florida

* Author, with Maxfield, Lind, and Calfee of *Federal Estate and Gift Taxation* (5th Ed. W. G. and L. 1983); with Freeland and Ferguson of *Income Taxation of Estates and Beneficiaries* (Little Brown and Co. 1970); with Freeland and Lind, of *The Fundamentals of Federal Income Taxation* (4th Ed., Foundation Press 1982); and of numerous articles in various legal periodicals.

TABLE OF CONTENTS

EFFECTIVE LEGAL WRITING
A STYLE BOOK FOR
LAW STUDENTS AND LAWYERS

*

CHAPTER ONE

Grammar and Meaning

Everyone except my law students thought that this chapter should be placed at the end, or hidden in the middle of this book, because grammar is at best a pedestrian subject. But because my law students considered its subject of great importance to them, it appears at the beginning. Many students arrive at law school with little grounding in the rudiments of grammar. They are aware of their deficiencies in this area and of the need to correct them.

As undergraduates, some law students majored in accounting or finance or other similar fields and therefore did little or no writing of essay examinations. They are rightly worried about taking law school essay final examinations on which their entire grade for the course will depend. Other law students, liberal arts majors as undergraduates, did a lot of writing, but a different kind of writing. They probably composed scholarly theses, replete with rhetorical flourishes and flights of fancy, and received high grades for creativity and imagination. Substandard grammar and incorrect spelling were not considered serious defects. Even clarity was not prized, obscurity being mistaken as profundity.

But students think—and they are right—that in law school things will be different. Here the ability to communicate ideas clearly in standard English and, yes, to spell correctly (even Latin terms) *is* important. Kudos are not awarded for these skills, but they are expected, and their absence invites the penalty of low grades.

For substandard English and poor spelling subject their users to the "can't even" theory. The (often unconscious) assumption of law professors and law professionals is that if a writer "can't even" couch his ideas in standard English, using correct spelling, he cannot be expected to understand and analyze complex legal problems. Therefore a final examination that is worth no more than a "D" in composition will almost never earn a "B" for its legal insights, no matter how profound they may be.

It is fortunate, since these skills are disproportionately important, that they are also easy to learn. For some readers, a review of this chapter will be sufficient to recall material once learned, but since forgotten. For other readers, who need practice in grammatical skills, the Appendix contains sentences (most of them from actual legal writing) to be corrected. Skim through this chapter to discover which group of readers you belong to; you may even find that you have no need to review this material and can move on at once to Chapter Two!

1

1. Punctuation of Restrictive and Non-restrictive Relative Clauses

Law students often admit with embarrassment that they do not know what a relative clause is, let alone what restrictive and non-restrictive relative clauses are. The fact is that such definitions are unimportant, and the only reason I will use these names to discuss punctuation of these clauses is to differentiate them.

A relative clause is a group of words introduced by a relative pronoun (which, that, who/whom) that modifies a preceding noun or pronoun. In each of the following examples the relative clause follows the relative pronoun:

> The lecture which I forgot to attend . . .

> The book that was open to page 65 . . .

> The defense attorney, who had left the courtroom . . .

> The plaintiff, to whom she had sent the letter . . .

Relative clauses are the source of two problems. One problem is which form of the pronoun "who/whom" to use. This problem will be discussed later.[1] The other problem is whether to use commas to set off the relative clause from the rest of the sentence. The usual explanation is somewhat circular and not very helpful: when the relative clause restricts the noun it modifies (as in the first two examples above) do not use commas. When the relative clause is already restricted by the language in the sentence (as in the last two examples above) use commas.

A better way to explain the difference between restrictive and non-restrictive relative clauses is by example. Note the difference in meaning and in punctuation between the two following sentences:

(1) People who live in glass houses should not throw stones.

(2) The Glassmans, who live in a glass house, should not throw stones.

Sentence (1) contains a restrictive relative clause. The clause does not need commas to separate it from the rest of the sentence because it identifies which people should not throw stones. The relative clause is therefore necessary to the meaning of the sentence; only those people who live in glass houses should not throw stones.

Sentence (2) contains a non-restrictive clause. The Glassmans are identified by name, not by the relative clause. The clause is not necessary to the meaning of the sentence; it merely adds information, and thus must be separated by commas from the main clause.

If you are a native speaker of English, you observe this distinction orally whether you realize it or not, whenever you use relative clauses. Listen to the sound of your voice as you read each sentence. The sound (intonation contour) of a spoken sentence containing a restrictive relative is like this:

---

1. See Section 2, infra.

People who live in glass houses should not throw stones.

The voice of the speaker rises during the vowel sound of the word "stones," then falls, to indicate the period at the end of the sentence. Contrast the sound (intonation contour) of the second sentence:

The Glassmans, who live in a glass house, should not throw stones.

In this sentence (because of its non-restrictive clause) the speaker's voice rises during the vowel sound in the first syllable of "Glassmans" and again during the vowel sound of "house," indicating the presence of a comma following those words. After the rise in pitch (indicated by the number 3) the voice falls to the normal pitch (indicated by the number 2) until the end of the sentence where the voice drops slightly (as indicated by the number 1). This intonation contour is represented by commas in writing. The commas indicate also a slight pause in the flow of words.

So one way to determine whether you are dealing with a restrictive clause (no commas) or a nonrestrictive clause (commas) is to "say" the sentence and listen to your voice. If your voice rises and then returns to normal pitch just before the relative pronoun, within the sentence, (2–3–2, 2–3–1), the sentence contains a non-restrictive relative clause. If your voice rises only at the end of the sentence, it contains a restrictive relative clause (2–3–1). Listen, also, for a slight pause at each comma. The test will be invariably accurate if you are a native American using standard English.

Now for the grammatical rule: if the relative clause identifies, restricts, or delimits the noun it modifies, the clause is restrictive and no commas are needed; if the relative clause is not necessary to identify, restrict, or delimit the noun it modifies, the clause is non-restrictive and commas are needed. Consider the following sentences. In sentence (3) there are two lakes near Joan's house; in sentence (4) there is only one lake near Joan's house.

(3) The lake which (or "that") is in front of Joan's house overflowed. (The relative clause explains *which* lake overflowed.)

(4) The lake, which is in front of Joan's house, overflowed. (Since there is only one lake near Joan's house, the relative clause merely provides additional information.) If you read sentence (4) aloud, it will sound like this:

The lake, which is in front of Joan's house, overflowed.

Note, too, the pause, indicated by a break in the contour line, that occurs in non-restrictive relative clauses where commas belong.

Whether or not to use commas in relative clauses may seem unimportant. But, especially in legal writing, the presence or absence of even one comma may be crucial. Note the opposite effect of the two news dispatches that follow:

(5) There is nothing being reported from the combat area which indicates the early cessation of hostilities.

(6) There is nothing being reported from the combat area, which indicates the early cessation of hostilities.

Sentence (5) is pessimistic; sentence (6) optimistic. The only difference is one comma.

In the following sentence, was the plaintiff deprived of five diamonds or only one? The presence or absence of one comma provides this crucial information:

> According to the terms of the contract, plaintiff had reason to expect the delivery of five carefully-selected diamonds, including one of rare color, of which he was deprived. (Plaintiff was deprived of five diamonds.)

> According to the terms of the contract, plaintiff had reason to expect the delivery of five carefully-selected diamonds, including one of rare color of which he was deprived. (Plaintiff was deprived of only one diamond.)

Exercises for those students who have difficulty recognizing the difference between restrictive and non-restrictive clauses are provided in the Appendix.

2. Case of the Relative Pronoun ("Who/Whom")

Needlessly confusing to many law students is the question of when to use "who" and when to use "whom." The decision can be reached easily by applying a formula. Substitute the personal pronouns "he/him," "she/her," "we/us," or "they/them" for "who/whom" and re-cast the clause in question into normal subject-verb-object order to determine whether who/whom is the subject or object of its own clause. If the relative pronoun functions as subject, "who" is correct; if the relative pronoun functions as object, "whom." A few examples should clarify this point:

(1) The attorney (who/whom) argued the case was the Public Defender.

Substitute: The attorney [he argued the case] was the Public Defender.

Since "he" is the subject of its own clause, "who" (the subjective form of the relative pronoun) is correct:

(1) The attorney who argued the case was the Public Defender.

(2) The attorney (who/whom) the defendant requested was the Public Defender.

Substitute: The attorney [the defendant requested him] was the Public Defender.

Since "him" is the object in its own clause, "whom" should be used:

(2) The attorney whom the defendant requested was the Public Defender.

The formula works equally well when the relative pronoun is the object of a preposition:

(3) The prisoner did not know (who/whom) he was talking to.

Substitute: The prisoner did not know [he was talking to her].

Since the objective form of "she" ("her") is proper, the objective form "whom" is also correct:

(3) The prisoner did not know whom he was talking to.

When a preposition is involved, merely re-casting the sentence so that the preposition immediately precedes the relative pronoun makes the choice clear:

Substitute: The prisoner did not know to whom he was talking.

(4) The judge, (who/whom) the plaintiff had done many favors for, asked to be removed from the case.

Substitute: The judge, for whom the plaintiff had done many favors, asked to be removed from the case.

See the Appendix for exercises on the choice of the proper case of the pronoun.

Regarding the use of relative pronouns in restrictive and non-restrictive clauses, there remains only the question of whether to use "that," "who/whom," or "which."

"That" is used only in restrictive clauses.

The dog that I bought for my son barks constantly.

If the dog was identified in a previous sentence, and thus a non-restrictive clause is used, "that" would be inappropriate; "which" would be the choice:

The dog, which I bought for my son, barks constantly.

Try using "that" with the intonation contour of a non-restrictive clause. If you are a native speaker, when you read the sentence aloud, the "sound" will indicate that it is non-idiomatic English usage:

*The dog, that I bought for my son, barks constantly.[2]

In restrictive clauses, "that" may be used to refer to all non-human nouns in both formal and informal usage, and, in informal usage, to refer to human beings individually and in groups as well.

(1) The books that I left on the table are missing.

(2) The man that borrowed the books has not returned them.

(3) The commission that promulgated the ordinance has convened.

---

2. Throughout this book, the asterisk placed before a cited sentence will indicate ungrammatical or nonidiomatic English usage.

In formal usage, "that" would be used in the first sentence, "who" and "which" in the second and third:

(2) The man who borrowed the books has not returned them.

(3) The commission which promulgated the ordinance has convened.[3]

In written English, groups of humans, (corporations, courts, institutions, and the like) are customarily referred to both by "which" and the singular verb form:

(1) Congress, which is in session . . .

(2) The committee, which meets in Room 10 . . .

(3) The Board of Directors, which makes the decision . . .

"That" is not used to refer to human beings in formal written English, although it has gained acceptability generally in spoken English.

(1) Anyone that wishes to comment may do so. (Spoken English)

(2) Anyone who wishes to comment may do so. (Spoken or written English)

In restrictive relative clauses, the pronouns "who," "which," and "that" may be deleted for succinctness when those pronouns function as objects in their own clauses.

(1) The dog that I bought for my son barks constantly.

Substitute, if you wish, for succinctness:

The dog I bought for my son barks constantly.

(2) The books which I placed on the table are missing.

Substitute, if you wish, for succinctness:

The books I placed on the table are missing.

(3) The person whom I just met is your friend.

Substitute, if you wish, for succinctness:

The person I just met is your friend.

However, if the restrictive pronoun functions as the subject in its own clause, it should not be omitted:

(4) The commission that promulgated the ordinance has convened.

(5) The person who just left was my attorney.

Do NOT substitute:

* The commission promulgated the ordinance has convened.

* The person just left was my attorney.

---

3. Since most legal writing requires the use of formal English (and indeed legal usage tends to be conservative and somewhat old-fashioned), the student is well-advised to avoid colloquial, casual usage in all of his law school writing assignments.

The exception to this rule is that when the verb is a form of "be," both the form of "be" and the relative pronoun may be omitted, for succinctness:

(5) The book which is on the table . . .

The book on the table . . .

(6) The person who is responsible . . .

The person responsible . . .

(7) The court that is sitting . . .

The court sitting . . .

3. Case of Personal Pronouns (I/Me, He/Him, She/Her, They/Them)

Somewhere in their past education, someone must have strongly impressed upon many law students the necessity of using the subjective case of personal pronouns in sentences like the following:

John and I are going out.

She and I were in the library.

We on the committee voted "yes."

It was he whom I wanted to meet.

Many law students seem to have been so well convinced to use the subjective form of personal pronouns in constructions like those cited that they do not use the objective forms of pronouns even when they should.   For example:

* Give it to Mary and I.

* For they who wished to study the library was open.

* Our study group is made up of John, Mary, and we two.

To decide whether to use the subjective or objective form of the pronoun, mentally revise the sentence so as to place the pronoun next to the verb.

(1) Give it to me (and Mary).

(2) The library was open for them (or "those") who wished to study.[4]

(3) Our study group is made up of us two, John, and Mary.

After "than" or "as" the personal pronoun takes the subjective or objective form depending upon whether it is the subject or object of the verb (in its own clause) either stated or implied.   Thus:

John admires Joe more than me.

(John admires Joe more than John admires me.)

John admires Joe more than I.

---

4.   "Them" is the objective form because it is the object of the preposition "for"; "who" is the subjective form because it is the subject of its own clause. These subject/object distinctions of personal and relative pronouns may in time be eliminated, but current good usage still requires they be made, especially in writing. The use of "those" avoids the problem in this locution and is probably a more felicitous choice.

(John admires Joe more than I do.)

College students socialize more than law students; law students study more than they (do).

Phil is younger than Jack but taller than he (is).

Jim is as tall as I (am).

For exercises dealing with case in relative and in personal pronouns, see the Appendix.

4. The Dangling Modifier

The most widespread grammatical error in law students' writing is, without doubt, the dangling modifier. Law students use dangling modifiers because in thinking ahead to what they are going to write next they forget what they have already written. Standard English requires that when a dependent clause has no subject, its implied subject be identical to the stated subject in the following independent clause; modifiers dangle when the implied subject is not the same as the subject stated in the following clause. To demonstrate, first using correct models, in the following sentences there are no dangling modifiers because in each sentence the unstated (but implied) subject of the first (dependent) clause is the same as the stated subject of the independent clause that follows:

(1) Being sick in bed, I missed class.

[I was sick in bed; I missed class.]

(2) Opening the jar, I took a pickle.

[I opened the jar; I took a pickle.]

(3) Followed by my dog, I left the house.

[I was followed by my dog; I left the house.]

(4) At age four I learned to read.

[I was age four; I learned to read.]

Contrast the following ungrammatical sentences, taken from legal writing:

(5) * When only four days old, the defendant abandoned her infant.

[The defendant was four days old.]

(6) * Viewing the issue from the proper perspective, a decision becomes easy.

[A decision views the issue.]

(7) * Having turned down the sound so as not to awaken others, the commercials blast with startling volume.

[The commercials turned down the sound.]

To eliminate the dangling modifier, give the dependent clause a subject:

When the infant was only four days old, the defendant abandoned her.

When the issue is viewed from the proper perspective, a decision becomes easy.

Although the sound was turned down so it would not awaken others, the commercials blast with startling volume.

It might be argued that because dangling modifiers appear so commonly in the writing of young educated persons and cause little confusion, such errors should be ignored rather than eliminated. The argument fails for at least two reasons: (1) lawyers are held to higher standards in language usage than other educated persons, and more important (2) dangling modifiers always reduce precision, and occasionally create ludicrous statements. The following examples, from actual writing, suffice to make the point:

(8) * Being filthy and infested with roaches, the defendant decided not to rent the apartment.

(9) * Lying on top of the large intestine, we can see a stringy, membranous material surrounding it.

An easy way to eliminate the dangling modifier is to add the missing subject to the dependent clause. Consider the following sentences:

(10) * If convicted of murder, the son's spouse would inherit his share of the mother's estate.

(11) * If convicted of murder, the son's share of his mother's estate would go to the spouse.

In (10), the spouse is convicted of murder; in (11) the "share of the mother's estate" is convicted of murder. Neither is the intended meaning. By putting the subject into the dependent clause, the sentence becomes clear and correct:

(12) If the son is convicted of murder, his share of the mother's estate would be inherited by his spouse.

5. Squinting Modifiers and Split Infinitives

Squinting modifiers were so-named because they "squint" in two directions, causing ambiguity. Here are a few examples:

(1) The trial that was postponed twice apparently will take place next month.

Was the trial apparently postponed twice? Or will it apparently take place next month? Either of the two sentences that follow will remove the guesswork:

The trial that was apparently postponed twice will take place next month.

The trial that was postponed twice will apparently take place next month.

(2) The attorney agreed eventually to aid the plaintiff in his suit.

Did the attorney eventually agree? Or did the attorney eventually aid the plaintiff? Read on, and find out:

The attorney eventually agreed to aid the plaintiff in his suit.

The attorney agreed to eventually aid the plaintiff in his suit.

Embedded in sentence (2) is a split infinitive.[5] Until fairly recently, split infinitives were considered sub-standard usage. But times have changed, and they are no longer considered anathema except by the most avid purists. They are, in fact, perfectly acceptable when, as in the last sentence above, they add clarity and smoothness to the statement. A safe rule is: avoid splitting infinitives except to avoid either ambiguity or awkwardness. Be especially reluctant to insert the negatives "not" and "never" between the "to" and the verb of the infinitive. The following constructions are illustrations:

(3) * She promised to never drive without a license again.

(4) * He was anxious to not be conspicuous in public.

Re-write these as:

She promised never to drive without a license again.

He was anxious not to be conspicuous in public.

(Or: He was anxious to be inconspicuous in public.)

6. Sentence Fragments

Occurring less frequently, but often enough to be included here, are errors involving incomplete sentences (sentence fragments).

The absence of a finite verb is responsible for most sentence fragments. A finite verb is the form of the verb that follows the first, second, and third persons singular and plural (I, you, he, she, it, we, they). In substituting the participial form of the verb (usually the present participle, ending in "-ing"), the writer creates a sentence fragment:

(1) * The defense attorney's motion for a directed verdict pending.

In order to change this sentence fragment to a complete sentence, add "is" or "was" (finite form of "be") to the present participle form, "pending."

The defense attorney's motion for a directed trial is pending.

You can also avoid sentence fragments by connecting the fragment to the preceding or following sentence if it belongs there semantically:

(2) Assumption of risk is a waiver of defects and dangers. * The employee consenting to assume them.

Assumption of risk is a waiver of defects and dangers, the employee consenting to assume them.

In example (2), by changing the period to a comma, the writer not only avoids an ungrammatical construction but joins two statements whose ideas are closely connected.

---

5. You "split" infinitives when you put an adverb between the word "to" and the verb; e.g., "to hardly move," "to apparently rely."

Law students sometimes fall into the trap of sentence fragments when they begin a sentence with the adverbs "whereas" or "although." These words are subordinating conjunctions and even though you use a finite verb with them the result will be a sentence fragment, because "whereas" and "although" introduce dependent clauses, not complete sentences. To avoid a sentence fragment, just attach the clause beginning with "whereas" either to the preceding or the following sentence, wherever the idea seems to belong:

> (3) The prosecutor asked that the accused be given a life sentence.
> * Whereas, the defense attorney asked for acquittal.
>
> The prosecutor asked that the accused be given a life sentence, whereas the defense attorney asked for acquittal.

7. Run-On Sentences

The run-on sentence is the reverse of the sentence fragment. Instead of half a sentence it is actually two sentences, improperly joined.[6] Correcting a run-on sentence involves several possibilities: the sentence may be divided into two sentences; it may be divided into two independent clauses joined by a semi-colon;[7] or it may be re-written as a compound sentence joined by a comma and a coordinating conjunction. For example:

> (1) * The victim of the attack was blind, he could not see the threatening gestures of his attackers.

This can be corrected in any of the following ways:

> The victim of the attack was blind. He could not see the threatening gestures of his attackers. (Division into two sentences)
>
> The victim of the attack was blind; he could not see the threatening gestures of his attackers. (Two independent clauses joined by a semi-colon)
>
> The victim of the attack was blind, so he could not see the threatening gestures of his attackers. (Comma plus the coordinating conjunction "so")

The coordinating conjunction "so," in the third example, indicates the causal relationship existing between the two parts of the sentence. The use of such causal conjunctions as "so," and "because" to indicate causal relationships is of course stylistically desirable for precision. The same causality may be indicated by conjunctive adverbs like "thus," "therefore," "hence," and "accordingly." But conjunctive adverbs are preceded by a semi-colon instead of a comma:

> (2) The victim of the attack was blind; thus he could not see his attackers.

---

6. Some grammarians discuss this problem under two headings, "comma splice" and "fused sentences." A comma splice is the improper combination of two sentences by a comma; a fused sentence combines two sentences with no punctuation at all. Since both sentences "run-on," they are here combined under that heading.

7. See the discussion of the semi-colon/comma choice, infra, § 8.

Whether to divide the run-on sentence into two sentences or to retain the single sentence with correct puctuation is a stylistic choice. The comma usually indicates two ideas more closely related than ideas joined by a semi-colon. The period shows even less connection between ideas.

The Appendix contains examples of dangling modifiers, squinting modifiers, split infinitives, sentence fragments and run-on sentences. Since the sentences were taken from students' unedited writing, they may contain other errors too. Re-write the sentences, eliminating all mistakes.

8. The Semi-Colon/Comma Choice

One grammatical error that has increased in incidence tremendously during the last ten years is the improper substitution of the comma for the semi-colon and the colon. The comma is a useful mark of punctuation, but it is not the only mark available, although the writing of law students often belies this fact. I sometimes think that no one in the elementary schools is bothering to tell little children that colons and semi-colons exist.

The semi-colon is used to join two closely-related sentences:

(1) The days were windy; the nights were cold and wet.

Using a coordinating conjunction, the writer may choose a comma instead. (Coordinating conjunctions are "and," "or," "for," "yet," "but," and "so.")

The days were windy, but the nights were cold and wet.[8]

A period between the two ideas creates two sentences and indicates a greater break in thought:

The days were windy. The nights were cold and wet.

You may also use a semi-colon to join two ideas separated by a coordinating conjunction. A semi-colon alone can also join two ideas, but a comma cannot. Joining two complete sentences by a comma with no coordinating conjunction or conjunctive adverb results in a run-on sentence:

(2) The suggestion has been made before; but I am not about to follow it. (semi-colon + coordinating conjunction)

The suggestion has been made before; I am not about to follow it. (semi-colon alone)

* The suggestion has been made before, I am not about to follow it. (comma alone: the result a run-on sentence)

Semi-colons or periods are the only marks of punctuation grammatically possible when two complete sentences are joined by conjunctive adverbs (words like "therefore," "hence," "nevertheless," "however," "thus," and "moreover.") [9] To distinguish a conjunctive adverb from a coordinating conjunction,

8. Commas are also used when a subordinate clause precedes a main clause; for example, "Since the evidence indicates that the defendant did not warn the plaintiff, the defendant is liable for negligence." For more on this subject, see Chapter 3, Section D(2).

9. This list is not complete. See *Harbrace Handbook*, 7th edition (1972), 474–475, for more.

move each around in the sentence. The coordinating conjunction can be used only at the beginning of its clause; the conjunctive adverb may be shifted to other positions:

(3) The decision was unsatisfactory; therefore an appeal is probable.

The decision was unsatisfactory; an appeal, therefore, is probable.

The decision was unsatisfactory; an appeal is therefore probable.

The decision was unsatisfactory; an appeal is probable, therefore.

But with a coordinating conjunction, only one order is possible:

The decision was unsatisfactory, so an appeal is probable.

* The decision was unsatisfactory, an appeal so is probable.

9. The Colon

The colon is another useful mark of punctuation that is largely ignored by some law students, except as part of the salutation in business letters (Dear Sir:). The colon can also be used as a signal that an explanation follows, as in:

(1) Both the public and criminals suffer from overcrowded jails: the public because criminals are often released prematurely; the criminals because the quality of life in overcrowded prisons suffers.

The colon introduces a list of statements or items:

(2) The following elements of assault are present in the instant case:

(1) the act was intentional and unconsented to; (2) the gesture reasonably caused apprehension of an imminent harmful touching; and (3) the actor was unprivileged to make the gesture.

(3) The contents of the glove compartment included: 30 quaaludes; 10 syringes; one rubber hose; 20 small packages of marijuana.

(In the third sentence, commas might separate the list since each item is brief and uncomplicated.)

10. The Possessive Apostrophe

Before learning how to use the possessive apostrophe, learn where *not* to use it.

A. Do *not* use the possessive apostrophe to indicate possession in inanimate nouns.[10] Use the longer form instead, called the periphrastic possessive. For example, write

the roof of the house (*not* the house's roof)

the contents of the course (*not* the course's contents)

the winner of the dispute (*not* the dispute's winner)

the long form of the possessive (*not* the possessive's long form).

---

10. This rule does not always apply to informal, colloquial writing.

Like all rules, this one has an exception: certain well-known phrases like "for argument's sake" are acceptable. And inanimate nouns, if they are composed of human beings, use the possessive apostrophe. For example,

> the committee's policy (but "the policy of the committee" is acceptable, too)

> the corporation's profits (but "the profits of the corporation" is acceptable, too)

> the alumni association's program (but "the program of the alumni" is acceptable, too).

B. Do *not* use the possessive apostrophe with personal pronouns. For example, the following are correct forms:

> The book is hers.

> The decision is theirs.

> The dog is ours.

> The luggage is yours.

Now for where the possessive apostrophe *is* used:

(1) In most singular animate nouns, add *'s* to form the possessive:

> the author's words

> the dog's tail

> Joe's house

> the professor's class.

In plural animate nouns ending in an *s* or *z* sound, add the possessive apostrophe after the final letter:

> boys' caps

> professors' classes

> ladies' clubs

> geniuses' problems

In one-syllable singular animate nouns that end in an *s* or a *z* sound, add *'s*:

> the boss's request

> the horse's legs

> James's appointment

> Alice's book

You may, of course, use the periphrastic possessive, if your prefer, for animate nouns, but not for proper nouns. That is, you can say "the classes of the professor," but not, "the book of Alice."

The following compounds add *'s* to form the possessive:

everybody's	someone's
anybody's	no one's (or noone's)
somebody's	everyone's
nobody's	anyone's

When two or more nouns are used to denote possession, only the last noun in the series takes the possessive form when possession is shared by all members of the group. For example:

John, Mary, and Bill's property (joint ownership)

Mary and Paul's will (only one will)

Joe and Joan's tax form (joint filing)

But when separate possession is indicated, every noun in the list must take the possessive form:

John's, Mary's, and Bill's property (three pieces of property)

Mary's and Paul's wills (two separate wills)

Joe's and Joan's tax forms (separate filing)

11. Number Errors

Errors in number occur so frequently that they deserve a separate section. One type of number error is a result of the disappearance of Latin from high school and college curricula. Since almost all English words indicate the plural by the addition of "s," the student who has never learned Latin does not recognize Latin plurals in words like "curricula," "addenda," "criteria," "media," "data," and other Latin words that have been adopted into English. All of those listed are plurals.)

The tendency of English speakers to add "s" for plurals has already created the composite form "medias"—a Latin plural form, with an English plural added for good measure. Since this hybrid is not yet acceptable as standard English, it behooves educated persons (and particularly attorneys, with their ready use of Latin terms) to use the correct singular and plural forms.[11] Listed below are the singular and plural forms of words descended from Latin and Greek:

Singular	**Plural**
criterion	criteria
addendum	addenda
curriculum	curricula
medium	media
datum	data [12]
stratum	strata
alumnus	alumni (male)
alumna	alumnae (female)
dictum	dicta

11. Ninety percent of the Usage Panel of the *American Heritage Dictionary of the English Language* (1973) calls "media" (as a singular noun) unacceptable, and the use of "medias" for the plural is even more severely condemned.

12. The singular form of the plural "data" and "strata" has all but vanished. Still, correct written usage requires the plural verb to follow. Thus, "the data are . . ."

The use of the grammatically correct "he" to refer to a singular subject of either sex has in recent years, been replaced by "they" in the writing and speech of persons who wish to avoid the impression that they are "sexist." [13] Whether to comply with grammatical correctness or to bow to social pressure is, of course, a choice each person must make, being aware that grammatical convention in formal writing still requires "he" in sentences like the following:

(1) Each physician is expected to comply with practices customary in his community.

(2) If one fails to pass the state bar examination, he may take it again.

(3) If a party is involved in a dispute in a state court, he is subject to state rules.

In these locutions, "he" refers to gender, not sex, and applies either to male or female. But for those persons who consider the above locutions unacceptable, yet hesitate to use incorrect English, there is an alternative. Change each singular noun to plural and use the non-gender plural pronoun "they." Thus:

All physicians are expected to comply with practices current and customary in their community.

If applicants fail to pass the state bar examination they may take it again.

If parties are involved in disputes in state courts, they are subject to state rules.

Another alternative for the second and third sentences is to change the construction to avoid the need for a referent pronoun:

An applicant who fails to pass the state bar examination may take it again.

A party who is involved in a dispute being tried in a state court is subject to state rules.

Law students often incorrectly use the plural pronoun "they" instead of the singular "it" when referring to a court, committee, institution, business or any entity composed of individuals. The Senate, for example, is an "it" (although its members are, of course, referred to as "they" in the plural).[14] The following sentences are correct:

(4) In Edwards v. California, the Court based *its* reaffirmation of the federal right of interstate travel upon the Commerce Clause.

(5) May a city limit *its* population by zoning laws?

(6) Congress *is* empowered to protect *its* constitutional right to travel by legislation.

13. For a discussion of this subject see my article, "Should the English Language Have a Sex Operation?" in *Illinois Quarterly*, Winter, 1977, Volume 40, Number 2, p. 24. See also my comments in the Introduction.

14. Since this is so, the singular verb must also be used. See, for example, sentence (6), following.

(7) The jury arrived at *its* decision after several days.

(8) The defense called as *its* first witness an expert chemist.

12. The Extra "That," Other Redundancies, and Some Deletions

The extra "that" is included in a written or spoken statement because the writer or speaker forgets that he has already used one "that," as in the following sentences:

(1) * The Court ruled in the earlier case that because quantity, price, and conditions were all stated that there was a valid offer.

(2) * It has been argued that because some students panic in an all-or-nothing final examination that tests should be given throughout the term.

In these two sentences there is one "that" too many. The simple way to correct them is to delete the second "that."

> The Court ruled in the earlier case that because quantity, price and conditions were all stated there was a valid offer.

> It has been argued that because some students panic in an all-or-nothing final examination, tests should be given throughout the term.

Similar to the extra "that" is the extra "is." This latter construction is a favorite of politicians being interviewed on television, and it appears less in writing than in speech:

(3) * The fact is is that . . .

(4) * The trouble is is that . . .

The speaker mistakenly considers the construction "the fact is" and "the trouble is" to be equivalent to a noun phrase, and therefore follows that construction with the verb "is." In fact, the noun phrases are "the fact" and "the trouble," and only one verb (in this case "is") should follow.

A word needs to be said about the redundant "would have . . . would have," as in:

(5) * If the defendant would have used his rear-view mirror he would have avoided the accident.

The proper combination is "had" plus "would have":

> If the defendant had used his rear-view mirror he would have avoided the accident.

Other redundancies in the writing of law students occur in phrases like "refer back," "return back," "reiterate again," and "repeat again," in which the first word of the term contains the meaning of the second, and the second word ought therefore to be deleted. Stylistic redundance will be discussed in Chapter Two.

On the other hand, sometimes words are deleted that should be included. Consider the following sentences:

(6) I enjoy corporate law practice and probably always will [enjoy corporate law practice].

(7) John has been employed by the city attorney and so has Jack [been employed by the city attorney].

In both of these sentences the bracketed words can be deleted, because they repeat words already present in the sentences. But in the following sentences, the deleted verb is not identical to the verb that remains:

(8) * I have and always will believe in the jury system.

(9) * He has and still does proclaim his innocence.

(10) * The company has in the past and continues to hire local residents.

Because the deleted verb is not identical to the retained verb in the sentence, it should not be omitted. The sentences should be rewritten as follows:

I always have believed and always will believe in the jury system.

(Or: I always have believed in the jury system and always will believe in it.)

He has proclaimed his innocence and still proclaims it.

The company has hired local residents in the past and continues to hire them.

In a profession known for its wordiness, lawyers, surprisingly, make other incorrect deletions. Sometimes they omit necessary prepositions:

(11) * The defense has considered which newspaper the advertisement should appear.

(12) * The Senate is the forum which he should make his case.

(13) * The controversy abounds the press.

(14) * The students browse the library.

With the prepositions included, the sentence would read:

The defense has considered which newspaper the advertisement should appear in.

The Senate is the forum which he should make his case in.

The controversy abounds in the press.

The students browse in the library.

In the first two sentences, the writer's reluctance to end sentences with a preposition may be the reason it was omitted. The final preposition can be avoided and the preposition retained, by a change in word order:

The defense has considered in which newspaper the advertisement should appear.

The Senate is the forum in which he should make his case.

But it is not necessary to torture syntax in order to avoid ending a sentence with a preposition. The "rule" forbidding such sentences was current *circa* the turn of the century and has long since been relaxed. Some readers may recall Winston Churchill's outburst (perhaps apocryphal) against a speechwriter who eliminated one of Churchill's terminal prepositions: "This is the sort of arrant nonsense up with which I will not put!"   When convenient, the preposition should be placed within the sentence, however, because the end of the sentence is too important to waste on a preposition.[15]

13.   Count and Non-count Nouns

Although you may not be able to identify the problem, you probably realize that something is wrong with each of the following sentences:

(1) * The amount of students in a class depends upon the teaching skill of the professor.

(2) * The feedback provided by tests are inadequate to discover what the students learned.

(3) * Law students have less chances to write than their counterparts in liberal arts.

The mistake in each of these sentences involves the improper treatment of count and non-count nouns.   In sentence (1), since "students" is a count noun, the word referring to it should be "number," not "amount."   In sentence (2), since "feedback" is a non-count noun, it does not have a plural and must therefore take a singular verb.   In sentence (3), since "less" must refer to a non-count noun, "chance" should be substituted for "chances."

> The number of students in a class depends upon the teaching skill of the professor.

> The feedback provided by tests is inadequate to discover what the students learned.

> Law students have less chance to write than their counterparts in liberal arts.

Count and non-count nouns are easily distinguishable.   For one thing, count nouns are divisible into units and can be counted.   "Cat" is a count noun: you can say "one cat, two cats, three cats."   Non-count nouns are indivisible into units and cannot be counted; they have no plurals.   "Information," "salt," "laziness," and "affluence" are a few examples of non-count nouns.

Another way to identify count and non-count nouns is by placing the indefinite article ("a" or "an") in front of them.   You can say "a box," "a chair," or "an orange," but not "a flour," or "an information."   Count nouns not only can be preceded by an indefinite article, but—in the singular—*must* have either a definite or indefinite article.   In their plural form, however, count nouns like non-count nouns, can be used without an article:

> * Umbrella is handy in a tropical climate.

> An umbrella is handy in a tropical climate.

> Umbrellas are handy in a tropical climate.

> * Alternative is available.

> The alternative is available.

15. For further discussion of this subject, see Chapter Two, § A(1).

Alternatives are available.

Recklessness is a required element of some torts.

Beauty is in the eyes of the beholder.

All nouns, both count and non-count, can be preceded by the definite article ("the"):

The advice is welcome.

The argument is valid.

The question is moot.

The briefs are due.

Count nouns are usually tangible: "father," "church," "lake," "feather." But "hope," "desire," and "ideal" are a few examples of count nouns that are intangible. Non-count nouns usually fall into one of two groups: they name bulky materials (like "dirt," "butter," "salt", or "rice") or they name states or qualities (like "peace," "cheerfulness," "nutrition," or "exuberance.") Some non-count nouns may occur as count nouns too. "Freedom," "democracy," "sin," and "bread" are a few words that are sometimes used as non-count nouns and sometimes as count nouns:

Freedom is precious.

Our freedoms are precious.

Democracy is under attack.

One new democracy is the state of Israel.[16]

The problem that law students have with count and non-count nouns is that they sometimes use the wrong words to refer to them.

With count nouns use:	With non-count nouns use:
many	much
few, fewer	little, less
number	amount

For example, "many joys" but "much happiness"; "few lakes" but "little water," "a number of dollars" but "an amount of money," "fewer headaches" but "less pain," "fewer chances" but "less chance."

The Appendix provides some sentences with which you can test your ability to distinguish between count and non-count nouns.

---

16. Non-count nouns frequently become count nouns but count nouns seldom become non-count. In Middle English (between about 1100 and 1500 A.D.) "peas," which is now a count noun, was a non-count noun, spelled "pease." Languages differ in what nouns they consider count and non-count, and even two dialects of English, American and British, differ on the word "hospital," which is a count noun in the U. S. and a non-count noun in England.

CHAPTER TWO

Legal Style

One need only consider the differences in the writing styles of James Joyce, Ring Lardner, Ernest Hemingway, and William Faulkner to realize that writing style is a combination of the subject matter and the writer's personality. In creative writing, the writer's personality brightly illuminates the subject matter; in legal writing, the writer's personality should appear only dimly, if at all. Matter, in legal writing, should dominate manner.

In fact, in legal writing, even style should not intrude. The reader should be left with the thought that the arguments are complete and convincing, not that the writer's style is clever or pleasing. The story is told of the appearance of Caesar and Cicero before the Roman Senate, which had met to decide what should be done about the bothersome Gauls. When Cicero finished his oration, the senators agreed that his speech was without equal—eloquent and brilliant. When Caesar finished his speech, however, the senators cried with one voice, "Let us fight the Gauls!" Good legal writing, like Caesar's oratory, should impel to action.

Since the essence of effective legal writing is communication, the ABC's are accuracy, brevity, and clarity. All of the writing techniques discussed in this chapter will make your writing more accurate, brief, and clear; all are included because they are often lacking in the writing of law students and legal professionals.

Accuracy is achieved by the most efficacious combination of ideas and language. The decision about what ideas to include and exclude is crucial for a written product both complete and selective. The stressing of important ideas and the subordination of less important ones may be the key to successful examinations and persuasive arguments. And the choice of the right word in the right place can change vagueness into clarity.

Brevity is equally important. Your writing will be more likely to be read, understood, and remembered if it is brief. But it takes time to be brief; a student once complained that his memo exceeded the word limit because he didn't have time to write a shorter one. To reduce verbiage careful editing is necessary, but the time spent is worthwhile, first because the person who reads what you write values his time at least as much as you do yours, and second because constant effort to reduce wordiness will help you eliminate the habit.

Writing that is brief and accurate has a good start toward clarity. But clarity also requires good organization of the entire product. Clear explanations and arguments take the reader by the hand and lead him logically and undeviatingly from point to point. There should be no gaps requiring leaps in imagination, no untoward digressions; clear legal writing resembles a roadmap with the route plainly charted, not a maze in which the reader must search out the way.

A. TECHNIQUES TO USE

1. Place Words in Their Best Order

Most writers are unaware that the placement of words in sentences is strategic. The most important ideas belong at the end of the sentence; the next most important ideas at the beginning; and into the middle goes everything else. But although they may be unaware of this "rule," good writers arrange their sentences in this order intuitively. In the following sentence the most important point is that the federal statute might override the state statute:

(1) If the defendant can prove that the state statute did not give adequate notice because it was vaguely written, the federal statute might override it.

Suppose that the writer wants to emphasize the possible vagueness of the state statute. Then the sentence should read:

The federal statute might override the state statute only if the defendant can prove that the state statute did not give adequate notice because it was vaguely written.

Here is a sentence from a student memo:

(2) The defendants had a duty under Florida law to have their truck inspected and by not stopping they were in violation of the statute; this gave the inspector the right to apply for a search warrant.

Three points are being made here: (1) the defendants had a legal duty under Florida law; (2) they violated that duty; and (3) therefore the inspector had the right to apply for a search warrant. If the important point is the violation of Florida law, that point should be placed at the end of the sentence:

The inspector had the right to apply for a search warrant because the defendants, in refusing to stop for inspection, violated Florida law.

If, however, the search warrant for the truck is of greatest importance, the sentence should end with that point

Because the defendants refused to stop for inspection, as Florida law requires, the inspector had the right to apply for a search warrant.

In another sentence from the same memo, the writer fails, because of improper word order, to achieve the emphasis he intends:

(3) The defendants could argue that they could not agree to the officer's request because they did not have access to the key, and not because they willfully refused this request and prima facie evidence of their violation of the statute should not be inferred by their non-compliance.

If the writer wants to emphasize the denial by the defendants of prima facie violation of the statute, that point should come at the end of the sentence:

> The defendants could argue that because they had no access to the key, their refusal to accede to the officer's request was not prima facie evidence of violation of the statute.

If, however, the important fact is that the defendants had no access to the key, the sentence should be recast to place this fact at the end:

> The defendants could argue that their refusal to accede to the officer's request was not prima facie evidence of violation of the statute, because their refusal was not willful since they had no access to the key.[1]

Another example comes from a brief in which the writer was arguing that a tire sold by the defendant to the plaintiff's father was not defective, although it had blown out, causing a fatal crash:

> (4) Certainly the defendant owed a duty to the plaintiff to sell him a tire which would withstand normal wear and tear. However, evidence indicates that a blow-out or a flat tire was possible due to the conditions of the road. Here the plaintiff failed to establish that there was a breach of duty by the defendant.

This argument suffers from gaposis, along with faulty arrangement. The three points to be made are (1) the defendant had a duty; (2) no breach of that duty has been proved; (3) therefore defendant should not be held liable. The first sentence deals with point (1) and can be left as it is, except for the placement of the first word.[2] The second sentence wastes valuable space by placing in the important first part words that do not carry much important meaning ("However, evidence indicates that"). The third sentence wastes space with a meaningless first word ("here"). One possible re-write:

> The defendant certainly owed a duty to the plaintiff to sell him a tire which would withstand normal wear and tear. However, since evidence indicates that the tire may have blown-out because of road conditions, no proof exists that the tire was defective. Thus the plaintiff has failed to establish that the defendant breached his duty.[3]

One more point; this will take you back to your elementary school days when your English teacher told you that there were three types of sentences: simple, compound, and complex. Note that when a point is to be stressed, in the re-writes above, it is not only placed at the end of the sentence; it is put into the main clause of a complex sentence. Recall that a complex sentence is made up of a main clause and one or more subordinate clauses, often adverbial clauses introduced by words like "after," "since," "when," "until," "because,"

---

1. Note that cause-effect relationships are clarified in both of these revisions by connectors like "since" and "because." More on this subject in Section 4, infra.

2. The first word is removed from the position of importance at the begin-

ning of the sentence and placed deeper into the sentence, as befits its less important status.

3. When possible, avoid the "there is" construction; see discussion of this point in Section B(5), under expletives.

"before," and "unless." **4** Placing the important idea in the main clause and also at the end of the sentence insures that the reader will understand its importance. This is done, for example, in the revision of the second sentence of example (4) above.

2. Make Lists

The arrangement of words or phrases in lists is more important than might at first be thought. Notice the ambiguity resulting from careless placement of words in the lists in the sentences that follow:

(7) His father, who died in 1973 at the age of 81, was a former county judge, state representative, and U. S. congressman for 22 years.

(Was 22 years the length of time he served as U. S. congressman, or in all three capacities?)

(8) The cause/effect relationship cannot be assumed in the absence of some interim connection or continuity.

(What kind of continuity is "interim continuity?")

(9) The director of nursing explained that the clinic had been closed because of the dilapidated condition of the building, lack of facilities and vermin. (Did lack of vermin cause the closing?)

In each sentence, ambiguity is prevented by changing the order of words in the list:

His father, who died in 1973 at the age of 81, was a former county judge and state representative, and, for 22 years, a U. S. congressman.

The cause/effect relationship cannot be assumed in the absence of continuity or some interim connection.

The director of nursing explained that the clinic had been closed because of vermin, lack of facilities, and the dilapidated condition of the building.

The benefits of list-making inhere not only to your readers however; like an outline, a list of the points you want to make will help you to marshall your arguments and call your attention to those you may have failed to include. So do yourself *and* your readers a favor: make lists. The Appendix for Section A(1) and (2) of Chapter Two contains sentences that can be written more effectively by revising word order or making lists. You may want to use them for practice.

3. Use Parallelism

In order to communicate clearly and effectively, you should place your lists in parallel structure. Surprisingly, not only law students but some lawyers

---

4. For those of you who have forgotten, a simple sentence has a single subject and predicate. (The boy has a ball.) A compound sentence has at least two main clauses. (She is going to class, and I am going to the library.) For more on this subject, see Chapter 3, Section D(2).

have never learned the knack of list-making. The following sentence, for example, was taken from the writing of a young lawyer:

> A valid banker's acceptance contains the following: (1) a time draft; (2) signature of an officer of a bank; (3) when and where the acceptance is payable; (4) statement of the underlying transaction; and (5) "accepted" written across the face of the instrument.

The list violates the two requirements of parallel structure:

(1) The word that introduces the list must be appropriate for all items on the list. (Here, the words "contain the following" are inappropriate for item (1), since a banker's acceptance "is" (not "contains") a bank draft. The introductory words also connect awkwardly with items (3) and (5).

(2) The grammatical structure of all the items must be similar. If the first item on the list begins with a verb, all items should begin with a verb; if a noun, all items should begin with a noun. But, in the example above, items (1), (2), and (4) begin with nouns; item (3) begins with an adverbial phrase; and item (5) begins with a past participle.

An improved version of the sentence complies with the requirements noted above; the introductory words ("time draft") are appropriate for all items on the list, and each item begins with the -ing form of a verb (the present participle):

> In order to be valid, a banker's acceptance must be a time draft: (1) containing the signature of an officer of the bank; (2) stating when and where acceptance is payable; (3) referring to the underlying transaction; and (4) bearing the word "acceptance" on its face.

The inability of educated persons to utilize parallel structure was brought sharply to my attention as I read the answers to tests taken by college graduates who hoped to enter law school. The students had been asked to paraphrase the following 16th century legal rule listing three criteria for the possession of wild animals:

> [A]ctual bodily seizure is not indispensable to acquire right to or possession of wild beasts, but .   .   .   the mortal wounding of such beasts by one not abandoning his pursuit may .   .   .   be deemed possession of them, since thereby, the pursuer [has] manifest[ed] an unequivocal intention of appropriating the animal to his individual use, has deprived it of his natural liberty, and [has] brought it within his certain control.[5]

Some of the students' answers follow. Can you re-write them using parallel structure?

(1) *A general rule in possession of wild animals can be that of one's being in actual power over that wild animal, and one must have deprived the wild animal of its natural liberty.

---

5. Pierson v. Post, Supreme Court of New York (1805). The language of the decision has been modernized slightly for use here.

(2) * We can also compare the elements of acquiring title to a wild animal, that an intent to possess, deprivation, reducing to a certain control must all be present.

(3) * To establish ownership of a wild animal, the hunter has to intend to capture it, deprivation of its liberty, actual possession, and all reasonable means must be used to bring the animal under control.

(4) * The criteria are (1) the animal must be deprived of its natural liberty, (2) pursuer must intend to deprive it of its liberty, and (3) be rendered to a state of certain control.

(5) * Pierson v. Post, gives a general rule of certain elements to look for in determining whether or not one has title to a wild animal. These are intent to possess, reduce to certain control, with an effort to deprive of natural liberty.

If your re-write looks something like the one that follows, you have used parallel structure. Note that the three requirements for possession are stated parallelly, introduced by a third person singular verb.

> The mortal wounding of a wild animal by one who continues to pursue the animal is deemed possession if the pursuer (1) manifests the intent to capture the animal, (2) deprives the animal of its natural liberty, and (3) brings the animal within certain control.

A diagram shows at a glance how parallelism works:

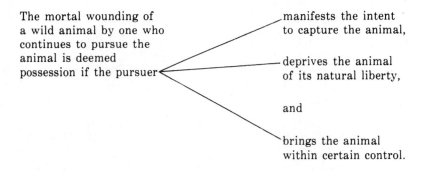

Diagramming will prevent non-parallel structures like the following:

> * A state statute requires bicyclists to either use bicycle paths or ride in the stream of traffic.

Diagrammed, the sentence would look like this:

Re-casting the sentence so that "either" is the introductory word produces the following parallel sentence:

> A state statute requires bicyclists either to use bicycle paths or to ride in the stream of traffic.[6]

Diagrammed, the sentence looks like this:

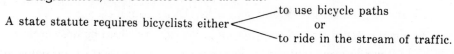

Parallelism has a place in all good writing, not only in lists. Nineteenth century writers, particularly, took great pains to present their thoughts in balanced sentences, giving their writing a grace and cadence not often present in that of twentieth century writers. This brief excerpt from Herbert Spencer's *The Philosophy of Style* provides an illustration:

> In proportion as the manners, customs and amusements of a nation are cruel and barbarous, the regulations of their penal codes will be severe. . . . In proportion as men delight in battles, bullfights, and combats of gladiators, will they punish by hanging, burning, and the rack.

Balance is achieved in these two sentences by the careful placing of parallel thoughts in parallel grammatical structure:

	Nouns	**Adjectives**
Idea One	manners	cruel
	customs	barbarous
	amusements of a nation	

	Nouns	**Gerunds & Noun**
Idea Two	battles	hanging
	bullfights	burning
	combats of gladiators	the rack

Parallel statement helps to make great ideas unforgettable. Consider Ecclesiastes:

> To every thing there is a season, and a time to every purpose under the heaven: a time to be born and a time to die; a time to plant and a time to pluck up that which is planted; a time to kill and a time to heal; a time to break down, and a time to build up. . . .

On a more mundane level, Erich Fromm's statement, "It is easier to love humanity than to get along with your neighbors," obtains its force as much by the parallelism of its structure as by the sentiments it expresses. Note the effectiveness of the re-stated infinitive form in "to love" and "to get along."

Simeon Potter, grammarian and linguist, asserts that balanced sentences satisfy "a profound human need for equipoise and symmetry." He is probably

---

6. The re-cast sentence also avoids a split infinitive. See discussion in Ch. One, Section 5.

right, but that need goes too often unsatisfied in modern writing, and even less so in the speeches of modern orators. Ralph Nader, one of today's more articulate speakers, recently remarked of a friend, "He is both a lawyer and has a Ph. D. in insurance." The following statement would have provided better balance, having the parallel structure lacking in the actual statement:

(1) He has both a law degree and a Ph. D. in insurance.

You can practice writing sentences to achieve parallelism by answering the writing problems in the Appendix, p. 182.

4. Choose Connectors Carefully

The increasing tendency to omit the final comma in a series is said to have been started by newspaper publishers who wanted to save ink. It is hard to fault this laudable motive in these energy-conscious times, but the final comma often needs to be included in legal writing to avoid ambiguity. Compare the following:

(1) Neither slavery nor involuntary servitude, unless for punishment of crime, shall be tolerated in this state.

(2) Neither slavery, nor involuntary servitude unless for punishment of crime, shall be tolerated in this state.

In (1) the state permits slavery for punishment of crime; in (2) slavery is prohibited, and involuntary servitude permitted only for punishment of crime. The difference in meaning is accomplished by the presence or absence of one comma.

The absence of a comma in § 21(1) of the Restatement of Torts creates unintended ambiguity. Assault is defined as

(3) an act other than the mere speaking of words which, directly or indirectly, is a legal cause of putting another in apprehension of an immediate and harmful or offensive contact . . .

Without the comma after "immediate," the question is whether the apprehension must be of "immediate and harmful" or else "offensive," or "immediate" and either "harmful or offensive" contact. If the former alternative is meant, the immediacy of an offensive contact would not be required. A comma after "immediate" would make it clear that the apprehension must be of immediate contact that is either harmful or offensive.

One more example of the need for the final comma in a series:

(4) The director of nursing explained that the clinic had been closed because of the dilapidated condition of the building, lack of facilities and vermin.[7]

This sentence indicates that the clinic was closed because of the lack of vermin, among other things, hardly the intended meaning. The added final

7. This sentence was also cited, supra, in Chapter Two, Section B(9). There, ambiguity was avoided by rearrangement of the list. Either method is acceptable.

comma makes it clear that the presence, not the absence, of vermin was the problem:

> The director of nursing explained that the clinic had been closed because of the dilapidated condition of the building, lack of facilities, and vermin.

Finally, be sure not to include a comma when a list is not intended:

(5) Israelis have announced the capture of five terrorists, three Lebanese, and two Syrians.

The comma after "Lebanese" makes the total number captured ten. Without the comma, the total would be five:

> Israelis have announced the capture of five terrorists, three Lebanese and two Syrians.[8]

Connecting words—conjunctions like "but," "for," "and," and "since," and adverbs like "hence," "therefore," "nevertheless," and "however"—provide nice distinctions which may be crucial. Use them indiscriminately and your ideas become fuzzy. Some law students use "and" as a handy catch-all to convey both causal and temporal relationships. Judiciously used, "and" indicates only accompaniment or sequence, as in:

(6) John and Mary are law students.   (accompaniment)

(7) I went home and went to bed.   (sequence) [9]

When "and" is used to express causation, as in the following sentence, the result is confusion:

(8) If the defendant can prove that the statute was vaguely written and did not give adequate notice, the federal statute might override it.

Words like "since," "because," "so," "thus," "hence," and "therefore" should be used to express causality:

> If the defendant can prove that the state statute was vaguely written because it did not give adequate notice, the federal statute might override it.[10]

Another example of the loose use of "and" comes from a student memo:

(9) Was plaintiff negligent in walking in the wooded area and having knowledge that it was an area frequently used by riflemen?

---

8. In this sentence, a colon after "terrorists" would also be acceptable. See Chapter One, Section 9, supra.

9. Used loosely to indicate purpose, as in "try and find it," "and" is acceptable in informal, spoken usage, but "to" or "in order to" should be used to indicate purpose in writing.

10. For further discussion of this sentence see the discussion of word order, Section 1, supra.

Here even the temporal connection, usually conveyed by "and" is lacking, since the "knowledge" must have preceded the "walking," and the student reverses this order.[11] Causal relationship can be shown in several ways:

> Was plaintiff negligent in walking in the wooded area although he knew that it was frequently used by riflemen?

The relative clause can also be used to indicate causality: [12]

> Was plaintiff, who knew that the wooded area was frequently used by riflemen, negligent in walking there?

> Was plaintiff negligent in walking in a wooded area that he knew was frequently used by riflemen?

Do not use a causal connector when you do not intend to express causality. For example, unintended causality is expressed in this sentence:

> (10) The judge should have instructed the jury that knowledge is very important because the appellant had no prior knowledge.

The causal relationship established in this sentence is that knowledge is important *because* the appellant did not have prior knowledge. This is not the relationship the student intended to express. A causal relationship should be expressed, however, that between the importance to the crime of prior knowledge and the judge's duty to make this clear to the jury. Note how the proper use of "because" expresses this relationship:

> Because prior knowledge was an important element of the crime, the judge should have informed the jury that the appellant had no prior knowledge.

Rearranging the ideas so that the most important idea is at the end of the sentence gives the sentence greater force.[13]

"Therefore," another word that expresses causal relationships, is sometimes casually tossed into sentences to mean "clearly," or sometimes to mean nothing at all, as the following paragraph reveals:

> (11) The appellant did testify to the fact that he had some LSD in the glove compartment of his car. (LSD is not a drug that has a penalty under the state's Penal Code.) Therefore the appellant's attorney can argue that the appellant had no prior knowledge of having heroin instead of LSD.

Besides the improper use of "therefore," this paragraph is almost unintelligible for two reasons: (1) the confusing "negative" construction;[14] and (2) gaposis in the reasoning. The paragraph gains clarity by the elimination of the nega-

---

11. This error, called "hysteron-proteron" (Greek for "the last before the first") is a common one in law students' writing. In literature it is sometimes used for rhetorical effect (as in Shelley's "I die, I faint, I fail," in his poem "Indian Serenade.") For discussion, see Chapter Three, Section C(3).

12. For a discussion of the relative clause, see Chapter One, Section 1.

13. See Chapter Two, Section A(1).

14. See Chapter Two, Section B(9).

tive construction, the use of the right connectors ("however," "since," "therefore," and "thus"), and the elimination of the gaps:

> The appellant testified that he was aware of the LSD in the glove compartment of his car. Possession of LSD is, however, not illegal under the state Penal Code; only possession of heroin and marijuana are illegal. The appellant's attorney can therefore argue that although appellant was aware of the presence of a drug in his glove compartment, he was unaware that the drug was heroin and thus cannot be said to have had prior knowledge of heroin possession.

This paragraph is longer than the first; it is also clearer. Succinctness is desirable in legal writing, but it should not be obtained at the expense of clarity. When your writing lacks connectors or suffers from gaposis, re-write until your meaning becomes clear. Someone said, with truth, that there is no great writing—only great re-writing.

The Appendix provides examples of ambiguity and vagueness caused by inadequate connectors and logical gaposis.

5. Match Nouns and Verbs

The misalliance of noun and verb, like other mismatches, results in an unhappy condition, as in the following examples of actual writing:

(1) The defendant's words were at a loss to express his meaning.

The verb phrase "to be at a loss" requires a human noun as subject: only persons can "be at a loss." A rewrite carries the intended idea:

> The defendant was at a loss to express his meaning. (The verb "express" includes the meaning of "words.")

In the next sentence the misalliance occurs because the verb requires a sentient being as object:

(2) The judge rebuked the language of the defense attorney.

The restatement makes the object of the verb a person, as it ought to be:

> The judge rebuked the defense attorney for his language.

Will a Supreme Court decision cause rapes to "disappear"? The next sentence seems to say so:

(3) A U. S. Supreme Court decision that will allow publication of rape victims' names may mean the disappearance of rapes reported to the police.

On closer inspection, one finds that the writer intends only to predict that the number of rapes *reported* will decrease. A more exact statement would be:

> A U. S. Supreme Court decision that will allow publication of rape victims' names may mean a reduction in the number of rapes reported to the police.

In the next sentence the noun/verb mismatch occurs because the verb "discriminate" requires a human noun as object.

(4) The employer should not discriminate against an employee's religion.

The sentence needs recasting to supply one:

> The employer should not discriminate against an employee because of his religion.

A noun/verb mismatch can also occur when one verb has two objects, but properly applies only to one:

(5) U.C.C. section 2–207 affords advantages and drawbacks to industrial sellers.

The verb "affords" properly refers to "advantages," but is improperly forced to apply to "drawbacks" as well. A more neutral verb would correct the statement:

> U.C.C. section 2–207 has advantages and drawbacks for industrial sellers.

The same problem arises when two verbs have only one object, and the object is appropriate for only one of the verbs:

(6) The evidence does conclude but does support the fact that the information conveyed to the defendants was incorrect.

(Evidence can "support" but not "conclude" facts.) A simple change will solve the problem:

> The evidence is not conclusive but it does indicate that the information conveyed to the defendants was incorrect.

To avoid noun/verb mismatches, read over what you have written and ask yourself, "Does the verb I have chosen really fit its subject? Is the object I have selected really the appropriate object for the verb?" More mismatches, for you to correct, are contained in the Appendix.

6. Prefer the Active Voice

The active voice is the construction most used in speech and in informal writing. In the active voice the subject comes first, followed by the verb and the object of the verb:

> Joan carried coals to Newcastle.
>
> James invited his client to lunch.
>
> The attorney read the statute to the clerk.

Unfortunately, law students and lawyers often prefer the passive voice to the active voice, perhaps because it "sounds more formal." What results, however, are statements that are ambiguous, indirect, and sometimes baffling. Do the following look familiar?

(1) The decision was arrived at by the committee . . .

(2) The holding was announced by the court . . .

(3) The argument was made by the attorney for the plaintiff . . .

The active voice produces fewer words and greater force:

(4) The committee decided . . .

(5) The court announced its holding . . .

(6) The plaintiff's attorney argued . . .

Here is a sentence from a student's answer to writing problem III on page 100:

> If the defendant's car is found to have been purchased for transportation to and from work, it will be found to be a necessity and the defendant's contract will not be voidable despite his minority.

When all the passive constructions are put into the active voice, the sentence becomes clearer and offers information the reader had to guess at in the sentence above:

> If the defendant purchased his car to provide transportation to his job, the court will consider the car a necessity and, despite his minority, the defendant will be unable to avoid the contract that he signed.

The active voice tells the crucial information. Because sentences written in the active voice provide a subject (who), a verb (the action of the subject), and a direct and indirect object (what was done and to whom), each ingredient necessary for communication of the writer's idea is present. On the other hand, the passive voice takes the former object and makes it the subject. The former subject is then made the object of the preposition "by"—or, even more confusing, is discarded completely.

(a) John applied force in leaving the building (active voice), or

(b) Force was applied by John in leaving the building (passive voice), or

(c) Force was applied in leaving the building (passive voice, with the former subject omitted).

The first sentence is clear; the second is clear but less forceful and direct; the third is neither clear nor forceful.

Therefore, in your writing, generally prefer the active voice to the passive. In editing what you have written, check sentences that seem unclear to see if their lack of clarity is due to the passive voice. Generally, be sure each sentence makes clear "who" did "what" to "whom."

However, the passive construction is not to be shunned completely; used with discrimination it is a valuable writing tool. You should use passive voice when

(a) the object of the verb in your sentence is more important than the subject, or

(b) the subject of your sentence is unknown, or

(c) you, the author of the statement, wish to dissociate yourself from the action of the verb.

For example, (a) would apply in an incident involving an unknown and a well-known public figure. When President Kennedy was assassinated, the newspapers quite legitimately headlined, "Kennedy Assassinated," not "Oswald Kills Kennedy."

In a news article about traffic congestion on Main Boulevard, (b) would probably apply, especially if the cause of the congestion was not known. The statement would properly emphasize the object, "congestion," and would therefore read, "Traffic was congested on Main Boulevard during rush hour yesterday."

Finally, a child might utilize (c) to report to his irate mother, "The vase was knocked off the table."

The sentences in the Appendix were taken from the actual writing of law students and may include errors other than the misuse of the passive construction. Re-writing these sentences will help you avoid such constructions in your own writing.

7. Use Concrete Language

Concrete words convey meaning more plainly than abstract words, yet lawyers' writing is notorious for vague abstractions. An anecdote, perhaps apocryphal, dating from Franklin Roosevelt's White House incumbency demonstrates this propensity. FDR instructed an aide to draft a memo asking White House employees to conserve energy, and the aide came up with, "It has been suggested that we minimize the utilization of excess illumination." When the memo arrived at his desk FDR added, "That is, turn out the lights."

Few lawyers follow FDR's example. One of their own profession has called them purveyors of "ponderous pomposity" [15] who are "blissfully unaware that the sounds they make are essentially empty of meaning." [16] Unfortunately the easy way to write is to reach for an abstraction. The *Harvard Magazine,* with tongue in cheek, published a handy guide for writers who wanted to sound erudite without saying anything precise. It was called an "extended Baffle-Gab Thesaurus," and contained three columns of words that would yield "125,000 portentous three-word phrases." Such mouth-filling abstractions as "theoretical operational conceptualization," and "counterproductive quantified initiatives" were available for immediate use to the writer who did not mind that his writing made no sense.[17] Some legal writing looks as if its authors had access to the lists.

Lawyers argue that they must use abstract words because the law itself contains so many abstractions. But for that very reason, the lawyer needs to use concrete language to clarify the law. For sheer clarity, compare the following examples:

> It is a false assumption that every graduate of a law school is, by virtue of that fact, qualified for ultimate confrontation in the courtroom. (Supreme Court Chief Justice Warren Burger)

---

15. F. Rodell, *Woe Unto You, Lawyers,* 1957, p. 128.

16. Id., p. 130.

17. June, 1974, p. 51.

> Lawyers, preachers, and tomtit eggs; there's more of them hatched
> than come to perfection. (Benjamin Franklin)

The vigor of Franklin's concrete language reaches across two centuries,
even though tomtit eggs are no longer easily identifiable. Chief Justice Bur-
ger's statement (though a jewel of clarity by comparison with some legal writing) pales in contrast. For real unintelligibility, consider this example, from a
book about crime and punishment written by prominent lawyers and law
professors:

> It may be possible to delineate the limits on magnitude better than we
> have done, but the foregoing should suffice to illustrate the basic idea;
> in deciding the magnitude of the scale, deterrence may be considered
> within whatever leeway remains after the outer bounds set by a scale of
> certain magnitude has been chosen; however, the internal composition
> of the scale should be determined by the principle of commensurate
> desserts.[18]

This kind of writing is not the exclusive preserve of the law, of course. The
writing of the educational establishment contains plenty of pretentious poppy-
cock, but, in their professional journals, its members speak largely to each other, while the legal profession should communicate clearly with the public it
serves. Law students can hardly be faulted for perpetuating and proliferating
legal gobbledegook: they read it in their casebooks and therefore believe that
is the way lawyers ought to write and talk. But the student who substitutes
clear concrete language for vague abstractions will produce writing that is better because it is precise, direct, and cogent. Furthermore, he will be able to
expose any banality, hidden by abstract language. This, too, is a benefit, for,
as Alice's King said, "If there is no meaning in it, that saves a world of trouble,
you know, as we needn't try to find it."

The Appendix contains examples of abstract language. Try your skill at re-
writing them in concrete language and note how communication improves.

8. Keep Your Sentences Clear

The writing of long, circuitous sentences is an occupational ailment among
lawyers, those who draft statutes having a particularly malignant form of the
disease. Lawyers seem almost compulsive about cramming as many facts as
possible between the capital letter and the period, and the result is often confusing, sometimes unintelligible. Law students unfortunately pick up the bug
almost at once, using this kind of writing because they believe that the cumbersome sentences they find in their casebooks are "lawyer-like."

The following sentence, taken from a student memo, illustrates that cumbersome sentences often confuse not only the reader but the writer as well.

---

18. Quoted by Goldfarb in "Lawyers and Their Language Loopholes,"
The Washington Post, June 8, 1977, p.
10. Note that the statement so confused its creator that he used a singular verb ("has") with a plural subject
("outer bounds").

Your search for the referent of "it" (third line from the end) will be in vain; the writer, lost in his ramifications, has omitted it:

(1) In Peairs v. Florida Publishing Company, where the court held the newspaper publisher liable for injuries resulting from a pedestrian tripping over a wire loop left on a public parking lot by a newsboy, if the publisher was aware of the conduct of the newsboys and failed to take proper action to remedy the situation, even though the newsboys and carriers were called independent contractors, if the publisher meddled or interfered, it was deemed an agent-principal relationship; accordingly we can establish a similar relationship between the principals in this case.

The problem here is that the writer is trying to say too many things at once. A good formula to follow is (1) if you have something to say, say it clearly and only once; (2) if you have two or more things to say, say them one at a time and in order; and (3) if you need to, for clarity, shorten your sentences. In the example above the writer is saying:

(1) The court in *Peairs* held that an agent-principal relationship existed between the defendant (Florida Publishing Company) and its newsboy/employee, despite the publisher's designation of its newsboy as an independent contractor.

(2) The agent-principal relationship existed because the publisher had the right to interfere in the activities of the newsboys.[19]

(3) As "principal" the employer has the duty to remedy a dangerous situation caused by the newsboy as "agent."

(4) Therefore the newspaper publisher is liable for the injuries of a pedestrian who tripped over a wire loop left on a public parking lot by a newsboy/employee.

These four sentences are clearer than the one sentence in which the writer attempted to say all four things.[20] They can be written (without the numbers, of course) as stated, or they can be combined into three sentences—but fewer would probably result in loss of clarity. In the following example, the order of the sentences is changed, so that the holding is given first, followed by the reasons for it:

The court held in *Peairs* that the Florida Publishing Company, a newspaper publisher, was liable for the injuries of a pedestrian who tripped over a wire loop left on a public parking lot by a newsboy, despite the claim of the publisher that newsboys were "independent contractors."

19. Note the deletion of "meddle" from the phrase "meddle or interfere." The use of two words conveying the same meaning is another unfortunate characteristic of legal writing, contributing to its general wordiness. Other common legalisms are "part and parcel," "each and every," "various and sundry," "good and sufficient." (See Chapter Two, Section B(1).)

20. It is true that each sentence contains more than one fact, but the facts in each sentence are closely related, and, combined, make up one "thing to say."

The court reasoned that the relationship between the publishing company and the newsboys was that of agent and principal because the publisher had the right to interfere in the newsboys' actions. Therefore the publishing company as principal should have taken appropriate action to remedy the dangerous situation of which it was aware and which was caused by the newsboy as agent.

In the sentence fragment below, from the same brief as the first sentence, the writer again lost his way in his own verbiage, this time failing to write a complete sentence:

(2) In summary, while one who engages a private contractor to perform a job for him will not become liable for the negligence of the independent contractor except by interfering or meddling with the job to the extent of assuming the detailed direction of it and thus becoming the master of the independent contractor's employer or by committing some act of negligence for which the prime employer would be liable, irrespective of the employer-independent contractor relationship.

Despite its length and complexity (or perhaps because of these) this example is a sentence fragment, a dependent clause introduced by the word "while." Omit "while," and you have a complete sentence, though hardly a clear one. Sort out the ideas, state them one at a time, provide words indicating causality and qualification, and the ideas become clear:

- Generally one who engages a private contractor to perform a job for him is not liable for the negligence of that contractor.

- However, one who engages a private contractor is considered the master of the independent contractor if (a) he interferes with the private contractor's work, to the extent of assuming the detailed direction of it, or (b) he commits some negligent act for which the prime employer would be liable.

Because there is no way to know whether "the employer-independent contractor relationship" mentioned in the final clause of the cited sentence refers to that between the prime contractor and his independent contractor or that between the employer of the private contractor and the private contractor, I have omitted this clause. The device of "listing" (above seen in (a) and (b)) is handy for sorting out ideas that would otherwise be confusing.

One more example, this from a legal textbook. (The first sentence of the example is included only to set the stage for the second):

Consider Lynch v. Household Finance, ante p. 229, in which a unanimous court ruled that a $10,000.00 minimum jurisdictional amount should not be imposed in § 1983 claims for property. Does the requirement that a federal district court judge spend time on a property claim which would, at best, be a state small claims court matter if state-action-conferred federal jurisdiction were not implicated, comport with

Rostow's suggestion that the Supreme Court should "avoid wasting its ammunition in petty quarrels"? [21]

Two points should be made about this example:

(1) The subject ("requirement") is too far from the verb ("comport"). To make it easy for the reader to follow your ideas, be sure that your subject and verb are close together, not separated by various explanations and qualifications.

(2) Avoid like the plague "adjective buildup," which occurs in this sentence in the phrase "state-action-conferred federal jurisdiction." [22] The four modifiers placed before the noun "jurisdiction" create almost complete obfuscation. Separate modifiers and place them in their own clauses, for example, "jurisdiction conferred upon the federal courts by state action." The succinctness obtained in the sample sentence should never be obtained at the expense of clarity in legal writing.

The Appendix contains cumbersome sentences taken from the writing of law students and lawyers. Practice re-casting to improve your own writing. Follow these rules:

- Say only one thing at a time; separate your ideas and place them in order;

- Begin at the beginning, not *in media res* as epic writers do; Start with the subject and put the verb as close to it as possible.

- Delete unnecessary "it" and "this" clauses; if you use them, be sure they refer to a clearly identifiable nearby noun.[23]

- To present a number of ideas, list them in order, stated parallelly.[24]

- When you have finished, be sure you have made clear "who" did "what" to "whom."

B. PITFALLS TO AVOID

1. Jargon

Errors in the use of the language of the law by law students occasion much merriment in the faculty lounge, but there is nothing funny about the damage such mistakes do to law students' grades. Avoidance of bloopers like "state statues," "malice aforesight," and the "law of imminent domain"—all recently seen in student briefs—is therefore well worth the effort it takes.

21. R. Aldisert, *The Judicial Process*, 1976, p. 513.

22. A letter to the *Federal Register* calls this kind of writing "verbal garbage" whose drafters are paid by "the volume of their verbiage." Cited in Block, "What Did You Mean? What Did You Say?" *Journal of Legal Education*, Vol. 28, 1977, p. 547.

23. See more in "Vague Referents," Chapter Two, B(5).

24. See more in "Use Parallelism," Chapter Two, A(3).

A general effect of either carelessness or ineptness is created also by abbreviating legal language. For example,

(1) A recent Pennsylvania case held . . . should be redrafted to read:

The court in a recent Pennsylvania case held . . . or

The holding in a recent Pennsylvania case was . . . or

In a recent Pennsylvania case the court decided . . .

(2) Plaintiff has a cause of battery . . . should be redrafted to read:

Plaintiff has a cause of action in battery . . . or

Plaintiff has a claim in battery . . .

(3) The issue before the court is that . . . should be redrafted to read:

The issue before the court is whether . . . .

(Issues are not facts, but questions to be considered before a decision can be made.)

(4) The defendant would raise consent as a defense . . . should be redrafted to read:

The defendant could argue that the plaintiff had consented . . . .

Archaic legal formulas are often tautological; they also give your writing a musty effect, like that of the formbooks from which they were probably taken. Such language has survived partly because of the legal profession's desire to make legal matters seem arcane and complex, comprehensible only by an "ordained priesthood." Medieval legal jargon is anachronous in today's world, and the enactment of "plain English" laws and the deletion by some large corporations of archiac, repetitious phrases from contracts may expedite the departure of legal tautology. To delete it from your own writing, examine every phrase you have joined with "and." Whenever the words on either side of "and" mean the same thing, or whenever one of the two words includes the meaning of the other (as in "first and foremost"), delete one. This rule also applies to words in a series.

For:	Substitute:
Last Will and Testament	Will
Null, void, and of no further effect	Null (or void)
Force and effect	Force (or effect)
Suffer and permit	Permit [25]
Kind or character	Kind
Full and complete	Full (or complete)
Clear and free	Clear (or free)

The list is far from complete. For more, and a discussion of the derivation of legal archaisms, see Mellinkoff, *The Language of the Law* (1963). Legal tautology, for example the phrase, "in any way, shape, manner or form

---

25. In Medieval English when "suffer" came into the language, it meant "permit." Now that "suffer" has come to mean "feel pain," it is needlessly confusing in this phrase.

. . ." and other such constructions, are intended to be reassuring. But legal redundancies more often appear insincere and pompous. It is good sense as well as good English to avoid them.

2. The Long Wind-Up

The long wind-up ought to be avoided for several reasons:

- It adds to verbiage, the foe of brevity.
- It is often redundant.
- It diminishes force and directness by filling the important first part of the sentence with language containing little or no content.

Lawyers love long wind-ups, perhaps because they provide time for thinking and are therefore valuable in extemporaneous argument. But that is no excuse to retain them in writing; they should be carefully edited out. Some examples of long wind-ups are:

- It is important to note that . . .
- I cannot fail to point out that . . .
- I intend to discuss . . .
- I should like to stress that . . .
- There can be no question but that . . .

Each of these preliminary postponers is intended to introduce important information, but the way to emphasize important information is to place it in a prominent part of your sentence (the beginning), instead of dumping it into the unimportant middle of the sentence.[26] If you simply must include wind-ups, put *them* into the middle of the sentence instead of at the beginning, as in the following sentence:

- Although the insanity plea has been available in Anglo-Saxon law for centuries, it is important to note that the plea is now being utilized more widely than ever before.

In the above sentence, the "wind-up" occupies the position of unimportance it deserves.

A favorite wind-up is "it is a true fact that." This expression should always be edited out because it is guaranteed to raise the hackles of persons sensitive to good usage. (A fact is something known with certainty, and is therefore, by definition, "true.") Other such combinations that should be deleted are:

- Due to the fact that . . . [27]
- It is due to the fact that . . .
- It is a well-known fact that . . .
- I might call your attention to the fact that . . .

---

26. For a discussion of this point, see Chapter Two, Section A(1).

27. Professor William Strunk (*The Elements of Style*, 1916) particularly detested "the fact that" and said it should be "revised out of every sentence." (Introduction, xiv).

- The fact that the defendant was negligent . . .
- The fact that this contention ignores is that . . .
- The unquestionable fact is that . . .

Each of the wind-up phrases in the left-hand column can be replaced by the single word in the right-hand column.

For:	**Substitute:**
The question as to wheth-er . . .	Whether . . .
There is no doubt but that . . .	Doubtless . . .
He is a person who . . .	He . . .
In a reckless manner . . .	Recklessly . . .
This is a subject that . . .	This . . .
For the purpose of . . .	For . . .
In the same way as . . .	Like . . .
Until such time as . . .	Until . . .
]During the time that . . .	While . . .

The following wind-ups can be shortened:

For:	**Substitute:**
It is not necessary for you to . . .	You need not . . .
It has been held by most courts that . . .	Most courts have held . . .
There are many points still to be considered . . .	Many points still need considera-tion . . .
There are a few states that have rejected . . .	A few states have rejected . . .

3. Metaphor-osis [28]

As damaging to your writing as jargon and the long wind-up are two other forms of language misuse: "metaphor-osis," and impossible comparisons.

Members of the legal profession seem more susceptible than their counter-parts in the general population to metaphor-osis, the tendency to mix or man-gle metaphors. The name is new, but the inclination is as old as language and as current as today's television interview. Among those who suffer from the malady is Hodding Carter, III, former state department spokesman, who com-mented about efforts to rescue Americans held hostage in Iran, "We are not going to play this game with all the cards face up on the deck." (He thus combined poker and ship metaphors, using the word "deck" as glue.)

28. This name was coined, to my best knowledge, by *Time* magazine, De-cember 17, 1979, p. 106, in an article dealing with the subject.

When lawyers become involved in political campaigns, mixed metaphors abound. One senator combined the images of poker and basketball when talking about the Massachusetts Presidential primary: "It's a new ballgame, and we're playing with a full deck." During the 1976 campaign, then-President Ford's campaign manager used an unfortunate metaphor in response to a suggestion that his political strategy be modified after a primary defeat: "I am not about to rearrange the deck chairs on the Titanic." (His statement called forth an image of President Ford's campaign as a sinking ship—and proved prophetic.)

The effect of an action may be ruined if the language that accompanies it destroys the intended image. When President Ford signed a bill establishing the Cuyahoga Valley Recreational Area, he hoped to endear himself to conservationists. However, he accompanied his action with the words, "This action paves the way for the preservation of thousands of acres of wilderness." The word "paves" evoked memories of his administration's huge expenditures for highway construction, thus diminishing the effect of the signing ceremony.

Incongruous images unintentionally juxtaposed are not always damaging, but are often comic, and should be avoided for that reason alone—if no humor is intended, as when Donald Nixon lamented, "People are using Watergate as a political football to bury my brother," and a Florida Comptroller-General commented that the record of a case spoke "louder than any smoke screen."

Unfortunately there is no vaccine to prevent metaphor-osis, but a few precautions should help to avoid the disease:

- Never use trite metaphors and indulge only sparingly in fresh ones.

- Delete from your writing all mixed metaphors that may have crept into your first draft.

- Be certain that those metaphors that remain illuminate rather than detract from your message.

4. Impossible Comparisons

Impossible comparisons occur more frequently in writing than mixed metaphors, probably because they are less noticeable. In the impossible comparison below, New York's laws are being compared to Connecticut—not to Connecticut's laws, as is intended:

(1) The laws of New York, unlike Connecticut, provide for restitution as an alternative to prison for first offenders.

The comparison can be made valid in either of two ways:

- New York's laws, unlike Connecticut's, provide for restitution as an alternative to prison for first offenders.

- The laws of New York, unlike those of Connecticut, provide for restitution as an alternative to prison for first offenders.

Here are some other examples from actual writing:

(2) The first public hearing on whether General Hospital should switch from control by the county to a non-profit corporation will be held on March 31.

(3) Like the over-eager young graduate student, the planner's dilemma is what to keep the nuclear reactor in.

In (2) county control is improperly compared to a non-profit corporation. In (3) a dilemma is compare to a graduate student. Here are revisions that convey the intended information:

(2) The first public hearing on whether the county should relinquish control of General Hospital preliminary to its becoming a non-profit corporation will be held on March 31.

(3) The planner's dilemma is like that of an over-eager young graduate student who wonders what to keep the nuclear reactor in.

The inability to make fine distinctions in language indicates an inability to make such distinctions in thinking. Some people maintain that language sloppiness is at the root of most inefficient behavior:

> To think, we must devise connected chains of predications, which, in turn, require fluency of language. Those who are fluent in no language just don't have the means for thinking about things. They may remember and recite whatever predications experience provides them, but they cannot manipulate them and derive new ones. Mostly therefore, they will think and do those things that the world suggests they think and do.[29]

Hyperbole is in evidence here. Nevertheless there is an obvious lesson for would-be lawyers: in a profession dependent upon the ability to think logically, practitioners must avoid the very appearance of mental confusion that sloppy language conveys. The Appendix provides some sentences, taken from actual writing, that contain awkward metaphors and impossible comparisons. These sentences should provide practice to help you avoid this kind of sloppy writing.

5. Vague Referents

The small, unimportant-looking pronoun "it" along with its companions "this" and "which," should refer to closely-adjacent antecedent nouns. If their antecedents are too far away, if they refer to some nebulous concept not actually mentioned in the sentence, or if they have no antecedent at all, "it," "this," and "which" become vague referents. Vague referents cause confusion in all

---

29. Mitchell, *Less Than Words Can Say*, (1979), pages 157–158, and passim.

kinds of writing, but they are dangerous in legal writing where precision is so important. These sentences were taken from law students' writing:

(1) Since defendants were playing a practical joke on the plaintiff, it shows intent on their part.

What shows intent? That is, what does the referent "it" refer to? The writer is aware that one of the elements of battery is "intent" and wants to say that the playing of the practical joke by the defendants indicates their intention to carry out the battery. In his sentence structure, however, the noun phrase that "it" refers to is "practical joke," and practical jokes cannot possess intent. The sentence needs recasting:

- The defendants showed intent when they decided to play a practical joke on the plaintiff.

(2) If one wishes to be free of liability, it must be clearly stated.

The writer intends "it" to refer back to "wish," but "wishes" here is a verb, not a noun, so the reference is unclear. The rewrite clarifies the meaning:

- In order to be free of liability, one must clearly disclaim it.

(3) The court held that since the petitioner believed he would be repaid, this was enough to prove a bona fide relationship.

Again, "this" refers back to a non-existent noun ("belief"). A re-write provides the noun and makes the vague referent unnecessary:

- The court held that the petitioner's belief that he would be repaid was enough to prove a bona fide relationship.

(4) The loss of sleep suffered by the plaintiff's daughter was caused by the accusations of the defendant, and this adds support to the plaintiff's claim of intentional infliction of emotional distress. (This sentence was part of a response to Writing Problem V, on pp. 154–155.)

What adds support? "This" refers to nothing in particular. The sentence is grammatically improved by adding "fact" after "this," avoiding the vague referent but doing nothing to reduce the vagueness itself. In order to get rid of the vagueness, the idea of causality needs to be added: [30]

- Because the accusations of the defendant caused the plaintiff's daughter loss of sleep, the daughter has a claim against the defendant for the intentional infliction of emotional distress.

In the re-write, it is clearly the daughter whose claim is validated by her loss of sleep. In the original sentence, the erroneous impression is that the mother's claim is based upon her daugher's sleeplessness. The claim of the daughter is given emphasis by placement, in the re-write, at the end of the sentence in the main clause, while the less important information is in a subordinate clause at the beginning of the sentence. If the accusations of the defendant were the most important information, the sentence positions would be reversed.[31]

---

30. Causality is discussed in Chapter Two, Section A(4).

31. More on this subject in Chapter Two, Section A(1).

One more illustration; the vague referent "which" is the culprit:

(5) In the Senate debate there are a number of good reasons for the passage of the Equal Rights Amendment, which should be considered.

As the sentence is cast, the antecedent of "which," is "Equal Rights Amendment." But the intended referent is "reasons." Recast, the sentence becomes clear:

- In the Senate debate about the Equal Rights Amendment, a number of good reasons for its passage should be considered.[32]

The Appendix provides more sentences containing vague referents. To correct the sentences, look for the noun or pronoun to which "it," "which," and "this" refer. If the antecedent is too far away, too vague, or non-existent, recast the sentence to provide an appropriate noun phrase antecedent closely adjacent to the referent. Or recast the sentence to delete "it," "which," and "this."

6. Expletives

Expletives are of two kinds. Some are profane or obscene exclamations; others are the kind to be discussed in this section, grammatical expletives. In English, grammatical expletives have virtually no meaning; they are added to the sentence merely to fulfill a grammatical requirement, i.e., to occupy the "subject" slot. For example, take the two following sentences:

- There is no reason to delay.
- It is easy to draft pleadings.

The expletives "there" and "it" add no meaning to the sentences in which they appear; they merely fill the subject slot, the true subject of the sentence being "reason" in the first sentence and "draft pleadings" in the second sentence. As in the sentences above, when the grammatical subject is not important, you can use the expletive construction to add variety to your writing.

But, perhaps because the expletive construction is more portentous and more mouth-filling, bureaucrats, lawyers, and therefore law students, overuse it. What is wrong with the expletive construction is that when the subject is important, the expletive either delays the subject, or, worse, eliminates it altogether, making the writing both vague and wordy. Notice how in each of the following sentences, eliminating the expletive construction clarifies the writer's meaning and reduces the number of words:

(1) There is a cause of action on behalf of the passenger, who suffered from the reckless conduct of the driver.

   Rewrite: The passenger, who suffered from the reckless conduct of the driver, has a cause of action.

(2) There is a possibility that the accused man could plead intoxication as a defense, if intent and knowledge are necessary elements of the crime.[33]

---

32. For a discussion of "there are," see the following section.

33. Since "could" indicates possibility, "it is possible" is redundant.

Rewrite: If intent and knowledge are necessary elements of the crime, the accused man could plead intoxication as a defense.

(3) It was indicated in *Zell* that there is almost universal acceptance of extrinsic parol evidence.

Rewrite: *Zell* indicates almost universal acceptance of extrinsic parol evidence.

7. Problem Words

a. Confusing Pairs

Certain word-pairs perplex even well-educated people. Most confusing are the look-alikes that have different meanings. Here are some:

- affect/effect

These two words are never interchangeable. The verb "affect" means "influence," "change," or "modify." "You can *affect* decision-making with your vote." This meaning of "affect" is its most frequent, but it also means "pretend" or "imitate"; you might *affect* uninterest in something in which you are actually very much interested.

The verb "effect" means "bring about," or "accomplish": "Legislation is designed to *effect* an end." Because of the phrase, "to effect a change," (i.e., to bring about a change), "effect" and "affect" are often confused. You can *effect* a change in your usage and *affect* your writing style by distinguishing between these words.

As nouns, this pair of words is not nearly as troublesome. Only "effect" is generally used as a noun: The *effect* of inflation is high prices. "Affect" is used as a noun only in the field of psychology, where it means "feeling" as distinguished from "cognition," "thought," or "action."

- principal/principle

Because as lawyers you will be using both of these words often, you should take care to distinguish between them. "Principles" are basic truths, rules or assumptions. Your legal arguments will often be based upon legal rules, also called theories or *principles*. "Principle" is never an adjective.

"Principal" can be either a noun or an adjective. As a noun it refers to the individual who is first in importance, rank, or degree. Thus schools employ principals and vice-principals. In legal usage, "principal," as a noun, means one who empowers another to act as his representative, or one who has prime obligation in a contract, or one who commits or is an accomplice in a crime. As an adjective, "principal" means "chief," or "first" or "of highest rank," as in "The Constitution is the *principal* defense of our rights."

- lie/lay

The discriminating writer maintains the distinction between these two words. The two words have become a shibboleth for educated usage. "Lay," the word more universally employed, is properly a transitive verb, which means that it must be followed by a noun as object. Thus you *lay* a book on the table, *lay* down a law, and *lay* bricks to make a wall. In all these phrases "lay" means "put," "place" or "set forth." ("Lay" has many other related meanings, for which consult your dictionary, but they all have in common some sort of placement, as in "lay a wager.")

"Lie" is an intransitive verb; that is, it does not take an object-noun. You *lie* on the bed, or you *lie* down, "lie" meaning, in general usage, "recline." In legal usage, it adds another meaning, "to be admissible," as in "an action *lies* in torts." (The third meaning of "lie" is one that confuses no one: "tell an untruth.")

The problem with "lie" and "lay" is that the past tense of "lie" is identical with the present tense of "lay." Although last night I *lay* on my bed, today I *lay* the books on my desk. The complete paradigm for each verb is:

> lay   laid   laid
> lie   lay   lain

- in/into

These prepositions are not interchangeable; "in" refers to a position, condition, or location, and "into" refers to a change of condition that indicates movement to another location. A person is sitting *in* a room, but when she leaves the room and enters another, she goes *into* another room. Both "in" and "into" have numerous other meanings (for which consult your dictionary), but the only confusion caused by the words is in this small but important distinction.

- bring/take

Although these words are not look-alikes, they are often mistakenly interchanged. They are distinguishable by the orientation of the speaker. Something is *brought* to the person speaking or to his residence (when he is there) or to a place identified with him (when he is there). Thus you, as speaker, would tell someone to *bring* his class notes to you when he comes to your home or to *bring* them to your home tonight, when you are there. But if you are at the law school you would tell him to *take* the notes to your home or to *take* them to another place. The distinction is like that between "come" and "go." (*Come* to me; *go* anywhere else.)

b. Words With More Than One Meaning

Some words, through years of use, have come to signify two different (sometimes opposite) meanings. Be sure that in your writing the context clearly denotes the meaning you intend. For example:

- oversight: can mean "unintentional error" or "intentional watchful supervision."

  The Brief was filed late due to an *oversight* on the attorney's part.

  (That is, the attorney made an error.)

The Foreign Relations Committee has *oversight* over its subcommittee's proceedings.

(That is, it has authority over its subcommittee's proceedings.)

- effectively: can mean either "well" or "actually."

The responsibility was *effectively* discharged.

(That is, it was carried out well or efficiently.)

The responsibility was *effectively* discharged.

(That is, it was actually carried out or was, in effect, carried out.)

- sanction: can mean "approval" or "penalty."

The *sanction* of violence should never be government policy.

(That is, government should never approve violence.)

Official *sanctions* are being considered against Argentina.

(That is, coercive measures are being considered.)

- presently: can mean "soon" or "right now."

I will join the group *presently*.

(That is, I will be there soon.)

I am *presently* without an apartment.

(That is, I am without one now.)

- cite: can mean "commend," "point out," or "summon before a court of law."

He was *cited* for his bravery.

(That is, he was commended for bravery.)

He was *cited* as a typical law student.

(That is, he was pointed out as typical.)

He was *cited* for a traffic violation.

(That is, he was summoned before a law court.)

- ultimately: can mean "at the end" or "at the beginning."

She *ultimately* reached her goal.

(That is, she finally got there.)

The two words are *ultimately* cognates.

(That is, they had the same ancestor.)

- address: can mean "call attention to" or "attempt to answer."

She *addressed* the question to the Chairperson.

(That is, she asked the Chairperson to supply an answer.)

She *addressed* the problem of unemployment.

(That is, she attempted to provide a solution to the problem.)

- may: can indicate either *permission* or *possibility*.[34]

  Students *may* adhere to the dress code.

  (That is, they are permitted to do so.)

  Students *may* adhere to the dress code.

  (That is, it is possible that they will.)

Other words, not listed here, are perhaps candidates for addition to this list, because English usage is constantly in flux, with words adding and changing meanings constantly. In the list above, the earliest meaning appears first.

c. Vague and Vogue Words

No living language can perfectly communicate because in no living language does each word contain only one meaning that is precise and understood by all. The problem of inherent inexactness in language is compounded, however, when people use language carelessly and unthinkingly. While this tendency is not confined to members of the legal profession, it is unfortunately common among them. Some of these words are:

- where

This formerly meaningful adverb has been rendered hopelessly vague by overuse. In its precise sense, "where" indicates only "place." As Weihofen says, one can speak of "states where the rule is followed," but "cases where the rule is followed" should be changed to "cases in which the rule is followed" or "cases that follow the rule." [35] In the following examples "where" is used as a catch-all, to mean "when," "if," "in which," and "that." The sentences are taken from actual legal writing.

(1) False imprisonment occurs where one party acts in a manner intending to confine another within fixed boundaries, succeeds in so doing, and the confined party is aware of his confinement.

(2) Where a person's house is searched without a search warrant, he has a cause of action against the officer who conducted the search.

(3) The defendant had reason to believe his life was in danger in a fight where the plaintiff had a knife.

(4) The defendant read in the newspaper where another man had been arrested for the robbery.

For greater precision, these sentences should be rewritten:

(5) False imprisonment occurs when one party acts intending to confine another within fixed boundaries, succeeds in so doing, and the confined party is aware of his confinement.

(6) If a person's house is searched without a search warrant, he has a cause of action against the police officer who conducted the search.

---

34. The meaning of "may" is an issue in In re Advisory Opinion of the Governor Civil Rights, S.Ct. of Fla., 306 So.2d 529, 531 (1975).

35. H. Weihofen, *Legal Writing Style*, 2d edition, 1979, p. 40.

(7) The defendant had reason to believe his life was in danger in a fight in which the plaintiff had a knife. (Better, show causality: The defendant had reason to believe his life was in danger in his fight with the plaintiff because the plaintiff had a knife.)

(8) The defendant read in the newspaper that another man had been arrested for the robbery.

Another overused favorite of lawyers is "as to," so typical of law jargon that it has been dubbed "the lawyerly as-to." Lawyers use "as to" as they use "where," to avoid thinking. They toss it indiscriminately into sentences in which it may mean "concerning," "of," "about," or sometimes (as in the phrase "as to whether") nothing at all. When one word can mean so many things, it should be replaced by a more specific one. Consider the following, all from legal documents:

(1) The requirement as to billing is to be observed. (Here "as to" means "concerning.")

(2) We can only conjecture as to the reasons for the break-in. ("As to" means "about.")

(3) There is no problem as to jurisdiction or as to whether to take this case. (The first "as to" means "of"; the second can be omitted: There is no problem of jurisdiction or whether to take this case.)

What applies to "where" and "as to" applies generally. Always replace vague words with specific ones. Be selective: never reach automatically for a term and use it without thinking what it means. For example, the verb "affects" should be replaced by one that says something exact: use "improves," or "worsens," or whatever word is most descriptive. Instead of the sensory "feel," use the more cerebral "think" or "believe." For "goes to," "look to" and "look at," all over-used and vague, substitute more precise language. A recent vogue verb, "pursue," which once meant "follow," is now used so indiscriminately that it no longer means much of anything.[36] Its adverbial form, "pursuant," is rapidly approaching the same condition.

Finally, never use a word because it "sounds right." It only sounds right because it is widely used (perhaps incorrectly).[37]

d. Words With Special Legal Meanings

Law students and lawyers should be sensitive to everyday meanings of these words, as well as their legal meanings, if for no other reason than to explain the difference to their clients. Some of these words are:

---

36. Recently "go forward" has begun to replace "pursue" in bureaucratic jargon. Now all those politicians who formerly "pursued" are "going forward."

37. I asked some of my students, who were addicted to the use of "goes to," exactly what it meant in their usage. Not one could provide a precise definition.

- cure

The everyday meaning of this verb is "heal," as in, "Medicine *cures* illness." But the legal meaning may be "correct," as in "The court held that the trial proceedings *cured* defects in the pleadings."

- constructive

The layman understands this adjective to mean "helpful," as in, "The review of the performance contained *constructive* criticism." But the legal meaning is more likely "to be considered as," as in "constructive notice," "constructive admission," "constructive fraud," "constructive possession," and other legal terms.

- facially

This refers in common speech to a portion of the human anatomy, but the legal meaning may well be "that which appears on the face of the document, with no explanation." A "facial defect" is more likely to be an imperfection in a legal document than an anatomical defect, as in, "The statute is *facially* unconstitutional."

- lie

For the everyday versus the legal meaning of this verb, see p. 47.

- issue

In everyday usage, this is a transitive verb (i.e., it must be followed by a noun-object) meaning "distribute." ("The Administration issued a policy-statement.") But in legal use it is sometimes an intransitive verb (i.e., it is not followed by a noun-object), meaning "come forth," as in, "The writ *issues*."

- material

The layman uses this word most frequently as a noun, meaning "substance," as in "The dress was made of flimsy *material*." To the lawyer, the word is more often an adjective meaning, "of the essence," as in, "The testimony of the eyewitness was *material*." [38]

e. Words Denoting Useful Distinctions

This list is shrinking even as I write, for there is a "law" of linguistics that when two words mean approximately the same thing, either they acquire different meanings or one disappears from the language. In the list of words that follow, the words of each pair did acquire different meanings. But careless users ignored the distinctions in meaning, and inevitably one word of each pair will ultimately disappear from the language unless educated users maintain the distinction. Perhaps you can help save these words from extinction. Here they are:

- prevalent/widespread

"Prevalent" connotes the wide occurrence of something unpleasant. Malnutrition in underdeveloped countries is *prevalent*. For all other wide occur-

---

38. Many other words have special legal meanings (e.g., "licensee," "invitee," and "trespasser," but these are clearly defined in legal casebooks. The words above, however, are often used without explanation.

rence use "widespread": Marriage during college has become *widespread* in the last 20 years.

- healthy/healthful

Only animate beings are healthy (i.e., in a state of good health); something that is good for you is healthful. *Healthy* adults need the *healthful* qualities of milk.

- sensuous/sensual

"Sensuous" means "having qualities that appeal to the senses, often esthetic qualities." "Sensual" means "appealing to the sexual appetites." A garden of roses is *sensous;* a strip-tease act may be *sensual.* (You may insult your client if you choose the wrong adjective.)

- historic/historical

An event of importance in history is a (or "an") "historic event." "Historical" refers to anything concerned with history, as in "historical fiction."

- economic/economical

"Economic" is the broader of these words, meaning relating to material wealth. Thus, inflation is viewed as an *economic* disaster. "Economical" means "thrifty." "*Economical* people put away money for a rainy day." The noun "economy" embraces the meanings of both members of this pair, contributing to the confusion regarding the difference in meaning of the adjectives.

- famous/notorious

If you are famous, it is because you have done something you can be proud of. If you are notorious, you have done something dishonorable. In both cases, you become well-known as a result of your act. (If you are notorious, you may be infamous.) The distinction is similar to that of "widespread" and "prevalent," above.

- unique/unusual

"Unique" means "one of a kind." But news commentators and others have prefaced it with "rather," "very" and "most," thinking of it as an adjective meaning "unusual." Unless users change their ways, "unique" will completely lose its uniqueness.

- uninterested/disinterested

Alas, the first member of this pair is disappearing. Please join the battle to save it. When it is correctly used, if you are *uninterested* in something, you are indifferent to it, one way or another. If you are *disinterested,* you may well be concerned about it, but you are also impartial about it. Thus a *disinterested* observer may be counted upon to report what is going on, without bias; an *uninterested* person will probably not observe what is going on at all.

- farther/further

"Farther," properly used, means literal distance in time or space. Cincinnati is *farther* from New York than from Louisville. "Further" is used in all other senses, especially to indicate degree or figurative space or time.

"America goes *further* into debt each year." It is the first member of this pair that is in jeopardy.

- discrete/discreet

The first word refers to individual, distinct parts: Civil procedure includes a number of *discrete* steps. The second word refers to a respect for reserve: Attorneys should be *discreet* in their client relationships.

- persuade/convince

This distinction has been all but lost, and now only old fuddy-duddies maintain it. Still, it is worth knowing: "persuade" means to cause someone to do something by argument or plea. "He *persuaded* me to go." "Convince" means to bring to relief by argument or reason: "He *convinced* me of the need to go."

See the Appendix (Chapter Two, Section B(7)) for exercises to help you to choose appropriate words.

8. Shifts in Viewpoint

Viewpoint shifts are especially confusing because writers implicitly promise that when they state a subject or an object in a sentence, that subject and object are retained until a new subject and object are stated. When a writer instead begins to discuss a different subject or object without letting the reader know his intentions, the reader becomes hopelessly confused—or, worse, assumes that the original subject and object still apply. Here is an illustration, from the office of an attorney:

(1) Although zoning ordinances should furnish owners of historic properties some relief from the financial burden of maintaining their property for public benefit, decline in market value value and diminished expectations are not sufficient injuries to constitute a taking of property without just compensation.

The sentence poses no problem until the phrase "diminished expectations" appears and the reader wonders *whose* diminished expectations about *what.* The writer does not say. Similarly, a little farther on, the phrase "a taking of property" has no stated subject; we wonder who took it and from whom and "without just compensation" to whom?

There is no need to be so cryptic; the writer only needs to indicate his shift in point of view:

- Zoning ordinances should furnish owners of historic properties some relief from the financial burden of maintaining their property for public benefit. However, the injury to the property owners due to a decline in the market value of their property or diminished expectation of income from their property is not considered sufficient to constitute a taking of private property by the state without compensation.

In the next illustration, only the seller is named; yet the point of view shifts to the buyer in the middle of the statement, and the reader is unable to tell from the context who is referred to in the final part of the statement:

(2) Consequential damages resulting from the seller's breach include (a) any loss resulting from general or particular requirements and needs of which the seller at the time of contracting had reason to know and which could not reasonably be prevented by cover or otherwise.[39]

Another illustration of unannounced viewpoint shift:

(3) In order to collect exemplary damages [who collects?] the conduct causing the injury [whose conduct?] must be wanton, malicious, or grossly negligent as to show heedless or willful disregard for the rights and safety of others.

A re-write, containing the necessary guideposts so that the reader can tell who did what to whom:

- In order for the victim of an injury to collect exemplary damages, the conduct of the person who caused the injury must have been so wanton, malicious, or grossly negligent as to show heedless or willful disregard for the rights and safety of others.

The addition of "so" before the phrase "wanton, malicious, or grossly negligent" is necessary to indicate the idea of "extent" that is important to the legal principle.

And, finally, from a student's paper:

(4) Defendant is guilty of driving recklessly, and with no opportunity to avoid the collision, the accident occurred.

A number of re-writes are possible which would improve this mangled sentence. Here are a few:

- By driving in such a manner that victim had no opportunity to avoid the collision, defendant is guilty of reckless driving and causing an accident.

- Defendant is guilty of driving recklessly and causing an accident because it was impossible for the victim to avoid the collision.

- Defendant's reckless driving caused the accident, for he made avoidance of it impossible for the victim.

- The victim had no opportunity to avoid the collision; defendant is therefore guilty of reckless driving to cause an accident.

You can probably think of other constructions to prevent the unannounced viewpoint shift in example (4). For practice, additional sentences are provided in the Appendix, Chapter Two, Section B(8).

9. The Ambiguous Negative

It is almost a truism that affirmative (positive) statements are more forceful and direct than negative ones. Negative statements do not assert anything; they merely deny. Therefore, when possible, even statements with negative

---

39. *Uniform Commercial Code,* § 2–715(2)(a). Note that the passive construction in the final clause omits the "by . . ." information, which would have denoted the subject and clarified the matter. For discussion of passive voice, see Chapter Two, Section A(6).

import should be phrased affirmatively. Note the greater forcefulness of the second statement in each of the following pairs:

(1) He did not carry out his responsibility.

He abrogated his responsibility.

(2) He did not fulfill his duty.

He failed in his duty.

(3) He did not carry out his part of the contract.

He breached the contract.

(4) Smoking in public areas is not permitted.

Smoking in public areas is prohibited. Or (still more forceful):

No smoking in public areas.

Negative statements are not only less forceful. They also often create an unintended ambiguity. Here are some actual examples taken from newspaper accounts. In each pair of possible meanings, "b" is the intended one:

(5) Billboards are not appearing along city streets due to loopholes in the law, as a city commissioner reported to the press.

Possible meanings:

     a. Loopholes in the billboard ordinance prevent billboards from appearing in the city streets, and a city commissioner reports this fact.

     b. The absence of billboards in city streets is due, not to loopholes in the ordinance, but to some other factor, and the city commissioner's report to the press is therefore inaccurate.

(6) In Pyle v. Pyle the Florida Supreme Court held that the lower court had abused its discretion by not acting on a petition purporting a marriage to be broken without considering all the facts.

     a. . . . all the facts of the petition.

     b. . . . all the facts regarding the breakup of the marriage.

(7) A's breach of duty was not established because A injured B.

     a. A's breach of duty was not established, for the reason stated.

     b. A's breach of duty was not established, but not for the reason given, but for some other reason.

Another problem with the negative construction is that it conveys not even one meaning very well. An illustration is § 5.01(2) of the Model Penal Code; an excerpt reads:

Without negativing the sufficiency of other conduct, the following, if strongly corroborative of the actor's criminal purpose, shall not be held insufficient as a matter of law . . .

Three negatives are crammed into this short passage. With the negatives removed, the statement becomes more clear:

> Although other conduct may also suffice, the following conduct, if it strongly corroborates the actor's criminal purpose, shall be held sufficient as a matter of law . . .

No discussion of negative ambiguity is complete without mention of that seemingless innocuous word "all." Beware when you use it with the negative, because the meaning you create may not be the meaning you intend. An illustration is the following announcement from the office of a dean:

> On Tuesday, June 8, all regularly scheduled courses will not meet.

What the dean meant was:

> On Tuesday, June, 8, no regularly scheduled classes will meet.

But what he *said* was that on June 8, some regularly scheduled classes would meet and some would not, just as

> "All blondes do not have blue eyes" means that some do, and

> "All web-footed animals are not birds" means that some are.

But after eliminating all unintentional ambiguity from your writing, you may want to insert some intentional ambiguity.[40] There will be times when you want to hedge, to be less than exact. The negative construction is a handy one to use on these occasions. You may wish to say "not unlawful" instead of "lawful," "not unwilling" instead of "willing," and "not unimportant" instead of "important."

Someone once defined a lady as a woman who never insulted anyone without intending to. Similarly, you should never select an ambiguous negative unless you intend to.

10. "Elegant Variation" and "Legerdemain With Two Senses"

These somewhat elaborate names were given to two opposite tendencies by a well-known grammarian, who recognized them as faults in his students' writing.[41] Both are even more damaging to legal writing than to ordinary writing. Elegant variation is the use of two or more different words to refer to the same thing. In ordinary writing, the habit may mislead or confuse the reader, but this same confusion may be fatal in a legal document. Here is elegant variation in an excerpt from an answer to the problem on page 157:

> (1) If the hunter had killed the animal and left it where the beast was slain
> . . .

In this sentence there is only one creature referred to, but the writer uses two words to do so ("animal" and "beast"). The reader looking for fine distinc-

---

40. For more on this subject, see Block, "A Fortunate Confusion," *Colorado Quarterly* Vol. XXIII, No. 4, Spring 1975.

41. H. M. Fowler, 1858–1933, whose *Modern English Usage*, has been a standard reference since its publication in 1926.

tions may assume that there is a good reason for the distinction in terminology. Here is another example:

(2) Students with writing deficiencies are required to take a course in basic writing prior to entering the regular legal writing program. After satisfactorily completing the basic program, they will continue in the regular writing course.

The "basic" course is first called a "course," and then a "program"; the "regular" course is first called a "program," then a "course." All this confusion can be avoided by assigning one name to each and referring to it throughout with that name.

(3) There are many possibilities for liability arising from this incident, but it does not appear that any of the three will succeed.

The writer employs elegant variation and confuses his reader because the reader assumes that "three" and "many" refer to different ideas, when in fact they are intended to be synonymous. He should have written:

There are three possibilities for liability arising from this incident, but it does not appear that any of the three will succeed.

So the rule should be: choose clarity over elegance. Use the same word to refer to the same thing each time you mention it.

"Legerdemain with two senses" is the writing fault opposite to "elegant variation." It is so-called because it involves a sort of rhetorical sleight-of-hand, the writer using the same word to mean two different things.[42] For example:

In this case, the issue is different from that in the case of Smith v. Jones.

The reader assumes that the two "case's" are synonymous, but he is wrong. The first "case" means "situation," (as in "in this situation") and the second "case" refers to a specific legal suit. Only momentary confusion will result from this language because the context soon makes evident that only one legal case is being discussed. Confusion does sometimes result, however, as in the well-known federal circuit court decision of United States v. Brawner, which contains a suggested jury instruction in which the word "responsible" is used twice with two different meanings:

[A] defendant is not responsible if at the time of his unlawful conduct his mental or emotional processes or behavior controls were impaired to such an extent that he cannot be held responsible for his act.[43]

Here, the first "responsible" means "able to discharge one's obligations," and the second, "accountable for one's actions." This proposed jury instruction was rejected by the majority of the drafters of the Model Penal Code, so juries are not being perplexed by it. Other words with legal meanings are

---

42. Another name for this fault is "ultraquistic subterfuge," an even more exotic term apparently coined by linguists Ogden and Richards.

43. 471 F.2d 969 (1972).

subject to two meanings; for example, "knowledge" may mean "specific information about something" or "general understanding."

The dual meaning of some legal terms has not escaped the attention of attorneys, some of whom have exploited it. For example, the attorney of a physician charged with procuring an abortion for a female patient, argued that the physician was protected by the Statute of Frauds, which states that no one shold be held for the debt, default or "miscarriage of another" unless evidenced by a memorandum in writing.[44] Phrases like "constructive fraud" (which means "innocent misrepresentation") lend themselves to exploitation by a devious attorney who might use the unsavory connotation of "fraud" to color an innocuous term.[45]

The Appendix for Chapter Two, Section B(10) contains sentences that can be improved by eliminating elegant variation and legerdemain with two meanings.

44. Cited in Chafee, "The Disorderly Conduct of Words," 41 Col.L.Rev. 381, 387 (1941).

45. *Id.*

CHAPTER THREE

Organization

A. THE OUTLINE

1. Preparing the Outline

As you have seen, the most important characteristic of legal writing is communication. To communicate what you intend to write is the reason you are careful to select correct grammar and punctuation, exact language, and appropriate sentence construction. But unless your writing is well-organized, your ideas may not be understood or appreciated, and your writing will fail in its purpose.

This chapter, therefore, deals with the organization of your legal paper. Because a good outline is basic to good organization, the chapter begins with the outline. An outline forces you to put your random thoughts in good marching order; once created, your outline is the skeleton of your paper, revealing to you what you may have forgotten to include, what you may have said twice, and where your ideas overlap. And, like a skeleton, the outline provides support for your writing, permitting the sentences and paragraphs to move along smoothly and effectively.

Fortunately, outlines for much legal writing follow a fairly standard formula. Therefore you probably can use the formula provided below to prepare your own outline, for in legal writing you are expected to be creative in ideas, not in format. Because your outline is a starting point and a guide, not an inflexible mold, you should prepare it before you have put anything down on paper, even before you have done much research on your subject. It can later be modified to suit your needs. The outline can be considered the first stage in the three-stage procedure for successful legal writing: pre-writing, writing, and re-writing.

Sample Outline [1]

I. Introduction

    A. Why you chose this subject

    B. What you intend to do with this subject

II. History

    A. The genesis of your subject

    B. The changes that have occurred during its development

    C. Why it has developed into its present state

---

1. This outline can be used for many legal essays. Outlines appropriate for answering examination questions are discussed in Chapter Five, Section A.

III. Status quo

    A. Its advantages

    B. Its defects

    C. Why it cannot (should not) continue

IV. Changes suggested (attempted) by others

    A. Advantages

    B. Defects

V. Your ideas for change

    A. Advantages

    B. Defects

VI. Conclusion

    A. Predictions

    B. Summary of ideas presented in paper

An outline like this is a skeleton that supports your writing. Unlike a skeleton, however, it can easily change its form. As you do your research and consider further the way you want to develop your subject, you can expand or otherwise modify the outline to include new ideas. You can use your outline to organize your research and use your research to re-organize and expand your outline.

The penalty for attempting to write a paper without an outline can be severe: you may have to re-write the entire paper, when on reading the first draft, you discover that it is hopelessly unorganized. The reward of outlining is that, once you have checked your outline to make sure the topics are in logical order, you can write the paper from the outline, simply adding the necessary transition between paragraphs.

2. Writing From the Outline

There are several ways to accumulate the data with which to flesh out your outline and write your paper. In "olden" days, before photocopiers, in order to gather information, writers laboriously covered large numbers of index cards with voluminous notes, indicating at the top of each index card where in the outline the notes on that particular card should go. Care had to be taken to copy verbatim whatever quotations might be used and to summarize carefully all of the other ideas succinctly enough to fit on the limited size of the index card. Furthermore, the source of all material had to be meticulously documented so that the writer could return to it for verification if necessary later. Many writers still use this method, although it is the method most apt to cause error and writer's cramp.

A second method also utilizes index cards, with the source of the data carefully indicated on the top of each card. Much less writing is necessary, however, because the writer also photocopies some, much, or all of the materials she has consulted.　Her index card references will be to valuable sections of photo-copied materials, and laborious notetaking is therefore minimized.　To verify or clarify, the writer need only check the photocopied material.

A third method of fleshing out an outline is to substitute a legal pad (or more than one if necessary) for index cards.　Separate pages, or groups of pages, in the legal pad will be assigned to each category of the outline.　The writer then reads her research materials, photocopies the portions she needs for quick reference, and notes on the photocopies where in the outline this material belongs.　She can use the legal paid to summarize briefly all useful material not photocopied, and place the summaries in the appropriate por-tions of the outline.

A big advantage of this last method is that all notetaking is in one or more legal pads, not on numerous index cards.　Precious research is not so apt to be misplaced, requiring annoying duplication of effort.　For the not-so-neat individual, this final method seems best.　Adding to the outline poses no prob-lem; a new page can be used for every new division or subdivision that is added.　A looseleaf notebook can be substituted for the legal pad, so that pages can be moved around if necessary.

So choose your own method, any one of the three discussed here, or one of your own choice.　All will serve the purpose of helping you organize your ideas, preventing you from discussing topics out of turn, wandering from one topic to another, and failing to develop topics fully.　Any of these defects can be fatally damaging to the finished product.

B.　PARAGRAPHING

1.　Why Paragraph?

Paragraphs break up your writing into units which, properly arranged, per-mit the orderly movement of ideas from the beginning of your manuscript to its conclusion.　Paragraphing is therefore important in all writing, but even more important in legal writing, in which the necessity for clear and logical reasoning is paramount.　The familiar paragraph indentation at intervals on each page of writing promise the reader that with each paragraph a new set of ideas is being introduced and developed.　Conversely, large blocks of unindented print discourage even the most interested reader from making the effort to learn what the writer has to say.

So paragraphing is psychologically important to the reader.　It is also im-portant to the writer.　The process forces him to develop fully the ideas he has introduced, since he knows that a paragraph of fewer than four to six sentences probably indicates incomplete idea development [2] and that a para-

---

2. In legal writing, in which sentences tend to be longer than in ordi-nary writing, the four-sentence mini-mum may sometimes be relaxed.　An-other criterion is the number of words: if your paragraphs have fewer than 50 or more than 250 words, you should check their content to see if you should combine or divide paragraphs.

graph of more than half a page of print is not only a fearful bore to read but a combination of too many ideas.   The four-to-six-sentence rule can (and should) be broken occasionally.   One-or-two-sentence paragraphs, sparingly used, are effective for summation of arguments, interjection of contrasting ideas, transition devices, or emphasis.   Here is an illustration:

> Many university students first came into contact with the word "ripoff" when, in 1971, it appeared on posters placed around campus announcing a "Ripoff Rally," at which students were invited "to see how many ways you are getting ripped off."   Included in the discussion at the rally were victims of injustice (black students) and the injustices themselves (e.g., a proposed tuition hike).   The context indicated that "ripped off" meant "cheated" or at least "treated with great unfairness."   But to a large majority of university students in 1971, the word "ripoff" was clearly new and indefinable.   Of the twenty students in my transformational grammar class, not one could provide a suitable definition.

> One year later—in March 1972—I asked my transformational grammar students to define "ripoff" again; all twenty students in that class could provide a working definition.[3]

Every paragraph should contain a central idea.   In most paragraphs that idea is expressed in one sentence, usually called a "topic sentence."   The topic sentence often comes first in a paragraph, sometimes following an introductory or transitional sentence.   Or it comes last, expressing in general the individual points made within the paragraph.   Rarely, the central idea of a paragraph is left unstated, implicit in the ideas contained in the paragraph, as in the following example:

> A factory survey of men all doing the same sort of work for the same length of time showed some were exhausted at day's end while others still seemed highly energetic.   What made this difference?   Analysts turned up one curious fact.   The tired ones expected to do nothing but rest after work.   The lively ones all had plans for the evening.[4]

2. Paragraph Organization and Development

Paragraphs can be developed by any of the following methods: definition; classification; process; illustration; cause and effect; comparison and contrast; induction; and deduction.   Frequently, more than one method of development occurs in a single paragraph.

Many books on English composition imply that you should choose among the methods of paragraph development before writing each paragraph.   This procedure would be stultifying and a waste of time, for you are no doubt using

3. Block, "A Year of Ripoffs," *American Speech*, Vol. 45, Nos. 3–4, 1970, p. 210.

4. The unstated topic sentence is, of course, that one's after-work plans affect the amount of energy he or she has at work.   Perhaps the idea is left implicit here because it is so vulnerable to attack.   It is arguable that only those workers who knew they would not be tired after work made plans for the evening.   From, *The Gainesville Sun*, April 27, 1982, p. 11B.

these methods quite intuitively as you write.   However, after you have finished writing the first draft of your manuscript, if any paragraphs seem undeveloped, overdeveloped, or badly developed, consider the various methods of paragraph development as one means of improving your writing.   Here they are:

a. Definition

Definition explains what something is by saying what it includes and what it excludes.   The item being defined is first put into a class of similar items and then is differentiated from those items.   The following paragraph exemplifies the process of definition:

> Historically, larceny was a common law felony, while embezzlement and false pretenses were statutory innovations.   Larceny, the trespassory taking and carrying away of another's personal property with the intent of depriving him permanently of it, is a crime against possession, not ownership. Thus, one commits larceny by stealing the ill-gotten gains of a thief, but not by taking property from its rightful possessor when the possessor parts with it voluntarily.   Therefore, larceny, under its strict definition, did not include fraud or the abuse of trust by a servant or another entrusted with one's possessions.

You can use definition, not only to explain, but to persuade, by deciding what to include and what to exclude.   For example, Model Penal Code sections 221.0 and 221.1 define burglary as the entering of a building or occupied structure with the purpose of committing a crime, unless the premises are open to the public at the time, or the actor is privileged to enter.   Whether the facts of the case you are considering are covered by the definition may depend on the meaning of "occupied structure."   Must the occupant be in general occupancy or only present when the burglary occurred?   What does "license to enter" include?   (Licensees have been defined by courts as persons using premises through the owner's "sufferance," [5] or "permission," [6] or as invitees who step beyond the limits of their invitation.[7])   You can persuade your reader to your point of view by arguing for the inclusion or exclusion of one of these definitions.

b. Classification

Classification categorizes items, either by their similarities or by their differences.   In legal writing, classifications are sometimes expanded, sometimes narrowed, by court decisions.   In his dissent in Roth v. Wisconsin State University, Supreme Court Justice Thurgood Marshall argues for the expansion of basic liberties protected by the Fourteenth Amendment so as to include the right to work.   That right, he says, is "the very essence of the personal freedom and opportunity that it was the purpose of the Amendment to secure." [8]

---

5. Boneau v. Swift & Co., 66 S.W.2d 172, 175 (Mo.App.1934).

6. Seabloom v. Krier, 219 Minn. 362, 18 N.W.2d 88, 91 (1945).

7. Wilson v. Goodrich, 218 Iowa 462, 252 N.W. 142 (1934).

8. 408 U.S. 564, 588, 92 S.Ct. 2701, 2714, 33 L.Ed.2d 548 (1972).

In the following paragraph, a Supreme Court decision expands the right to privacy by placing unmarried persons in the same classification as married persons:

> If under *Griswold* the distribution of contraceptives to married persons cannot be prohibited, a ban on distribution to unmarried persons would be equally impermissible. It is true that in *Griswold* the right of privacy in question inhered in the marital relationship. Yet the marital couple is not an independent entity with a mind and heart of its own, but an association of two individuals each with a separate intellectual and emotional make-up. If the right of privacy means anything, it is the right of the *individual,* married or single, to be free from unwarranted governmental intrusion into matters so fundamentally affecting a person as the decision whether to bear or beget a child . . .[9]

Note that, to argue his point, the writer of the opinion interprets "the marital couple" not as an entity but as two individuals, who are thus classifiable with unmarried cohabiting individuals. In your own case analyses, be aware of the possibilities of classification in arguing a point.

c. Process

Process involves orderly, step-by-step explanation. The ability to describe procedures and events in the proper order and without omissions is valuable in legal writing because of the importance of detail, accuracy, and completeness in legal matters. In the following excerpt the process to be followed in a lawsuit is described:

> The first step in a lawsuit is the decision to sue someone. In making this decision intelligently, the potential litigant must discover whether the grievance he has suffered is one for which the law furnishes relief, whether it is probable that he will win the lawsuit, and whether the time, effort, and expense of bringing the suit will be worth the gain if he does win. The second step is to determine in which court to bring the action, and the choice of court will depend not only upon the preference of the litigant but upon which court has jurisdiction both over the subject matter and over the person against whom the suit is being brought, and which court has proper venue.[10]

You will find that competence in the use of process is well rewarded in law school final examinations, in which detailed and orderly explanations are demanded. (See Chapter Five, Section A.)

d. Illustration

Illustration utilizes concrete examples to explain an abstract concept or persuade the skeptic of its truth. Several examples might be used, or one striking

---

9. Eisenstadt v. Baird, 405 U.S. 438, 452, 92 S.Ct. 1029, 1038, 31 L.Ed.2d 349 (1972).

10. These two steps are, of course, only the first two in a long and complicated procedure.

example. The following definition of constructive possession uses several examples:

> Constructive possession is the possession that the law annexes to the title, distinguishing constructive possession from in fact or in deed possession, achieved by actual occupancy. Courts have found constructive possession to exist in several situations, as when (1) an employer delivers property to his employee; (2) the owner delivers property to another for a transaction to be completed in his presence; (3) a bailee breaks bulk; (4) a wrongdoer obtains possession but not title to the property by lies; (5) a wrongdoer finds lost or mislaid property; or (6) property is delivered to a wrongdoer by mistake.[11]

The paragraph above uses six examples. However, in some situations one striking example might suffice. For example in arguing that capital punishment is unwise, the writer might use as an example a man convicted of murder but later found innocent, who would have been executed had capital punishment been in effect.

You will find illustration not only useful but necessary in your law practice to make legal concepts comprehensible to your clients.

e. Cause and Effect

In legal writing, one way to make your argument effective is to indicate clearly and completely whatever causal relationship you consider important. Yet this method of development is often overlooked or ineptly attempted by law students.[12] Paragraphs utilizing cause and effect development raise the question of why something occurs and provide the answer. In the following paragraph, for example, the reason for the development of the *mens rea* doctrine in criminal law is explored:

> The concept of *mens rea* was not always part of common law. Anglo-Saxon law had held that intent was not a necessary element of crime. The act itself was considered rather than the intent behind it, and reparation was demanded of the actor for the consequences of his act. But beginning in the ninth century, this objective standard of criminal responsibility was increasingly rejected by the church. Concern for the eternal soul of the criminal and belief in the Augustinian doctrine of free will led the church to adopt instead a subjective standard of responsibility: if the actor intended freely to commit the crime, he should be punished not only in heaven but on earth. Thus was born the modern doctrine of *mens rea.*[13]

11. LaFave and Scott, *Criminal Law*, West Publishing Company (1972), p. 622.

12. For discussion of this topic, see Chapter Two, Section A(4).

13. Block, "The Semantic Delusion of the Insanity Defense," *University of Pittsburgh Law Review*, Volume 44, Issue 3 (1982).

f. Comparison and Contrast

In legal writing, comparison and contrast are often employed to show substantial similarities between things that are superficially different and to show significant distinctions between things that are seemingly similar. You will use this method of paragraph development when you analogize and distinguish cases, because the judicial system relies upon the doctrine of precedent. That is, courts "reason from precedent" basing decisions in the cases at hand upon decisions with similar facts handed down previously.[14] As law students you will do this kind of reasoning when you write interoffice memoranda, appellate briefs, and final examinations, and you will continue to utilize this method of reasoning throughout your legal career.

Since prior cases seldom contain facts exactly like those in the case you are considering, you will have to decide whether the facts in your case are similar enough to those of previous cases to warrant the same decision or whether differences in the facts are significant enough for precedent not to apply.

In applying comparison and contrast, the memo writer (or the law student writing a final examination) will attempt, without bias, to reach the appropriate conclusion. But the brief writer is an advocate for a client. In order to reach the best result for his client, he therefore tries to show that despite seeming similarities, the facts of his client's case can be distinguished from those of prior cases or that despite seeming differences the facts are similar enough to warrant the same decision. Here is the way one student used comparison and contrast in his brief for a defendant businessman being sued by a visitor to the premises who had been injured. The facts in the instant case:

> A customer visiting a business was walking in the business parking lot and was hit and injured by a truck negligently operated by a driver employed by the owner of a business.

In a similar case, a superior court in the same jurisdiction had held the owner of a business liable for injuries to a pedestrian. The facts in that case were:

> A pedestrian crossing a business parking lot was hit and injured by a truck negligently operated by a driver employed by the owner of the business.

These facts are facially similar. In the one aspect in which they differ, the relationship between businessman and visitor in the instant case seems even closer than in the prior case. Here the visitor was a customer; there a mere pedestrian crossing the premises. The brief writer, as he searched for distinguishing facts, found, however, that in the prior case construction in the parking lot created a hazardous condition, whereas in the instant case the premises were safe for visitors. Further research revealed that, in the prior case, the owner of the business knew that the parking lot was unsafe, yet failed to warn visitors of that fact. The brief writer was able, therefore, to distinguish the

---

14. This process is discussed more completely in Chapter Four.

facts of his case from those of the earlier case, and to argue that the differences were material.

g. Induction

Inductive reasoning utilizes specific relevant details in order to arrive at a general truth. It is the method of the scientific researcher, who must collect sufficient data from experiments to arrive at a generalization based upon these data. The trial attorney uses induction when he asks a witness a series of questions orchestrated to lead the witness to a conclusion desired by the attorney. As lawyers and law students you will often use inductive reasoning to derive a general conclusion from individual bits of relevant evidence.

As law students, perhaps your most important use of induction is in examination questions, when you apply pertinent legal theories to a set of facts, hoping to persuade your professor that you have reached a reasonable conclusion (even though your conclusion may differ from his). One law student used induction in the following hypothetical fact situation:

A pedestrian was attacked by rowdies, who knocked him down, beat him with sticks, and ran away, but were subsequently apprehended.

Question: Has the pedestrian a cause of action in torts against the attackers?

Relevant facts: The rowdies *intended* to cause *harmful* and *offensive contact* with the pedestrian.

Harmful and offensive contact did result from their action: the pedestrian was bruised by the contact and he was frightened by the attack.

Possible defenses: Since the pedestrian had not consented to the conduct of the rowdies and the rowdies had no privilege to make the harmful and offensive contact, these possible defenses are inapplicable.

Legal doctrine: Battery is the intentional, harmful or offensive contact of another person if the actor is not privileged to make the contact and the victim has not consented to it.

Conclusion: Because the actions of the rowdies satisfy the elements of battery, the pedestrian has a cause of action in battery against them.[15]

In the course of progression from facts to a generalization based upon those facts (induction), what the seventeenth century philosopher Blaise Pascal called "the leap of faith" must occur. In logic this leap is an "inductive leap." The more complete the specific evidence, the shorter the leap, the more cogent your argument will be.

• The facts you present as proof should irrevocably lead to the conclusion you reach;

• The facts you offer should be complete enough to justify your conclusion;

---

15. This answer was written in essay form, not in the format used here.

Problems in assault and battery can be found on pp. 149–157.

- Any exceptions to your facts should not be substantial enough to invalidate your conclusion.

h. Deduction

Deduction is the opposite of induction. As shown above, when you reach a conclusion by examining pertinent details, you are using induction. Conversely, when you reason from an accepted truth, such as a legal doctrine, you are using deduction.

The syllogism is perhaps the best-known form of deduction. Described by Aristotle, it is a three-step construction consisting of a major premise, a minor premise, and a conclusion. The major premise is a general presumption accepted as true (e.g., a legal principle), the minor premise identifies the item under consideration as within the class described by the major premise (e.g., a fact situation), and the conclusion then follows that the minor premise should be governed by the same reasoning that governs the major premise. The classic example bears repeating:

Major premise: All men are mortal. (Class is described.)

Minor premise: Socrates is a man. (Individual under consideration belongs to class described.)

Conclusion: Socrates is mortal. (Major premise applies to individual.)

Deductive reasoning can be applied to legal problems, e.g.:

Defendant drove into an empty carwash after it had closed for the night, intending to commit a theft. The carwash consisted of wash stalls open at each end, a roof, a concrete floor, and a coin box. The defendant forced open the coin box, removed the contents, and fled. The applicable section of the burglary statute in your jurisdiction reads:

A person commits burglary when, without authority, he knowingly enters or remains within a building, housetrailer, watercraft, motor vehicle, railroad car or any part thereof, with intent to commit therein a felony or theft.

Assuming that all other elements of burglary are present, the issue is whether a carwash is defined as a building, under the terms of this statute. If you believe it should be, you might construct the following syllogism:

Major premise: Buildings are constructions containing at least two walls, a floor, and a roof.

Minor premise: A carwash has two walls, a floor, and a roof.

Conclusion: A carwash is a building.[16]

---

16. If you did not want the carwash to be considered a building, your major premise would define a building as having four walls.

Court decisions often create legal principles that become precedent, binding upon inferior courts of the same jurisdiction.[17]   Then the legal principle can become the major premise of a syllogism like the following:

Major premise: To establish liability for negligence, it must be proved that but for the actor's negligence, the victim would not have been injured. (Class is described.)

Minor premise: The victim received a broken leg because of the negligence of the actor.   (Victim is a member of the class.)

Conclusion: The actor is liable for negligence to the victim.   (The major premise applies to the victim.)

Note, however, that this major premise is fallacious because liability for negligence requires elements other than the "but for" responsibility stated. When the major premise is fallacious, the conclusion is invalid, and the syllogism fails.

You can use the syllogism to expose faulty reasoning, as in this paragraph from an appellate brief:

Contracts in Florida between physicians and patients have been held legally enforceable wherein the physician agreed to withhold the use of artificial methods to postpone a patient's death, when the patient was suffering from an incurable and painful illness.   Dr. X, a Florida physician, contracted with his patient, a Florida resident, to withhold, at his patient's request, artificial methods to maintain life.   The patient, terminally ill, told the physician not to use artificial methods to prolong his life, and the physician complied with the patient's request.   Since the physician was fulfilling the terms of a legally enforceable contract, he can not be held liable for malpractice.

To discover the fallacy in the syllogism, look at the major premise, seen in the first sentence of the paragraph.   Unless the major premise contains an accepted legal principle, the entire syllogism will be invalid.   The statement does not reveal whether the legal principle stated in the first sentence is valid in Florida, since we do not know whether a majority of Florida courts have adopted the principle or whether only some courts have done so.   Furthermore, the individual described in the minor premise may not be a member of the class described in the major premise, for the facts do not indicate that his illness was "painful."

The syllogism can also be used to expose specious logic.   Suppose, for example, that a powerful group of individuals in your city wish to raze an old neighborhood so as to construct a shopping center, which you oppose.   The argument this group advances is that the old buildings in the neighborhood, though not unattractive, present a hazard, old buildings often being decrepit

17. For a discussion of this point, see Chapter Four.

and rodent-infested. You can discredit this argument by showing that the underlying syllogism is based upon specious logic:

Major premise: All old buildings are decrepit and rodent-infested.

Minor premise: These buildings are old.

Conclusion: These buildings are decrepit and rodent-infested.

You could point out the fallacy of the major premise and build your opposing argument on the following syllogism:

Major premise: Unless old buildings are decrepit or rodent-infested they should be preserved if they are beautiful or of historical interest.

Minor premise: These old buildings are not decrepit or rodent-infested, and they are beautiful and historically interesting.

Conclusion: These old buildings should be preserved.

If the minor premise can occur outside the boundaries of the major premise, the syllogism is also fallacious:

Major premise: Attorneys are skilled in syllogistic reasoning.

Minor premise: Jane Doe is skilled in syllogistic reasoning.

Conclusion: Jane Doe is an attorney.

Even if the major premise is a generally-accepted truth, the syllogism is faulty because persons other than attorneys may be skilled in syllogistic reasoning, and Jane Doe may be one of those persons.

Specious reasoning is most easily hidden in the **enthymeme**, a syllogism stated in a reduced form, with one step missing (usually the major premise). The comment, "He must be a panhandler: he's dirty and he's loitering on the street corner," is an enthymeme, the unstated major premise of which is fallacious: All dirty people who loiter on street corners are panhandlers. Here is an enthymeme-containing excerpt from a political speech:

> During his years in the state legislature, Representative Quagmire has often spoken out in favor of federal handouts, even though he himself has profited from the free enterprise system which is about to be undermined by federal handouts. Communists in Russia and China also favor handouts and oppose the free enterprise system upon which this nation was founded. Let's replace Quagmire with John Dogood, a man of strong ideals and get the communists out of state government.[18]

This paragraph is loaded with enthymemes that are invalid because they contain fallacious major premises. Some of these are:

- People who have profited from the free enterprise system should not speak out in favor of federal handouts.

- Federal handouts are incompatible with free enterprise.

- People with "strong ideals" oppose federal handouts.

18. The use of slanted language, as used in this paragraph, is discussed in Chapter Five, Section A(3).

- Handouts are bad because communists in Russia and China favor them.
- All persons who favor federal handouts are communists.

You might be able to discover more enthymemes in this short paragraph. The ability to discern fallacious logic is important for attorneys. See the Appendix, pp. 203–204, for exercises containing missing enthymemes.

C. COHERENCE

At least as important to successful writing as development by one or more of the methods just discussed is organization to provide coherence within and between paragraphs. In legal writing, particularly, the natural and orderly connection between your ideas ought to be obvious. Each sentence should proceed logically from the previous sentence and logically precede the sentence that follows. Each paragraph should flow naturally from its predecessor, with no ideas repeated or omitted.

1. Use Chronological Development

If your subject lends itself to chronological development, that organization best insures coherence. Your reader follows without difficulty events discussed in the order in which they occurred. Yet often writers fail to use this simple method of development. Note the difference in the two paragraphs that follow, both taken from the "Facts" portion of memos on the same subject. The first paragraph is hard to follow, the second easy; the difference is that the second paragraph is developed chronologically: [19]

> * D. W. Indy now files a motion to suppress evidence that he refused to take a breathalyzer test in compliance with Florida's implied consent statute. D. W. I. was arrested on June 13, 1981, by Officer Gettum for driving under the influence of alcohol to the extent that his normal faculties were impaired. D. W. I. refused the breathalyzer test at the police station. He was read the *Miranda* rights and Florida Statute § 322.261, providing that a refusal to take the test would result in a three-month suspension of his driver's license. Officer Gettum says he also showed Indy the implied-consent statement on Indy's driver's license. Prior to trial, Indy filed a motion to suppress evidence of his refusal to take the breathalyzer test, claiming that Officer Gettum told him that he had the right to refuse to do so. Officer Gettum denies that he did so.

Chronological development makes the following paragraph easier to comprehend:

> On June 13, 1981, Officer Jones arrested D. W. Indy for driving while under the influence of alcohol to the extent that his normal faculties were impaired. When taken to the police station, D. W. I. was read his *Miranda*

19. Some students tell me that they prefer not to read "bad" examples of writing, because when they do, they tend to copy them. If you have this tendency, skip the paragraphs preceded by the asterisk; these are the "bad" examples.

rights and Florida Statute § 322.261, providing that a refusal to take a breathalyzer test in compliance with Florida's implied consent statute would result in a three-month suspension of his driver's license. Officer Gettum says he also showed D. W. I. the implied-consent statement on his driver's license. D. W. I. claims, however, that Officer Gettum told him at the police station that he had the right to refuse to take the breathalyzer test. Officer Gettum denies this. D. W. I. now files a motion to suppress any evidence of his refusal to take the breathalyzer test.[20]

Here are two more paragraphs, taken from the "Facts" sections of memos. Note how chronological development improves the second paragraph:

* K. R. owns a pawnshop in a high-crime area of El Dorado. When he arrived at his shop on October 8, 1981, he saw two teenaged girls hurriedly leaving. K. R.'s clerk said that a ring worth about $1,000 was missing from its usual place. On his car radio K. R. heard that a number of jewelry thefts had occurred in the neighborhood. This especially concerned K. R. because his insurance coverage had recently been cancelled. He pursued the girls, who were running down the street.

While driving to his pawnshop, located in a high crime area of El Dorado, K. R. heard on his car radio that a number of jewelry thefts by teenaged girls had recently occurred in the neighborhood. This news especially concerned K. R. because his insurance had recently been cancelled. As K. R. arrived at his shop, he saw two teenaged girls hurriedly leaving his shop. K. R.'s clerk said that a ring worth about $1,000 was missing from its usual place. K. R. pursued the girls, who were running down the street.

2. Use Logical Development

Even without chronological development, if your ideas develop logically and consistently, fulfilling the expectations you have aroused in your readers, coherence will result. Develop one point at a time; your thoughts should appear to focus on a single analysis until it is complete rather than seeming to dash about in many directions. The writer of the following paper at first failed to organize her ideas properly. When she wrote a second draft, using logical development, her writing became more effective. Her first draft was:

* Much of the dispute about the purpose of the equal protection clause centers on whether it should be interpreted as prohibiting the consideration of race in governmental decision-making or whether the equal protection clause should be interpreted as imposing upon government an affirmative duty to remove the effects of past discrimination against minorities. The Supreme Court has struggled to resolve the conflict about whether illicit motive or disparate impact is the touchstone in constitutional violations, whether de jure or de facto segregation is condemned by the equal protection clause. This conflict is seen in the phenomenon of suburbia.

---

20. The repetition in the first and next to last sentences is avoided when chronological order is used.

This paper will argue that the equal protection clause should be concerned with the substance of governmental decision-making as it affects minorities. Motivation is largely irrelevant as a constitutional basis for a violation of the equal protection clause if the effect is further subordination of victims of discrimination. As the white middle class has abandoned the cities, the tax base has decreased, and the familiar minority ghettos have burgeoned.

The logical development of ideas in this later draft improves it greatly:

Much of the conflict about the purpose of the equal protection clause centers on whether it should be interpreted as prohibiting the consideration of race in governmental decision-making or whether the equal protection clause should be interpreted as imposing upon government an affirmative duty to remove the effects of past discrimination against minorities. This conflict is seen in the Supreme Court's struggle to resolve the question of whether illicit motive or disparate impact is the touchstone in constitutional violations, whether de jure or de facto segregation is condemned by the equal protection clause.

This paper will argue that, although color-blind decision-making is necessary, if the results of such decision-making nevertheless discriminate against minorities, the equal protection clause should be interpreted as prohibiting such results. In such cases, motivation is irrelevant. The phenomenon of suburbia illustrates de facto discrimination against minorities, occurring along with color-blind decision-making.[21]

3. Avoid Hysteron-Proteron

The habit of hysteron-proteron produces disorganized writing. The term means "the last before the first" in Greek. I am fond of it, not because of its venerable past, but because it proved very useful to me when I taught freshman English composition. Whenever I found an example of the error on a student's theme, I would write "hysteron-proteron" in the margin where the error occurred. Then I would wait. If the student did not come to me and ask "What does *that* mean?" I would know he had not taken the time to read any of my comments on his paper, but had just checked the grade at the end.

Hysteron-proteron is a device frequently used in poetry. Recall Shelley's "I die, I faint, I fail," which is effective although the order of incidents must surely have been reversed. But it is quite inappropriate, and often confusing, in legal writing, where it creates the same problem as illogical development of ideas. Here are some examples of the error from students' writing:

* Congress enacted § 666 to curb the increased use of tax shelters that followed the *Baxley* holding. Before § 666, taxpayers received all the benefits of their investments but none of the risks. That is, a non-recourse

21. The re-draft also eliminates the "elegant variation" of the first draft, caused by the author's referring to the "conflict" first as a "dispute," leading the reader to think she was referring to two different things. See discussion of elegant variation, Chapter Two, Section B(10).

mortgage could be used as the basis for depreciation deductions. In order to limit the deductions the taxpayer could claim, Congress enacted § 666.

As occurred in this excerpt, when the writer falls into the trap of hysteron-proteron, he often attempts to extricate himself from the resulting confusion by repeating the idea in its proper place. Therefore, the following re-write is both shorter and clearer than the previous draft:

> After the *Baxley* holding, taxpayers received all the benefits of their investments but none of the risks. That is, a non-recourse mortgage could be used as the basis for depreciation deductions. In order to limit the deductions the taxpayer could claim and to curb the increased use of tax shelters that followed the *Baxley* holding, Congress enacted § 666.

Here is another example of hysteron-proteron. See if you can untangle it:

> * In Jones v. Jones, involving a man and woman who had just been divorced, the man had signed a note evidencing a loan from his wife, while they were still married. Then, after the divorce, by mutual consent, the former wife released the former husband from the debt. Since she was not repaid by her former husband, she took a bad debt deduction.

Your re-write may look something like this:

> In Jones v. Jones, a man signed a note evidencing a loan from his wife. Then the couple were divorced and, by mutual consent, the man was released from his debt. The woman took a bad debt deduction because she had not been repaid by her former husband.

The topsy-turvy character of the original paragraphs above may seem so apparent that you are saying to yourself, "I'd never get that mixed up!" But you should beware of hysteron-proteron even so, because it can occur in a subtler form. You can recognize it as a reader when you are disappointed in your expectation of what is coming next. In the following paragraph, for example, stop after sentence one and consider what you expect to follow forthwith; then read on to discover whether your expectation is fulfilled.

> * In some instances the Roman commander would delegate the authority to decide the death sentence. But in any case, the commander's *lictors* were probably the executioners. This authority would sometimes be granted to the military tribunes who were next in command to the commanders. Or the delegation of the punishment would be awarded to the *centurions*.

The first sentence promises that the author will next discuss the instances in which the Roman commander would delegate authority. Instead, he begins another idea in the second sentence, returning in the following sentences not to the *instances* of delegation, but to the groups who would administer it. (A couple of paragraphs later, the writer does get around, belatedly to telling the reader what he promises to tell him here.)

Here is another paragraph from the same paper—and it contains the same problem:

> * Ancient Roman military success was based on the fact that those chosen to take part in military operations had something to fight for. The soldiers knew that the outcome of their battles would determine whether they had something to come home to. Since the Republican military establishment required, from the start, that all those in its ranks own some property and/or be citizens of Rome, the soldiers knew that battles would determine whether they kept their homeland of Rome free from external conquerors and internal subversives. They had property and positions to lose if their defense of Rome was weak.

The first sentence promises the reader he will learn what it was the Roman soldiers had to fight for. In the last sentence, the reader does learn. Why not rearrange the paragraph so that the information promised appears in sentence two? The result might look something like this:

> Ancient Roman military success was based on the fact that those chosen to take part in military operations had something to fight for. All soldiers had either property or position to lose if their defense of Rome was weak, for the Republican military establishment required from the start that all those in its ranks own some property and/or be citizens of Rome. Thus the soldiers knew that whether they had something to come home to would be determined by the outcome of their battles.[22]

When the sentences are placed in their proper order, one sentence can be omitted. This is often true when disorganized sentences are rearranged because unnecessary repetitions and *non sequiturs* are more apt to creep into illogically-arranged paragraphs. The material omitted will often be found to belong somewhere else in the paper.

4. Use Transition Words and Phrases

Transition language makes clear the relationship between what you have said and what you are about to say; it is the language you use to show your reader where you are taking him. We all use transition, most of us without thinking about it. Good writers probably make more use of transition language than poor writers. But as a writer you should be moderate in the use of transition language. Writing replete with transition language, which insistently reiterates relationships, may seem to insult your reader's intelligence or appear simplistic. On the other hand, in legal writing, which often deals with complex subjects, proper transition is needed to make comprehensible what would otherwise be confusing. And lack of transition makes writing appear to jerk rather than to flow. If you have been told that your writing is "choppy,"

---

22. The term "and/or" might better be avoided because many legal commentators abhor it.

you should probably add transitions.   The paragraph that follows is an example:

> * Taxpayers and Congress play games with tax laws.   Congress enacts a tax law disallowing deductions for certain activities.   Taxpayers' lawyers find loopholes in the law so as to provide deductions for their clients. Congress promulgates an amendment to the law to close the loophole. The depreciation deduction allowed under Sections 167 and 169 permitted taxpayers to include borrowed amounts in determining the adjusted basis of property.   When taxpayers reduced their tax liability by depreciation deductions through heavily mortgaged property, tax shelters resulted.   Congress enacted § 465 in 1976 to close the loophole.

Here is the same paragraph, with transitional words and phrases added:

> Taxpayers and Congress play games with tax laws.   First, Congress enacts a tax law disallowing deductions for certain activities.   Then taxpayers' lawyers find loopholes in the law so as to provide deductions for their clients.   Next Congress promulgates an amendment to the law to close the loophole.   And so it continues.   For example, the depreciation deduction allowed under Sections 167 and 168 permitted taxpayers to include borrowed amounts in determining the adjusted basis of property.   This depreciation resulted from depreciation deductions through heavily mortgaged property.   Therefore, in 1976, Congress enacted § 465 in order to close that loophole.

The transitional language in the second paragraph lengthens it, but the gain in clarity justifies the added length.   You can easily identify the transition language.

Although you will probably never consult a list to select transition language, here are some of the words most commonly used to express the following relationships:

Temporal relationships: Then, meanwhile, next, before, later, in a few days, until, then, when, after, following . . .

Spatial relationships: Above, below, nearby, beyond, opposite, adjacent to, adjoining, far from . . .

Addition: Furthermore, moreover, besides, also, again, in addition to, further . . .

Causal relationships: Because, since, consequently, so that, in order to, for that reason . . .

Logical relationships: Nevertheless, however, therefore, hence, thus, despite, but . . .

Comparison and contrast: Similarly, likewise, in a like manner, yet, but, on the contrary, notwithstanding . . .

Another way to provide transition is to repeat a word or phrase used at the end of the previous sentence or paragraph.   This device should be used with restraint, for it can lead to repetitiousness. The repetition of "theories" in the following excerpt is an illustration:

> * Several theories regarding the intent of the equal protection clause are discussed in this section of the paper. Differences in these theories, their weaknesses and strengths, and a proposal for alternative theories to avoid the unfavorable results of these theories will also be discussed.

Between paragraphs, transition is even more important than between sentences within a paragraph, for the reader expects that all sentences in a paragraph are somehow connected and transition merely shows him *how*. But the new paragraph signals either a new topic or a new direction for the previous topic. In the following excerpt, the repetition of "decision" tells the reader to expect a new direction for the previous topic:

> In its decision in Smith v. Bagwell, the Florida Supreme Court described punitive damages as recompense to the sufferer as well as punishment to the offender and an example to the community. It described compensatory damages as those which arise from actual and indirect pecuniary loss, mental suffering, medical expenses, and bodily pain and suffering.
>
> The court, in this decision, seemed to confuse the principle of compensatory damages—the means of compensating the victim for injury to his person—with the principle of punitive damages—punishment for the offender and a deterrent to the community.

The first draft of any writing is apt to lack transition, particularly when the writer knows his subject so thoroughly that he is unaware that transition language is missing. The problem is compounded when, as is often true in legal writing, the subject is complex. So as you read your first draft, be alert to the need for providing guideposts to your reader so that he can follow you to your destination.

D. SENTENCE CONSTRUCTION

Your ability to construct clear and cogent sentences will determine whether your readers will understand and care about what you are saying—even whether they will read what you have written. Long, circuitous sentences may irritate and even baffle your readers.[23] A succession of such sentences may cause them to stop reading. So it is well to recognize and use sentence structure to good advantage in your writing. Sentences are classified in three ways: functionally, grammatically, and stylistically.

1. Classification by Function

Functionally, sentences are of four kinds: the statement, the command-wish, the question, and the exclamation. Because in writing on legal subjects you will use the statement almost exclusively, this classification is the least im-

---

23. For more on circuitous sentences, see Chapter Two, Sections A(8) and B(2).

portant kind. The command-wish, chiefly exhortatory, may be appropriate in addressing the jury but should be used with caution in writing. The rhetorical question ("Can anyone doubt the defendant's guilt?") should generally be avoided. And the question posed and immediately answered ("Is the defendant guilty? No, he is not.") should be redrafted as a statement ("The defendant is not guilty"). Variety in your sentences will therefore be gained by application of the two other sentence classifications.

2. Classification by Grammar

Grammatically, sentences are either simple, compound, or complex.[24] The simple sentence is the least complicated and usually the shortest. It is composed of a single subject-predicate unit. The following are all simple sentences:

I know John.

Democracy lives!

Our neighbors and their friends are active in politics.

Mary spends her time studying and thus has little time for socializing.

Compound sentences are merely two or more simple sentences joined by a coordinating conjunction like "and," "but," "for," and "so" or by a semi-colon either with or without a conjunctive adverb like "however," "moreover," or "nevertheless." [25] When you want to make several points of equal importance or join ideas that are closely connected, you will probably choose compound sentences to do so. The following are some compound sentences:

I have known John for some time, but I do not know his brother.

Democracy lives, and it will survive its present threats.

Our neighbors and their friends are active in politics; they urge us to get involved.

Mary spends her time studying; therefore she has little time to socialize.

Complex sentences contain at least one main clause and one subordinate clause. The main clause could stand by itself as a simple sentence and is therefore sometimes called the "independent" clause; the subordinate clause, often introduced by an adverb (like "when," "while," "because," or "since"), cannot stand alone and is therefore sometimes called the "dependent" clause. You will use complex sentences when you want to stress an important idea and subordinate a less important one. [26] The following are some complex sentences:

Because John is ethical and considerate, [subordinate clause] he is well liked. [main clause]

24. See also Chapter Two, Section A(1).

25. See Chapter One, Sections 7 and 8 for a discussion of these kinds of sentences.

26. For more on this subject see Chapter Two, Section A(1).

Although Joe has retired from practice, [subordinate clause] he is still politically active. [main clause]

After the trial ends but before sentencing the defendant, [subordinate clause] the court will consider mitigating circumstances. [main clause]

The judicious use of grammatical structure lends variety to your sentences. Occasional interpolation of a short, simple sentence among compound and complex sentences also provides emphasis to the idea stated in the short sentence, just as does the occasional one or two-sentence paragraph. [27]

3. Classification by Style

Stylistically, sentences are of three kinds: periodic, loose, and balanced.

The periodic sentence is fine for creating suspense and is used for that effect by skilled writers. Reading the sentence, one is kept in mystery until the climax is reached in the final words, for no stopping places are provided which contain the full idea until the end. Edward Gibbon uses the periodic sentence to describe how the idea for his *History* came to him:

> In Rome, on the 15th of October, as I sat musing amidst the ruins of the Capital, while the barefooted friars were singing vespers in the temple of Jupiter, it was that the idea of writing the decline and fall of the city first started to my mind.

But for writing when suspense is not sought or desirable, the periodic sentence construction is not so useful. The clarity and communicability of a loose sentence is preferable when the subject is complicated. But most legal writers seem to love the periodic sentence and use it much too often, with resultant obfuscation. Following is an example; it is a proposed constitutional amendment, placed on the ballot for citizens' approval. It is written in the periodic style, with no stopping place provided at which the reader can understand a full idea until after the 74th word ("laws") in the eighth line of the sentence. Would you, after a careful reading, feel sure that you understood what you were being asked to consider?

> No moneys derived from any fees, excises, or license taxes, levied by the state, relating to registration, operation, of use of vehicles upon the public highways, except a vehicle-use tax imposed in lieu of a sales tax, and no moneys derived from any fee, excises, or license taxes, levied by the state, relating to fuels used for propelling such vehicles except pump taxes, shall be used for other than cost of administering such laws, statutory refunds and adjustments allowed therein, cost of construction, reconstruction, maintenance and rights-of-way, payment of highway obligations, the cost of traffic regulation, and the expense of enforcing state traffic and motor vehicle laws.

This is a horrendous example, to be sure, for it imposes a burden upon the hapless reader so heavy as to cause her to give up the effort to understand

---

27. See discussion in Chapter Three, Section B(1).

what is being said before she is halfway through the ridiculously-long sentence. But this sentence is unfortunately similar in kind, if not in degree, to much legal writing. And even this sentence can be made comprehensible if written in loose sentence construction, with stopping points along the way at which the ideas thus far presented are complete. Here is the proposed constitutional amendment written in loose sentence construction:

> Certain sources of revenue will be used exclusively for the administration of these laws. The sources include all fees, excises, or license taxes which are levied by the state and relate to the registration or use of vehicles on public highways or to the fuel used in propelling these vehicles, and exclude pump taxes and vehicle-use taxes imposed in place of sales taxes; the costs of administration of these laws include the cost of refunds and adjustments that the laws allow, the cost of construction and maintenance of public highways and bridges, the cost of highway rights-of-way, the payment of highway obligations, the cost of traffic regulation, and the expense of enforcing state traffic and motor vehicle laws.

Even revised, this paragraph is no literary gem, but it is clearer than the original because it provides stopping places where the reader can understand what has been said thus far (and draw a breath) before proceeding. In the revision, the first stopping place occurs after the 14th word ("laws"), in the second line. Subsequent stopping places occur after "state" in line three, "vehicles" in line five, "taxes" in line six, "allow" in line eight, "bridges" in line nine, "rights-of-way" in line 10, "obligations" in line 11, and "regulation" in line 12.

You will notice, of course, that other changes were made to improve clarity. Instead of one sentence, the paragraph now contains two—and would be improved if further divided. The division into two sentences separates the "sources of revenue" from the "costs of administration." The negative statements were replaced by positive statements,[28] and unnecessary (in fact ungrammatical) and confusing commas were deleted.

So give your readers a break. Edit the first draft of whatever you write to eliminate any periodic sentences that will prevent your readers from understanding what you are trying to communicate. Even without the plain language laws that make understandability a requirement in consumer contracts,[29] you will want your good ideas to be understood and appreciated.

Once your writing is clear, consider using balanced sentences for grace and polish. The balanced sentence uses parallel structure or repetition of similar structure to call attention to similarities or contrasts in ideas.[30] The balanced

---

28. For a discussion of this point, see Chapter Two, Section B(9). The use of lists, typical of loose construction, is discussed in Chapter Two, Section A(2).

29. See G. Block, "Plain Language Laws: Promise v. Performance," *Mich-*

igan Bar Journal, Vol. 59, No. 11, November 1980, p. 762.

30. For a discussion of parallelism, see Chapter Two, Section A(3).

sentence is also most quotable: the maxims "first come, first served," "nothing ventured, nothing gained," and others you can think of utilize parallel structure (and brevity) to make their point. Those legal writers whose comments are most often repeated use balanced sentences to add equipoise to their writing. For example,

> [L]aw consists of all the ways in which a politically organized society through its politically created organs aims to and does influence the conduct of members of society and maintains its own organization. It consists of commands and sanctions to be sure; but it also consists of admonitions and rules without coercive sanctions.[31]

The balanced pairs of this excerpt add interest: balance in the first sentence in the pairs "politically organized" and "politically created," and "aims to and does"; and in the second sentence the pairs "consists of" and "also consists of," and "commands and sanctions," and "admonitions and rules."

The most skilled writers combine the kinds of sentence structure: they mix long and short; simple, compound, complex; and periodic, loose, and balanced sentences. They combine several kinds in the same sentence. Note the mingling of periodic, loose, and balanced constructions in the following excerpt:

> Judges have the power   . . .   though not the right, to ignore the mandate of a statute, and render judgment in despite of it. They have the power, though not the right, to travel beyond the walls of the interstices, the bounds set to judicial innovation by precedent and custom. None the less, by that abuse of power, they violate the law.[32]

The safest course for the legal writer is to use loose sentence structure whenever it is necessary for clarity. When clarity is certain, add the intricacy of the periodic structure and the polish of the balanced structure to make your writing memorable as well as clear.

---

31. C. Breitel, "The Lawmakers," 65 *Columbia Law Review* 749, 753 (1965).

32. Benjamin Cardozo, *The Nature of the Judicial Process* (1921), p. 129.

CHAPTER FOUR

Case Analysis and Argumentation

(Briefing, Analogizing, Synthesizing)

As soon as law school classes begin, your professors are sure to suggest that you brief the opinions in your casebooks.[1] That is because if you brief the opinions you will understand and remember them better than if you merely read them. You can then intelligently answer the professor's questions and participate in class discussions. Unfortunately, few professors explain carefully how to brief opinions. So at the beginning of each semester a large number of students come to my office wearing the woebegone expression that immediately identifies them as first semester law students wanting to know how to brief cases.

One method of case-briefing is suggested and illustrated in the following pages. But *how* you brief is less important than *that* you brief. Briefing fixes the opinions securely in your mind; analogizing and synthesizing opinions help relate cases to one another. All are excellent preparation for final examination study. Although you can buy briefs in paperback outline form, "canned" briefs do not substitute for the do-it-yourself variety, because the ability to brief cases is an essential legal skill. You can, however, use the "canned" briefs against which to check your own.

Briefing involves three steps: (1) carefully reading an opinion, (2) selecting salient data from the plethora that the opinion contains, and (3) inserting the data in an outline. The process is explained below. The suggested outline contains ten items, but as you become experienced you may find that an outline of as few as five items is sufficient. You can start with the ten-point outline and eliminate or combine items as you gain skill in briefing.

Analogizing cases involves selecting information from your case briefs and applying it to other cases or fact situations in order to make predictions about the decision a court will reach in considering the new facts. This process is essentially what you will be doing in your final examinations in law school.

A case synthesis is a summary of two or more cases, describing their similarities and differences. Using synthesis you can discover why appellate courts sometimes reach similar conclusions in cases with seemingly different facts and different conclusions in seemingly similar cases. Case syntheses also illustrate how legal rules are expanded, narrowed, or abandoned by court opinions.

---

1. As you have probably already discovered, professors and others in the legal profession use the word "case" to mean "opinion." Thus, when you are told to brief cases, you are usually being asked to brief the appellate court opinions in your "casebooks," which are actually "opinion" books.

A. BRIEFING

Various authors suggest different techniques for briefing cases,[2] and your law professors may have their own preferences. If you are free to choose, you should adopt the method most comfortable and helpful to you. The ten-point brief below is a suggested starting point. You may want to delete or combine some of the items. But the "briefest" brief should include at least: facts, legal theories, issues, holding, and reasoning.

The first step in briefing is to read the opinion carefully. Then list the ten items below on the left side of a legal-sized sheet, leaving enough room opposite each item for appropriate information from the opinion. Re-read the opinion, indicating in pencil in the margin what should be included opposite each item on your legal sheet. Transfer this information to your legal pad, paraphrasing it succinctly but retaining the relevant legal language. Check the meaning of any legal terms you do know, and footnote your brief with these definitions. (See, for example, the brief for *Transatlantic Financing Corporation,* below, at 94.)

Here is the suggested outline:

1. Parties, their relationship, and how the matter reached this court.
2. Cause(s) of action
3. Facts
4. Relief requested
5. Legal theories relied upon
6. Issue(s)
7. Holding(s)
8. Reasoning
9. Resulting legal rule(s)
10. Dicta

Here is an explanation of each item:

1. *Parties, their relationship, and how the matter reached this court:*

The names of the parties usually appear in the caption at the beginning of the opinion. Their relationship also appears there, the plaintiff(s) first, followed, after the "v." (for "versus"), the defendant(s). When multiple parties are involved, list only the last name of the first litigant on each side. These are the names that appear in the body of the opinion. Even in captions reading, "In re . . ." or "In the Matter of . . ." there are at least two opposing parties, and their names should appear in your brief. In this section of your brief, indicate as well the status of each party, e.g., "employer" and "employee," "appellant" and "appellee," "petitioner" and "respondent."

2. For example, Statsky & Wernet, *Case Analysis and Fundamentals of Legal Writing* (1977), Chapter 16 and passim; M. Rombauer, *Legal Problem Solving* (Third Edition, 1978), 112–13.

In "how the matter reached this court," briefly note any prior proceedings and explain why this court is now involved. Most of the cases you will brief are appellate court cases whose previous history appears at the beginning of the opinion. The headnote (syllabus) also contains this information, but be aware that errors may be present in this material since notes that precede the opinion are written by the reporter, not by the judge who wrote the opinion. A story, perhaps apocryphal, is told of a legal principle established over the years by *stare decisis,* whose original citation was from an erroneous headnote, the information never having appeared in the opinion itself!

2. *Cause(s) of action:*

The cause of action explains why the appellant is in court, i.e., what he seeks to obtain by his suit. Usually the appellant wants to obtain something from the appellee, who wants to prevent him from doing so, but sometimes the appellee also wants to obtain something for himself. (See, for example, Northern Corporation v. Chugach Electric Association, briefed below, at 112.) When this is the case, both sides of the dispute will present a cause of action.

3. *Facts:*

The fact section of your brief contains a succinct summary of the salient information, often called "key facts," of the opinion. Key facts are those facts upon which the court based its holding. Thus no facts that could be omitted or altered without changing the decision are key facts. (For example, in *Transatlantic Financing Corporation v. United States,* at 86, below, the fact that the Egyptian government had nationalized and taken over operation of the Suez Canal is not a key fact, since it could be deleted without changing the opinion of the court; however, the fact that the Suez Canal had been closed to traffic as a result of the takeover is a key fact.)

4. *Relief requested:*

This item might well be included in the cause of action. However, since in the opinion, the relief requested usually follows the facts, I have listed it as a separate item. The relief requested is the specific remedy the appellant is seeking. In the sample briefs (pp. 93, 100, and 112), that remedy is in the form of money. The amount of money is a key fact in *American Trading and Production Corporation* (see p. 98), since it influenced the court in its decision-making. The kind of relief requested was a key fact in *Transatlantic Financing Corporation,* the court stating that the appellant's theory of relief was inappropriate (see pp. 92–93).

5. *Legal theories relied upon:*

The legal theories relied upon are the relevant rules of law which are cited by the appellant as legal basis for obtaining the desired objectives. The plaintiff always advances one or more legal theories; the defendant also does so when, instead of merely denying the validity of the plaintiff's cause of action, he raises a separate claim (called a counterclaim). (See, for example, the counterclaim of Chugach in Northern Corporation v. Chugach, below, at 104.)

6. *Issue(s):*

Issues are the precise legal questions that must be resolved by the court in order to reach its decision in the case at hand. Often the issues are expressly stated in the opinion, but when they are not, you can identify them by reading the holding and the reasons given to support it. The complete issue derives from the rule of law as it applies to the key facts.[3]

7. *Holding(s) and disposition:*

The holding is stated as a negative or affirmative response to an issue. In its entirety, however, the holding, like the issue, depends upon the rule of law and the facts to which the rule is being applied.

The disposition is whatever the court says it will do procedurally as a result of its holding. The disposition usually comes at the end of the opinion, stated in a few words (e.g., "vacated and remanded").

8. *Reasoning:*

In its reasoning, the court justifies its holding on each issue. When the case presents more than one issue, the court may intermingle the reasoning behind its holding on several issues, but you should separate the court's statements so as to apply its reasoning to each issue. To identify the reasoning of the court, look for its reasons for agreeing with one party and disagreeing with the other, for accepting some legal precedents and rejecting others, for extending or limiting other courts' opinions. Also look for the court's citation of enacted law and its interpretation of the intent of that law.

9. *Resulting legal rule(s):*

The legal rule is a broad statement of principle developed by or applied in *this* decision. The rule may then become precedent for analogous cases, in future decisions. Few decisions enunciate a new legal rule; many cite a rule previously developed, which was applied in the case at hand. This item and item 10, which follows, are often omitted from briefs, but they are helpful in placing the case under consideration into perspective with respect to cases that have preceded or will follow it.

10. *Dictum* (dicta):

Dictum (the plural of which is dicta) is official but incidental and gratuitous language, unnecessary to the decision of the case under consideration. Since courts are supposed to reach decisions only on the narrow questions before them, decisions theoretically should not contain dicta, but they sometimes do. You will recognize as dictum any statement a court makes based on facts other than those presented in *this* controversy or any conclusion a court reaches based upon law not applicable to *this* controversy. You should identify dictum because later courts may agree with the view expressed as dictum, although dictum is not binding on later courts any more than the minority decision is binding. (In *Transatlantic Financing Corporation,* for example, the

---

3. See also the discussion of issues in the use of the IRAC formula, pp. 131–133.

dictum expressed by the court could result in a later court's extension of this court's holding.)

Following are briefs of three cases, prepared according to the suggested ten-point outline. You may wish to use these briefs as models as you prepare briefs for the cases you are studying in your casebooks. The cases briefed are:

(1) Transatlantic Financing Corporation v. United States,

(2) American Trading and Production Corporation v. Shell International Marine LTD,

(3) Northern Corporation v. Chugach Electric Association.

A copy of the opinion of the court precedes each brief.

TRANSATLANTIC FINANCING CORPORATION v. UNITED STATES

United States Court of Appeals, District of Columbia Circuit, 1966.
363 F.2d 312.

J. Skelly Wright, Circuit Judge:

This appeal involves a voyage charter between Transatlantic Financing Corporation, operator of the SS CHRISTOS, and the United States covering carriage of a full cargo of wheat from a United States Gulf port to a safe port in Iran. The District Court dismissed a libel filed by Transatlantic against the United States for costs attributable to the ship's diversion from the normal sea route caused by the closing of the Suez Canal. We affirm.

On July 26, 1956, the Government of Egypt nationalized the Suez Canal Company and took over operation of the Canal. On October 2, 1956, during the international crisis which resulted from the seizure, the voyage charter in suit was executed between representatives of Transatlantic and the United States. The charter indicated the termini of the voyage but not the route. On October 27, 1956, the SS CHRISTOS sailed from Galveston for Bandar Shapur, Iran, on a course which would have taken her through Gibraltar and the Suez Canal. On October 29, 1956, Israel invaded Egypt. On October 31, 1956, Great Britain and France invaded the Suez Canal Zone. On November 2, 1956, the Egyptian Government obstructed the Suez Canal with sunken vessels and closed it to traffic.

On or about November 7, 1956, Beckmann, representing Transatlantic, contacted Potosky, an employee of the United States Department of Agriculture, who appellant concedes was unauthorized to bind the Government, requesting instructions concerning disposition of the cargo and seeking an agreement for payment of additional compensation for a voyage around the Cape of Good Hope. Potosky advised Beckmann that Transatlantic was expected to perform the charter according to its terms, that he did not believe Transatlantic was entitled to additional compensation for a voyage around the Cape, but that Transatlantic was free to file such a claim. Following this discussion, the CHRISTOS changed course for the Cape of Good Hope and eventually arrived in Bandar Shapur on December 30, 1956.

Transatlantic's claim is based on the following train of argument. The charter was a contract for a voyage from a Gulf port to Iran. Admiralty principles and practices, especially stemming from the doctrine of deviation, require us to imply into the contract the term that the voyage was to be performed by the "usual and customary" route. The usual and customary route from Texas to Iran was, at the time of contract, via Suez, so the contract was for a voyage from Texas to Iran via Suez. When Suez was closed this contract became impossible to perform. Consequently, appellant's argument continues, when Transatlantic delivered the cargo by going around the Cape of Good Hope, in compliance with the Government's demand under claim of right it conferred a benefit upon the United States for which it should be paid in *quantum meruit.*

The doctrine of impossibility of performance has gradually been freed from the earlier fictional and unrealistic strictures of such tests as the "implied term" and the parties' "contemplation." Page, *The Development of the Doctrine of Impossibility of Performance,* 18 Mich.L.Rev. 589, 596 (1920). See generally 6 Corbin, Contracts §§ 1320–1372 (rev. ed. 1962); 6 Williston, Contracts §§ 1931–1979 (rev. ed. 1938). It is now recognized that " 'A thing is impossible in legal contemplation when it is not practicable; and a thing is impracticable when it can only be done at an excessive and unreasonable cost.' " Mineral Park Land Co. v. Howard, 172 Cal. 289, 293, 156 P. 458, 460, L.R.A. 1916F, 1 (1916). *Accord,* Whelan v. Griffith Consumers Company, D.C.Mun. App., 170 A.2d 229 (1961); Restatement, Contracts § 454 (1932); Uniform Commercial Code (U.L.A.) § 2–615, comment 3. The doctrine ultimately represents the ever-shifting line, drawn by courts hopefully responsive to commercial practices and mores, at which the community's interest in having contracts enforced according to their terms is outweighed by the commercial senselessness of requiring performance.[1] When the issue is raised, the court is asked to construct a condition of performance[2] based on the changed circumstances, a process which involves at least three reasonably definable steps. First, a contingency—something unexpected—must have occurred. Second, the risk of the unexpected occurrence must not have been allocated either by agreement or by custom. Finally, occurrence of the contingency must have rendered performance commercially impracticable.[3] Unless the court finds these three requirements satisfied, the plea of impossibility must fail.

---

1. While the impossibility issue rarely arises, as it has here, in a suit to recover the cost of an alternative method of performance, compare Annot., 84 A.L.R.2d 12, 19 (1962), there is nothing necessarily inconsistent in claiming commercial impracticability for the method of performance actually adopted; the concept of impracticability assumes performance was physically possible. Moreover, a rule making nonperformance a condition precedent to recovery would unjustifiably encourage disappointment of expectations.

2. Patterson, *Constructive Conditions in Contracts,* 42 Colum.L.Rev. 903, 943–954 (1942).

3. Compare Uniform Commercial Code § 2–615(a), which provides that, in the absence of an assumption of greater liability, delay or non-delivery by a seller is not a breach if performance as agreed is made "impracticable"

The first requirement was met here. It seems reasonable, where no route is mentioned in a contract, to assume the parties expected performance by the usual and customary route at the time of contract.[4] Since the usual and customary route from Texas to Iran at the time of contract[5] was through Suez, closure of the Canal made impossible the expected method of performance. But this unexpected development raises rather than resolves the impossibility issue, which turns additionally on whether the risk of the contingency's occur-

by the occurrence of a "contingency" the non-occurrence of which was a "basic assumption on which the contract was made." To the extent this limits relief to "unforeseen" circumstances, comment 1, see the discussion below, and compare Uniform Commercial Code § 2–614(1). There may be a point beyond which agreement cannot go, Uniform Commercial Code § 2–615, comment 8, presumably the point at which the obligation would be "manifestly unreasonable," § 1–102(3), in bad faith, § 1–203, or unconscionable, § 1–302. For an application of these provisions see Judge Friendly's opinion in United States v. Wegematic Corporation, 2 Cir., 360 F.2d 674 (1966).

4. Uniform Commercial Code § 2–614, comment 1, states: "Under this Article, in the absence of specific agreement, the normal or usual facilities enter into the agreement either through the circumstances, usage of trade or prior course of dealing." So long as this sort of assumption does not necessarily result in construction of a condition of performance, it is idle to argue over whether the usual and customary route is an "implied term." The issue of impracticability must eventually be met. One court refused to imply the Suez route as a contract term, but went on to rule the contract had been "frustrated." Carapanayoti & Co. Ltd. v. E. T. Green Ltd., [1959] 1 Q.B. 131. The holding was later rejected by the House of Lords. Tsakiroglou & Co. Ltd. v. Noblee Thorl G.m.b.H., [1960] 2 Q.B. 348.

5. The parties have spent considerable energy in disputing whether the "usual and customary" route by which performance was anticipated is defined as of the time of contract or of performance. If we were automatically to treat the expected route as a condition of performance, this matter would be crucial, and we would be compelled to choose between unacceptable alternatives. If we assume as a constructive condition the usual and customary course always to mean the one in use at the time of contract, any substantial diversion (we assume the diversion would have to be substantial) would nullify the contract even though its effect upon the rights and obligations of the parties is insignificant. Nor would it be desirable, on the other hand, to assume performance is conditioned on the availability of *any* usual and customary route at the time of performance. It may be that very often the availability of a customary route at the time of performance other than the route expected to be used at the time of contract should result in denial of relief under the impossibility theory; certainly if *no* customary route is available at the time of performance the contract is rendered impossible. But the same customarily used alternative route may be practicable in one set of circumstances and impracticable in another, as where the goods are unable to survive the extra journey. Moreover, the "time of performance" is no special point in time; it is every moment in a performance. Thus the alternative route, in our case around the Cape, may be practicable at some time during performance, for example while the vessel is still in the Atlantic Ocean, and impracticable at another time during performance, for example after the vessel has traversed most of the Mediterranean Sea. Both alternatives, therefore, have their shortcomings, and we avoid choosing between them by refusing automatically to treat the usual and customary route as of any time as a condition of performance.

rence had been allocated and, if not, whether performance by alternative routes was rendered impracticable.[6]

Proof that the risk of a contingency's occurrence has been allocated may be expressed in or implied from the agreement. Such proof may also be found in the surrounding circumstances, including custom and usages of the trade. See 6 Corbin, supra, § 1339, at 394–397; 6 Williston, supra, § 1948, at 5457–5458. The contract in this case does not expressly condition performance upon availability of the Suez route. Nor does it specify "via Suez" or, on the other hand, "via Suez or Cape of Good Hope."[7] Nor are there provisions in the contract from which we may properly imply that the continued availability of Suez was a condition of performance.[8] Nor is there any-

6. In criticizing the "contemplation" test for impossibility Professor Patterson pointed out:

"'Contemplation' is appropriate to describe the mental state of philosophers but is scarcely descriptive of the mental state of business men making a bargain. It seems preferable to say that the promisee *expects* performance by [the] means . . . the promisor expects to (or which on the facts known to the promisee it is probable that he will) use. It does not follow as an inference of fact that the promisee expects performance by *only* that means . . . ." Patterson, supra Note 2, at 947.

7. In Glidden Company v. Hellenic Lines, Limited, 2 Cir., 275 F.2d 253 (1960), the charter was for transportation of materials from India to America "via Suez Canal or Cape of Good Hope, or Panama Canal," and the court held performance was not "frustrated." In his discussion of this case, Professor Corbin states: "Except for the provision for an alternative route, the defendant would have been discharged, for the reason that the parties contemplated an open Suez Canal as a specific condition or means of performance." 6 Corbin, supra, § 1339, at 399 n. 57. Appellant claims this supports its argument, since the Suez route was contemplated as usual and customary. But there is obviously a difference, in deciding whether a contract allocates the risk of a contingency's occurrence, between a contract specifying no route and a contract specifying Suez. We think that when Professor Corbin said, "Except for the provision for an alternative route," he was referring, not to the entire *provision* —"via Suez Canal or Cape of Good Hope" etc.—but to the

fact that *an alternative route* had been provided for. Moreover, in determining what Corbin meant when he said "the parties contemplated an open Suez Canal as a specific condition or means of performance," consideration must be given to the fact, recited by Corbin, that in *Glidden* the parties were specifically aware when the contract was made the Canal might be closed, and the promisee had refused to include a clause excusing performance in the event of closure. Corbin's statement, therefore, is most accurately read as referring to cases in which a route is specified after negotiations reflecting the parties' awareness that the usual and customary route might become unavailable. Compare Held v. Goldsmith, 153 La. 598, 96 So. 272 (1919).

8. The charter provides that the vessel is "in every way fitted for *the voyage*" (emphasis added), and the "P. & I. Bunker Deviation Clause" refers to "the contract voyage" and the "direct and/or customary route." Appellant argues that these provisions require implication of a voyage by the direct and customary route. Actually they prove only what we are willing to accept— that the parties expected the usual and customary route would be used. The provisions in no way condition performance upon nonoccurrence of this contingency.

There are two clauses which allegedly demonstrate that time is of importance in this contract. One clause computes the remuneration "in steaming time" for diversions to other countries ordered by the charterer in emergencies. This proves only that the United States wished to reserve power to send the goods to another country. It does not imply in any way that there was a thing in custom or trade usage, or in the surrounding circumstances generally, which would support our constructing a condition of performance.   The numerous cases requiring performance around the Cape when Suez was closed, see, e.g., Ocean Tramp Tankers Corp. v. V/O Sovfracht (The Eugenia), [1964] 2 Q.B. 226, and cases cited therein, indicate that the Cape route is generally regarded as an alternative means of performance.   So the implied expectation that the route would be via Suez is hardly adequate proof of an allocation to the promisee of the risk of closure.   In some cases, even an express expectation may not amount to a condition of performance.[9]   The doctrine of deviation supports our assumption that parties normally expect performance by the usual and customary route, but it adds nothing beyond this that is probative of an allocation of the risk.[10]

rush about the matter.   The other clause concerns demurrage and dispatch.   The charterer agreed to pay Transatlantic demurrage of $1,200 per day for all time in excess of the period agreed upon for loading and unloading, and Transatlantic was to pay despatch of $600 per day for any saving in time. Of course this provision shows the parties were concerned about time, see Gilmore & Black, *The Law of Admiralty* § 4–8 (1957), but the fact that they arranged so minutely the consequences of any delay or speedup of loading and unloading operates against the argument that they were similarly allocating the risk of delay or speed-up of the voyage.

9.   Uniform   Commercial   Code § 2–614(1) provides: "Where without fault of either party . . . the *agreed* manner of delivery . . . becomes commercially impracticable but a commercially reasonable substitute is available, such substitute performance must be tendered and accepted." (Emphasis added.)   Compare Mr. Justice Holmes' observation: "You can give any conclusion a logical form.   You always can imply a condition in a contract.   But why do you imply it?   It is because of some belief as to the practice of the community or of a class, or because of some opinion as to policy . . . ." Holmes, *The Path of the Law*, 10 Harv. L.Rev. 457, 466 (1897).

10.   The deviation doctrine, drawn principally from admiralty insurance practice, implies into all relevant commercial instruments naming the termini of voyages the usual and customary route between those points.   1 Arnould, *Marine Insurance and Average*, § 376,

at 522 (10th ed. 1921).   Insurance is cancelled when a ship unreasonably "deviates" from this course, for example by extending a voyage or by putting in at an irregular port, and the shipowner forfeits the protection of clauses of exception which might otherwise have protected him from his common law insurer's liability to cargo.   See Gilmore & Black, supra Note 8, § 2–6, at 59–60.   This practice, properly qualified, see *id.* § 3–41, makes good sense, since insurance rates are computed on the basis of the implied course, and deviations in the course increasing the anticipated risk make the insurer's calculations meaningless.   Arnould, supra, § 14, at 26.   Thus the route, so far as insurance contracts are concerned, is crucial, whether express or implied. But even here, the implied term is not inflexible.   Reasonable deviations do not result in loss of insurance, at least so long as established practice is followed.   See Carriage of Goods by Sea Act § 4(4), 49 Stat. 1210, 46 U.S.C. § 1304(4); and discussion of "held covered" clauses in Gilmore & Black, supra, § 3–41, at 161.   Some "deviations" are required.   E.g., Hirsch Lumber Co. v. Weyerhaeuser Steamship Co., 2 Cir., 233 F.2d 791, cert. denied, 352 U.S. 880, 77 S.Ct. 102, 1 L.Ed.2d 80 (1956).   The doctrine's only relevance, therefore, is that it provides additional support for the assumption we willingly make that merchants agreeing to a voyage between two points expect that the usual and customary route between those points will be used.   The doctrine provides no evidence of an allocation of the risk of the route's unavailability.

If anything, the circumstances surrounding this contract indicate that the risk of the Canal's closure may be deemed to have been allocated to Transatlantic. We know or may safely assume that the parties were aware, as were most commercial men with interests affected by the Suez situation, see The Eugenia, supra, that the Canal might become a dangerous area. No doubt the tension affected freight rates, and it is arguable that the risk of closure became part of the dickered terms. Uniform Commercial Code § 2–615, comment 8. We do not deem the risk of closure so allocated, however. Foreseeability or even recognition of a risk does not necessarily prove its allocation.[11] Compare Uniform Commercial Code § 2–615, Comment 1; Restatement, Contracts § 457 (1932). Parties to a contract are not always able to provide for all the possibilities of which they are aware, sometimes because they cannot agree, often simply because they are too busy. Moreover, that some abnormal risk was contemplated is probative but does not necessarily establish an allocation of the risk of the contingency which actually occurs. In this case, for example, nationalization by Egypt of the Canal Corporation and formation of the Suez Users Group did not necessarily indicate that the Canal would be blocked even if a confrontation resulted.[12] The surrounding circumstances do indicate, however, a willingness by Transatlantic to assume abnormal risks, and this fact should legitimately cause us to judge the impracticability of performance by an alternative route in stricter terms than we would were the contingency unforeseen.

We turn then to the question whether occurrence of the contingency rendered performance commercially impracticable under the circumstances of this case. The goods shipped were not subject to harm from the longer, less temperate Southern route. The vessel and crew were fit to proceed around the Cape.[13] Transatlantic was no less able than the United States to purchase insurance to cover the contingency's occurrence. If anything, it is more reasonable to expect owner-operators of vessels to insure against the hazards of war. They are in the best position to calculate the cost of performance by alternative routes (and therefore to estimate the amount of insurance re-

11. See Note, *The Fetish of Impossibility in the Law of Contracts*, 53 Colum.L.Rev. 94, 98 n. 23 (1953), suggesting that foreseeability is properly used "as a *factor* probative of assumption of the risk of impossibility." (Emphasis added.)

12. Sources cited in the briefs indicate formation of the Suez Canal Users Association on October 1, 1956, was viewed in some quarters as an implied threat of force. See N. Y. Times, Oct. 2, 1956, p. 1, col. 1, noting, on the day the charter in this case was executed, that "Britain has declared her freedom to use force as a last resort if peaceful methods fail to achieve a satisfactory settlement." Secretary of State Dulles was able, however, to view the state-

ment as evidence of the canal users' "dedication to a just and peaceful solution." *The Suez Problem* 369–370 (Department of State Pub. 1956).

13. The issue of impracticability should no doubt be "an objective determination of whether the promise can reasonably be performed rather than a subjective inquiry into the promisor's capability of performing as agreed." Symposium, *The Uniform Commercial Code and Contract Law: Some Selected Problems*, 105 U.Pa.L.Rev. 836, 880, 887 (1957). Dealers should not be excused because of less than normal capabilities. But if both parties are aware of a dealer's limited capabilities, no objective determination would be complete without taking into account this fact.

quired), and are undoubtedly sensitive to international troubles which uniquely affect the demand for and cost of their services. The only factor operating here in appellant's favor is the added expense, allegedly $43,972.00 above and beyond the contract price of $305,842.92, of extending a 10,000 mile voyage by approximately 3,000 miles. While it may be an overstatement to say that increased cost and difficulty of performance never constitute impracticability, to justify relief there must be more of a variation between expected cost and the cost of performing by an available alternative than is present in this case,[14] where the promisor can legitimately be presumed to have accepted some degree of abnormal risk, and where impracticability is urged on the basis of added expense alone.[15]

We conclude, therefore, as have most other courts considering related issues arising out of the Suez closure,[16] that performance of this contract was not rendered legally impossible. Even if we agreed with appellant, its theory

14. Two leading English cases support this conclusion. The Eugenia, supra, involved a time charter for a trip from Genoa to India via the Black Sea. The charterers were held in breach of the charter's war clause by entering the Suez Canal after the outbreak of hostilities, but sought to avoid paying for the time the vessel was trapped in the Canal by arguing that, even if they had not entered the Canal, it would have been blocked and the vessel would have had to go around the Cape to India, a trip which "frustrated" the contract because it constituted an entirely different venture from the one originally contemplated. The lower court agreed, but the House of Lords (see Lord Denning's admirable treatment, [1964] 2 Q.B. at 233), "swallowing" the difficulty of applying the frustration doctrine to hypothetical facts, reversed, holding that the contract had to be performed. Especially relevant is the fact that the case expressly overruled Societe Franco Tunisienne D'Armement v. Sidermar S. P. A. (The Massalia), [1961] 2 Q.B. 278, where a voyage charter was deemed frustrated because the Cape route was "highly circuitous" and cost 195s. per long ton to ship iron ore, rather than 134s. via Suez, a difference well in excess of the difference in this case.

In Tsakiroglou & Co. Ltd. v. Noblee Thorl G.m.b.H., supra Note 4, the difference to the seller under a C.I.F. contract in freight costs caused by the Canal's closure was £ 15 per ton instead of £ 7.10s. per ton—precisely twice the cost. The House of Lords found no frustration.

15. See Uniform Commercial Code § 2–615, comment 4: "Increased cost alone does not excuse performance unless the rise in cost is due to some unforeseen contingency which alters the essential nature of the performance." See also 6 Corbin, *supra*, § 1333; 6 Williston, *supra*, § 1952, at 5468.

16. Appellant seeks to distinguish the English cases supporting our view. The Eugenia, supra, appellant argues, involved a time charter. True, but it overruled The Massalia, supra Note 14, which involved a voyage charter. Indeed, when the time charter is for a voyage the difference is only verbal. See Carver, *Carriage of Goods by Sea* 256–257 (10th ed. 1957). More convincing is the argument that *Tsakiroglou & Co. Ltd.*, supra Note 4, involved a contract for the sale of goods, where the seller agreed to a C.I.F. clause requiring him to ship the goods to the buyer. There is a significant difference between a C.I.F. contract and voyage or time charters. The effect of delay in the former due to longer sea voyages is minimized, since the seller can raise money on the goods he has shipped almost at once, and the buyer, once he takes up the documents, can deal with the goods by transferring the documents before the goods arrive. See *Tsakiroglou & Co. Ltd.*, supra Note 4, [1960] 2 Q.B. at 361. But this difference is not so material that impossibility in C.I.F. contracts is unrelated to impossibility in charter parties. It would raise serious questions for a court to require sellers under C.I.F. contracts to perform in circumstances under which

of relief seems untenable. When performance of a contract is deemed impossible it is a nullity. In the case of a charter party involving carriage of goods, the carrier may return to an appropriate port and unload its cargo, The Malcolm Baxter, Jr., 277 U.S. 323, 48 S.Ct. 516, 72 L.Ed. 901 (1928), subject of course to required steps to minimize damages. If the performance rendered has value, recovery in *quantum meruit* for the entire performance is proper. But here Transatlantic has collected its contract price, and now seeks *quantum meruit* relief for the additional expense of the trip around the Cape. If the contract is a nullity, Transatlantic's theory of relief should have been *quantum meruit* for the entire trip, rather than only for the extra expense. Transatlantic attempts to take its profit on the contract, and then force the Government to absorb the cost of the additional voyage.[17] When impracticability without fault occurs, the law seeks an equitable solution, see 6 Corbin, supra, § 1321, and *quantum meruit* is one of its potent devices to achieve this end. There is no interest in casting the entire burden of commercial disaster on one party in order to preserve the other's profit. Apparently the contract price in this case was advantageous enough to deter appellant from taking a stance on damages consistent with its theory of liability. In any event, there is no basis for relief.

Affirmed.

Case Brief

1. Parties/their relationship/how matter reached this court: Transatlantic Financing Corporation, Plaintiff/Appellant/Charter Operator v. United States, Defendant/Appellee/Charterer. Appeal from dismissal of a libel action [a] by the United States District Court for the District of Columbia. 363 F.2d 312, (1966).

2. Cause of action: Recovery for expenses caused by diversion of voyage from normal sea route due to closing of Suez Canal.

3. Facts: In July 1956, Egypt nationalized and took over the operation of the Suez Canal. In October 1956, a contract was executed between Transatlantic and the United States for a voyage from the United States

the sellers could be refused performance by carriers with whom they have entered into charter parties for affreightment. See The Eugenia, supra, [1964] 2 Q.B. at 241. Where the time of the voyage is unimportant, a charter party should be treated the same as a C.I.F. contract in determining impossibility of performance.

These cases certainly are not distinguishable, as appellant suggests, on the ground that they refer to "frustration" rather than to "impossibility." The English regard "frustration" as substantially identical with "impossibility." 6 Corbin, supra, § 1322, at 327 n. 9.

17. The argument that the Uniform Commercial Code requires the buyer to pay the additional cost of performance by a commercially reasonable substitute was advanced and rejected in Symposium, supra Note 13, 105 U.Pa.L.Rev. at 884 n. 205. In Dillon v. United States, 156 F.Supp. 719, 140 Ct.Cl. 508 (1957), relief was afforded for some of the cost of delivering hay from a commercially unreasonable distance, but the suit was one in which the plaintiff had suffered losses far in excess of the relief given.

a. Libel: an initial pleading in a suit in admiralty, equivalent to a petition.

to Iran. No route was stipulated in the contract, although the usual route for such a voyage was through the Suez Canal. When Egypt closed the Suez Canal to traffic in November 1956, Transatlantic delivered the cargo by travelling around the Cape of Good Hope.

4. Relief requested: $43,972.00 above the contract price, the amount representing the added cost to the appellant over its expected cost of performing the contract by the usual route through the Suez Canal.

5. Legal theory relied upon:

   (1) Admiralty principles and practices require by implication in the contract the term that the voyage was to be performed by the "usual and customary" route (i.e., through the Suez Canal). When this route became unavailable the contract became impossible to perform and in delivering the cargo by the alternative route, appellant conferred a benefit upon appellee for which it should be paid in *quantum meruit.*[b]

6. Issue: Did the closing of the Suez Canal render performance by appellant legally impossible under the circumstances of this case?

7. Holding: No. Disposition of case: Decision of lower court affirmed.

8. Reasoning: For a contract to be rendered legally impossible, three conditions must prevail:

   (1) a contingency[c] must occur;

   (2) the risk for this contingency must not have been allocated by agreement or by custom;

   (3) occurrence of the contingency must render performance commercially impracticable. Here, only the first requirement is met. Regarding (2), no express condition of performance via the Suez Canal is a term of this contract, nor is there a constructive condition of performance either in custom or trade usage or in the surrounding circumstances generally. Nor is condition (3) present, for the crew was not subject to harm from the longer route, the vessel and crew were fit to proceed around the Cape, and appellant could have purchased insurance as easily as appellee to protect against the unexpected occurrence.

9. Resulting legal rule: When legal impracticability is urged on the basis of added cost alone, there must be more variation between the expected cost and the actual cost than is present here, where promisor can be presumed to have accepted some abnormal risk and could have insured against it.

---

b. *Quantum meruit:* "As much as it is worth," i.e., the amount deserved.

c. Contingency: an unexpected occurrence. (Definition supplied by the court.)

10. Dicta:

    (1) Even an expressed expectation that the route would be via the Suez Canal may not amount to a condition of performance. (U.C.C. § 2–614(1) cited in footnote.)

    (2) If anything, owner-operators of vessels can be more reasonably expected to insure against the hazards than those who hire their services since owner-operators are in the best position to calculate the cost of performance by alternate routes and to estimate the cost of the insurance required.

AMERICAN TRADING AND PRODUCTION CORP. v. SHELL INTERNATIONAL MARINE LTD.

United States Court of Appeals, Second Circuit, 1972.
453 F.2d 939.

MULLIGAN, CIRCUIT JUDGE:

This is an appeal by American Trading and Production Corporation (hereinafter "owner") from a judgment entered on July 29th, 1971, in the United States District Court for the Southern District of New York, dismissing its claim against Shell International Marine Ltd. (hereinafter "charterer") for additional compensation in the sum of $131,978.44 for the transportation of cargo from Texas to India via the Cape of Good Hope as a result of the closing of the Suez Canal in June, 1967. The charterer had asserted a counterclaim which was withdrawn and is not in issue. The action was tried on stipulated facts and without a jury before Hon. Harold R. Tyler, Jr. who dismissed the claim on the merits in an opinion dated July 22, 1971.

We affirm.

The owner is a Maryland corporation doing business in New York and the charterer is a United Kingdom corporation. On March 23, 1967 the parties entered into a contract of voyage charter in New York City which provided that the charterer would hire the owner's tank vessel, WASHINGTON TRADER, for a voyage with a full cargo of lube oil from Beaumont/Smiths Bluff, Texas to Bombay, India. The charter party provided that the freight rate would be in accordance with the then prevailing American Tanker Rate Schedule (ATRS), $14.25 per long ton of cargo, plus seventy-five percent (75%), and in addition there was a charge of $.85 per long ton for passage through the Suez Canal. On May 15, 1967 the WASHINGTON TRADER departed from Beaumont with a cargo of 16,183.32 long tons of lube oil. The charterer paid the freight at the invoiced sum of $417,327.36 on May 26, 1967. On May 29th, 1967 the owner advised the WASHINGTON TRADER by radio to take additional bunkers at Ceuta due to possible diversion because of the Suez Canal crisis. The vessel arrived at Ceuta, Spanish Morocco on May 30, bunkered and sailed on May 31st, 1967. On June 5th the owner cabled the ship's master advising him of various reports of trouble in the Canal and suggested delay in entering it pending clarification. On that very day, the Suez Canal was closed due to the state of war which had developed in the Middle East. The owner then communicated with the charterer on June 5th through the broker who had negotiated the charter party, requesting approval for the diversion of the WASHINGTON TRADER which then had proceeded to a point about 84 miles northwest of Port Said, the entrance to the Canal. On June 6th the charterer responded that under the circumstances it was "for owner to decide whether to continue to wait or make the alternative passage via the Cape since Charter Party Obliges them to deliver cargo without qualification." In response the owner replied on the same day that in view of the closing of the Suez, the WASHINGTON TRADER would proceed to Bombay via the Cape of Good Hope and "[w]e [are] reserving all rights for extra compensation." The vessel proceeded westward, back through the Straits of Gibraltar and around the Cape and eventually arrived in Bombay on July 15th (some 30 days later than initially expected), traveling a total of 18,055 miles instead of the 9,709 miles which it would have sailed had the Canal been open. The owner billed $131,978.44 as extra compensation which the charterer has refused to pay.

On appeal and below the owner argues that transit of the Suez Canal was the agreed specific means of performance of the voyage charter and that the supervening destruction of this means rendered the contract legally impossible to perform and therefore discharged the owner's unperformed obligation (Restatement of Contracts § 460 (1932)). Consequently, when the WASHINGTON TRADER eventually delivered the oil after journeying around the Cape of Good Hope, a benefit was conferred upon the charterer for which it should respond in *quantum meruit.* The validity of this proposition depends upon a finding that the parties contemplated or agreed that the Suez passage was to be the exclusive method of performance, and indeed it was so argued on appeal. We cannot construe the agreement in such a fashion. The parties contracted for the shipment of the cargo from Texas to India at an agreed rate and the charter party makes absolutely no reference to any fixed route. It is urged that the Suez passage was a condition of performance because the ATRS rate was based on a Suez Canal passage, the invoice contained a specific Suez Canal toll charge and the vessel actually did proceed to a point 84 miles northwest of Port Said. In our view all that this establishes is that both parties contemplated that the Canal would be the probable route. It was the cheapest and shortest, and therefore it was in the interest of both that it be utilized. However, this is not at all equivalent to an agreement that it be the exclusive method of performance. The charter party does not so provide and it seems to have been well understood in the shipping industry that the Cape route is an acceptable alternative in voyages of this character.

The District of Columbia Circuit decided a closely analogous case, Transatlantic Financing Corp. v. United States, 124 U.S.App.D.C. 183, 363 F.2d 312 (1966). There the plaintiff had entered into a voyage charter with defendant in which it agreed to transport a full cargo of wheat on the CHRISTOS from a United States port to Iran. The parties clearly contemplated a Suez passage, but on November 2, 1956, the vessel reduced speed when war blocked the

Suez Canal. The vessel changed its course in the Atlantic and eventually delivered its cargo in Iran after proceeding by way of the Cape of Good Hope. In an exhaustive opinion Judge Skelly Wright reviewed the English cases which had considered the same problem and concluded that "the Cape route is generally regarded as an alternative means of performance. So the implied expectation that the route would be via Suez is hardly adequate proof of an allocation to the promisee of the risk of closure. In some cases, even an express expectation may not amount to a condition of performance." Transatlantic Financing Corp. v. United States, supra, 363 F.2d at 317 (footnote omitted).

Appellant argues that *Transatlantic* is distinguishable since there was an agreed upon flat rate in that case unlike the instant case where the rate was based on Suez passage. This does not distinguish the case in our view. It is stipulated by the parties here that the only ATRS rate published at the time of the agreement from Beaumont to Bombay was the one utilized as a basis for the negotiated rate ultimately agreed upon. This rate was escalated by 75% to reflect whatever existing market conditions the parties contemplated. These conditions are not stipulated. Had a Cape route rate been requested, which was not the case, it is agreed that the point from which the parties would have bargained would be $17.35 per long ton of cargo as against $14.25 per long ton.

Actually, in *Transatlantic* it was argued that certain provisions in the P. & I. Bunker Deviation Clause referring to the direct and/or customary route required, by implication, a voyage through the Suez Canal. The court responded "[a]ctually they prove only what we are willing to accept—that the parties expected the usual and customary route would be used. The provisions in no way condition performance upon non-occurrence of this contingency." Transatlantic Financing Corp. v. United States, supra, 363 F.2d at 317 n. 8. We hold that all that the ATRS rate establishes is that the parties obviously expected a Suez passage but there is no indication at all in the instrument or *dehors* that it was a condition of performance.

This leaves us with the question as to whether the owner was excused from performance on the theory of commercial impracticability (Restatement of Contracts § 454 (1932)). Even though the owner is not excused because of strict impossibility, it is urged that American law recognizes that performance is rendered impossible if it can only be accomplished with extreme and unreasonable difficulty, expense, injury or loss.[1] There is no extreme or unreasonable difficulty apparent here. The alternate route taken was well recognized, and there is no claim that the vessel or the crew or the nature of the cargo made the route actually taken unreasonably difficult, dangerous or onerous. The owner's case here essentially rests upon the element of the additional expense involved—$131,978.44. This represents an increase of less than one

1. This is the formula utilized in the Restatement of Contracts § 454 (1932).

third over the agreed upon $417,327.36. We find that this increase in expense is not sufficient to constitute commercial impracticability under either American or English authority.

Mere increase in cost alone is not a sufficient excuse for non-performance (Restatement of Contracts § 467 (1932)). It must be an "extreme and unreasonable" [2] expense (Restatement of Contracts § 454 (1932)).[3] While in the *Transatlantic* case supra, the increased cost amounted to an increase of about 14% over the contract price, the court did cite with approval [4] the two leading English cases Ocean Tramp Tankers Corp. v. V/O Sovfracht (The Eugenia), [1964] 2 Q.B. 226, 233 (C.A.1963) (which expressly overruled Société Franco Tunisienne D'Armement v. Sidermar S.P.A. (The Messalia), [1961] 2 Q.B. 278 (1960), where the court had found frustration because the Cape route was highly circuitous and involved an increase in cost of approximately 50%), and Tsakiroglou & Co. Lt. v. Noblee Thorl G.m.b.H., [1960] 2 Q.B. 318, 348, aff'd, [1962] A.C., 93 (1961) where the House of Lords found no frustration though the freight costs were exactly doubled due to the Canal closure.[5]

Appellant further seeks to distinguish *Transatlantic* because in that case the change in course was in the mid-Atlantic and added some 300 miles to the voyage while in this case the WASHINGTON TRADER had traversed most of the Mediterranean and thus had added some 9000 miles to the contemplated voyage. It should be noted that although both the time and the length of the altered passage here exceeded those in the *Transatlantic,* the additional compensation sought here is just under one third of the contract price. Aside from this however, it is a fact that the master of the WASHINGTON TRADER

---

2. The Restatement gives some examples of what is "extreme and unreasonable"—Restatement of Contracts § 460, Illus. 2 (tenfold increase in costs) and Illus. 3 (costs multiplied fifty times) (1932); compare § 467, Illus. 3. See generally G. Grismore, Principles of the Law of Contracts § 179 (rev. ed. J. E. Murray 1965).

3. Both parties take solace in the Uniform Commercial Code which in comment 4 to Section 2–615 states that the rise in cost must "alter the essential nature of the performance . . . ." This is clearly not the case here. The owner relies on a further sentence in the comment which refers to a severe shortage of raw materials or of supplies due to "war, embargo, local crop failure, unforeseen shutdown of major sources of supply or the like, which either causes a marked increase in cost . . . ." Since this is not a case involving the sale of goods but transportation of a cargo where there was an alternative which was a commercially reasonable substitute (see Uniform Commercial Code § 2–614(1)) the owner's reliance is misplaced.

4. Transatlantic Financing Corp. v. United States, supra, 363 F.2d at 319 n. 14.

5. While these are English cases and refer to the doctrine of "frustration" rather than "impossibility" as Judge Skelly Wright pointed out in *Transatlantic,* supra, 363 F.2d at 320 n. 16 the two are considered substantially identical, 6 A. Corbin, Contracts § 1322, at 327 n. 9 (rev. ed. 1962). While *Tsakiroglou* and *The Eugenia* are criticized in Schegal, Of Nuts, and Ships and Sealing Wax, Suez, and Frustrating Things—The Doctrine of Impossibility of Performance, 23 Rutgers L.Rev. 419, 448 (1969), apparently on the theory that the charterer is a better loss bearer, the overruled *Sidermar* case was previously condemned in Berman, Excuse for Nonperformance in the Light of Contract Practices in International Trade, 63 Colum.L.Rev. 1413, 1424–27 (1963).

was alerted by radio on May 29th, 1967 of a "possible diversion because of Suez Canal crisis," but nevertheless two days later he had left Ceuta (opposite Gibraltar) and proceeded across the Mediterranean. While we may not speculate about the foreseeability of a Suez crisis at the time the contract was entered, there does not seem to be any question but that the master here had been actually put on notice before traversing the Mediterranean that diversion was possible. Had the WASHINGTON TRADER then changed course, the time and cost of the Mediterranean trip could reasonably have been avoided, thereby reducing the amount now claimed. (Restatement of Contracts § 336, Comment *d* to subsection (1) (1932)).

In a case closely in point, Palmco Shipping Inc. v. Continental Ore Corp. (*The "Captain George K"*), [1970] 2 Lloyd's L.Rep. 21 (Q.B.1969), *The Eugenia,* supra, was followed, and no frustration was found where the vessel had sailed to a point three miles northwest of Port Said only to find the Canal blocked. The vessel then sailed back through the Mediterranean and around the Cape of Good Hope to its point of destination, Kandla. The distances involved, 9700 miles via the initially contemplated Canal route and 18,400 miles actually covered by way of the Cape of Good Hope, coincide almost exactly with those in this case. Moreover, in *The "Captain George K"* there was no indication that the master had at anytime after entering the Mediterranean been advised of the possibility of the Canal's closure.

Finally, owners urge that the language of the "Liberties Clause," Para. 28(a) of Part II of the charter party [6] provides explicit authority for extra com-

___

6. "28. Liberty Clauses. (a) In any situation whatsoever and wheresoever occurring and whether existing or anticipated before commencement of or during the voyage, which in the judgment of the Owner or Master is likely to give rise to risk of capture, seizure, detention, damage, delay or disadvantage to or loss of the Vessel or any part of her cargo, or to make it unsafe, imprudent, or unlawful for any reason to commence or proceed on or continue the voyage or to enter or discharge the cargo at the port of discharge, or to give rise to delay or difficulty in arriving, discharging at or leaving the port of discharge or the usual place of discharge in such port, the Owner may before loading or before the commencement of the voyage, require the shipper or other person entitled thereto to take delivery of the Cargo at port of shipment and upon their failure to do so, may warehouse the cargo at the risk and expense of the cargo; or the owner or Master, whether or not proceeding toward or entering or attempting to enter the port of discharge or reaching or attempting to reach the usual place of discharge therein or attempting to discharge the cargo there, may discharge the cargo into depot, lazaretto, craft or other place; or the Vessel may proceed or return, directly or indirectly, to or stop at any such port or place whatsoever as the Master or the Owner may consider safe or advisable under the circumstances, and discharge the cargo, or any part thereof, at any such port or place; or the Owner or the Master may retain the cargo on board until the return trip or until such time as the Owner or the Master thinks advisable and discharge the cargo at any place whatsoever as herein provided or the Owner or the Master may discharge and forward the cargo by any means at the risk and expense of the cargo. The Owner may, when practicable, have the Vessel call and discharge the cargo at another or substitute port declared or requested by the Charterer. The Owner or the Master is not required to give notice of discharge of the cargo, or the forwarding thereof as herein provided. When the cargo is discharged from the Vessel, as herein provided, it shall be at its own risk and expense; such dis-

pensation in the circumstances of this case. We do not so interpret the clause. We construe it to apply only where the master, by reason of dangerous conditions, deposits the cargo at some port or haven other than the designated place of discharge. Here the cargo did reach the designated port albeit by another route, and hence the clause is not applicable. No intermediate or other disposition of the oil was appropriate under the circumstances.

Appellant relies on C. H. Leavell & Co. v. Hellenic Lines, Ltd., 13 F.M.C., 76, 1969 A.M.C. 2177 (1969) for a contrary conclusion. That case involved a determination as to whether surcharges to compensate for extra expenses incurred when the Suez Canal was closed after the commencement of a voyage, were available to a carrier. The Federal Maritime Commission authorized the assessment since the applicable tariffs were on file as provided by section 18(b) of the Shipping Act (46 U.S.C. § 817(b)) and also on the basis of Clause 5 of the bill of lading which is comparable to the Liberties Clause in issue here, except for the language which authorized the carrier to "proceed by any route . . . ." (*Leavell,* supra, 13 F.M.C. at 81, 1969 A.M.C. at 2182). This is the very language relied upon by the Commission in finding the surcharge appropriate (*Leavell,* supra, 13 F.M.C. at 89, 1969 A.M.C. at 2191) where the carrier proceeded to the initially designated port of destination via the Cape of Good Hope. Utilization of an alternate route contemplates berthing at the contracted port of destination. There is no such language in the clause at issue. Its absence fortifies the contention that the Liberties Clause was not intended to be applicable to the facts in litigation here.

Matters involving impossibility or impracticability of performance of contract are concededly vexing and difficult. One is even urged on the allocation of such risks to pray for the "wisdom of Solomon." 6 A. Corbin, Contracts § 1333, at 372 (1962). On the basis of all of the facts, the pertinent authority and a further belief in the efficacy of prayer, we affirm.

Case Brief

1. Parties/their relationship/how matter reached this court: American Trading and Production Corporation, Plaintiff/Appellant/Owner v. Shell International Marine LTD., Defendant/Appellee/Charterer. Appeal from a judgment of U. S. District Court for the Southern District of New York, which had dismissed the claim. 453 F.2d 939 (1972).

2. Cause of action: Claim for additional compensation for transportation of cargo from Texas to India via the Cape of Good Hope, due to closing of Suez Canal.

3. Facts: Appellant entered into a contract of a voyage charter with appellee to hire owner's tank vessel to deliver oil from Texas to India, the freight rate to be in accordance with the prevailing rate schedule, with an additional charge per ton for passage through the Suez Canal.

charge shall constitute complete delivery and performance under this contract and the Owner shall be freed from any further responsibility. For any service rendered to the cargo as herein provided the Owner shall be entitled to a reasonable extra compensation."

Closing of Suez Canal resulted in decision to travel to India via the Cape of Good Hope, resulting in a voyage of 18,095 miles instead of 9,709 miles. Owner billed $131,978.44 in extra costs.

4. Relief requested: Owner seeks $131,978.44 in extra compensation from charterer.

5. Legal theories relied upon:

(1) In *quantum meruit* liability for benefit conferred upon charterer by Owner's performance by other than agreed-upon methods, since contract was legally impossible to perform.

(2) Commercial impracticability excused owner from performance because delivery had to be performed by a more expensive alternate route.

(3) "Liberties Clause" of the charter party provides explicit compensation for the circumstances of this case.

6. Issues:

(1) Was contract legally impossible to perform, subsequent delivery by owner thus conferring upon charterer a benefit for which it should respond in *quantum meruit?*

(2) Was owner excused from performance on the theory of commercial impracticability?

(3) Did the Liberties clause of the charter party provide explicit compensation for the circumstances of this case?

7. Holdings:

(1) No.

(2) No.

(3) No.

Disposition of case: Lower court dismissal affirmed.

8. Reasoning:

(1) In order for benefit in *quantum meruit* to be obtained, the parties to the contract must have contemplated or agreed that the Suez passage was to be the exclusive method of performance. No such agreement was a part of the contract here. The Cape route is well understood in the shipping industry to be an acceptable alternative route. (Citation to Transatlantic Financing Corporation, as "closely analogous.")

(2) The theory of commercial impracticability is premised upon only extreme or unreasonable difficulty, expense, injury or loss resulting from performance. No such circumstances present here, only an increased cost to owner of less than one-third of the contracted price for performance of the contract, an amount insufficient to constitute commercial impracticability.

(3) The Liberties Clause applies only where the master, because of dangerous conditions, deposits the cargo at a port other than the one designated. Here the cargo did reach the designated port, although by another route. Hence, the clause is inapplicable here.

9. Resulting legal rules:

(1) For in *quantum meruit* liability to lie, parties must have agreed in contract that the specific method of performance be one which subsequently became legally impossible to perform.

(2) For commercial impracticability to apply, cost of performance must be extremely and unreasonably in excess of that contemplated, or there must be unreasonable difficulty or injury caused by performance. Increased cost of one-third above the contracted price is not sufficient to constitute commercial impracticability.

10. Dicta: None

NORTHERN CORPORATION v. CHUGACH ELECTRIC ASSOCIATION

Supreme Court of Alaska, 1974.
518 P.2d 76.

BOOCHEVER, JUSTICE.

We are here presented with issues concerning the alleged impossibility of performing a public contract. Northern Corporation (hereafter referred to as Northern), appellant and cross-appellee, entered into a contract with Chugach Electric Association (hereafter Chugach), appellee and cross-appellant, on August 3, 1966 for the repair and protection of the upstream face of the Cooper Lake Dam. The contract was awarded to Northern on the basis of its low bid in the sum of $63,655.

The work to be performed was described as follows:

It is required that the upstream face of Cooper Lake Dam be regraded and riprap and filter layer stone quarried, hauled and placed on the upstream face and all other appurtenant work accomplished as required, all in accordance with these plans and specification [sic]. There are about 1750 cubic yards of filter material and 3950 cubic yards of riprap to be placed. The Contractor shall furnish all labor, equipment, materials, etc. required for this project.

The contract called for completion of the work within 60 days of notice to proceed, which was given on August 29, 1966.

The major expense in performing the contract was to be the procurement and placing of riprap. The bidders on the contract were advised with respect to quarry areas from which rock could be obtained:

A quarry area, with suitable rock outcropping on the stream bank, has been located approximately 2500 feet downstream from the dam. A haul road will have to be constructed, either down the stream bed or along the left bank. The quarry area is shown on the vicinity map.

.   .   .

The Contractor may, at his option, select a quarry different from the site shown on the drawings. In this event, the Contractor shall pay the costs of all tests required to verify the suitability of the rock for this project.

Northern first discovered boulders in the stream bed which would be more economical than the designated quarry and received permission to use this source. According to Northern, approximately 20 percent of the contract requirements were fulfilled before Northern exhausted the supply located in the stream bed. Then in the first week of September, Northern moved to the designated quarry site and commenced shooting rock. On September 19, 1966, Northern wrote to Chugach informing them that the rock in the designated quarry was unusable, but was directed in a letter the following day from Chugach's engineering firm to proceed with further blasting and exploration of the designated areas. By September 27, however, Chugach conceded that suitable rock was not available at the designated site and reformed the agreement accordingly.

Alternate quarry sites were found at the opposite end of the lake from the dam. As a result of negotiations, Chugach wrote to Northern on September 27, 1966 authorizing completion of the contract by use of these alternate quarry sites. The authorization provided for amendments to reflect the circumstance that suitable rock was not available in the stream bed for mining, nor in the quarry which had been designated in the original contract documents. Paragraph 3 of the letter of authorization specified:

Rock will be quarried in suitable sizes and quantities to complete the project and will be stockpiled in or near the quarry, or quarries, mentioned above for transport across Cooper Lake to the dam site when such lake is frozen to a sufficient depth to permit heavy vehicle traffic thereon.

The contract price was increased by $42,000. Subsequently, the contract was formally amended in accordance with the September 27, 1966 authorization. Work commenced in the new quarry in October 1966; and within about 30 days, all of the required rock was drilled and shot.

Although there is some question as to who first suggested it or how it came about, it was the agreement of the parties that the rock from the new quarry site would be transported in winter across the ice of Cooper Lake. In December 1966, Northern cleared a road on the ice to permit deeper freezing of the ice. By the time the ice was thought to be sufficiently thick to begin hauling, however, a water overflow on the ice one to two feet in depth prohibited crossings by the trucks. Northern complained to Chugach of unsafe conditions on the lake ice, but Chugach insisted on performance. In March 1967, one of Northern's Euclid loaders went through the ice and sank, and a small crawler tractor subsequently broke through but was recovered. Neither incident involved loss of life. Despite these occurrences, Chugach and its engineering firm continued to insist on performance, threatening default. On March 27, 1967, Chugach again threatened to consider Northern in default unless they immediately commenced hauling operations. Northern attempted to commence operations but continued to meet with difficulties, finally ceasing operations on March 31, 1967, apparently with the approval of Chugach.

On January 8, 1968, Chugach advised Northern that it would consider Northern in default unless all rock was hauled by April 1, 1968. On January 20, Northern informed Chugach that they were returning to Cooper Lake, and wrote on January 30 that they anticipated favorable conditions to start hauling rock on January 31. The ice conditions were apparently different from those encountered in 1967—there was very little snow cover and no overflow problem. The ice varied from $23\frac{1}{2}$ inches to 30 inches thick, and for several days the temperature had been 30 degrees below zero and clear.

On February 1, 1968, Northern started hauling with half-loaded trucks; but within the first few hours, two trucks with their drivers broke through the ice, resulting in the death of the drivers and loss of the trucks. Northern at this point ceased operations; and on February 16, 1968, informed Chugach that it would make no more attempts to haul rock across the lake. On March 28, 1968, Northern advised Chugach that it considered the contract terminated for impossibility of performance.

Northern commenced legal action against Chugach in September 1968, seeking recovery for costs incurred in attempted completion of the contract less revenues received. The case was tried in superior court without a jury in December 1971. Northern contended that in the original contract there were express and implied warranties that the designated quarry contained sufficient quantities of suitable rock for the job, and that breach of the warranties entitled Northern to damages. In the alternative, Northern argued that the modified contract was impossible of performance, justifying an award to Northern of reasonable costs incurred in attempted performance. Chugach counterclaimed, contending that it overpaid Northern for work performed under the contract, and that it was entitled to liquidated damages for the period between the date of completion specified in the amended contract and the date of its termination by Northern. The superior court discharged the parties from the contract on the ground of impossibility of performance, but denied both parties' claims for damages and attorney's fees. From that decision, Northern appeals and Chugach cross-appeals.

The issues on this appeal may be summarized as follows:

1. Is Northern entitled to damages for breach of alleged express and implied warranties contained in the original contract pertaining to available quantities of rock?

2. In the alternative, was the contract as modified impossible of performance?

3. If the modified contract was impossible of performance, is Northern entitled to reasonable costs incurred in endeavoring to perform it?

4. Is Chugach entitled to liquidated damages for delays in performance of the contract, and to costs and attorney's fees? [1]

Our analysis of the events preceding the lawsuit leads us to the conclusion that the dispositive issues pertain to the question of impossibility of performance. It appears clear to us that the original agreement between Chugach and Northern was superseded as a result of Chugach's letter to Northern, dated September 27, 1966, and the subsequent formal amendment of the contract in accordance therewith. The amendment recognized that the quarries originally specified did not provide a sufficient quantity of riprap. The original contract price of $63,655 was increased by $42,000 to cover the additional costs incurred and to be incurred by Northern in exploration of the quarry originally designated, in securing rock at the redesignated quarries, in hauling the rock to the dam site, in stockpiling it, and in cleaning up the redesignated quarry areas. The amendment was executed by both parties to the contract. Since the amendment provided for the additional costs incurred by Northern as a result of the absence of a suitable rock supply at the quarry originally designated, we need not concern ourselves with whether express or implied warranties were breached with reference to the quantity of rock available at the originally designated quarry.[2] There is no contention here that the amended contract did not designate quarries containing suitable quantities of rock.

IMPOSSIBILITY

The focal question is whether the amended contract was impossible of performance. The September 27, 1966 directive specified that the rock was to be transported "across Cooper Lake to the dam site when such lake is frozen to a sufficient depth to permit heavy vehicle traffic thereon," and the formal amendment specified that the hauling to the dam site would be done during the winter of 1966–67. It is therefore clear that the parties contemplated that the rock would be transported across the frozen lake by truck. Northern's repeated efforts to perform the contract by this method during the winter of 1966–67 and subsequently in February 1968, culminating in the tragic loss of life, abundantly support the trial court's finding that the contract was impossible of performance by this method.

Chugach contends, however, that Northern was nevertheless bound to perform, and that it could have used means other than hauling by truck across the ice to transport the rock. The answer to Chugach's contention is that, as the trial court found, the parties contemplated that the rock would be hauled by truck once the ice froze to a sufficient depth to support the weight of the vehicles. The specification of this particular method of performance presupposed the existence of ice frozen to the requisite depth. Since this expectation of the parties was never fulfilled, and since the provisions relating to the means

1. Chugach's contention that it overpaid Northern has apparently been abandoned on appeal.

2. See Cooperative Refinery Ass'n v. Consumers Public Power Dist., 190 F.2d 852, 856–857 (8th Cir. 1951); Johnson v. Mosley, 179 F.2d 573, 588 (8th Cir. 1950); In re Swindle, 188 F.Supp. 601, 604 (D.Or.1960).

of performance was clearly material,[3] Northern's duty to perform was discharged by reason of impossibility.[4]

There is an additional reason for our holding that Northern's duty to perform was discharged because of impossibility. It is true that in order for a defendant to prevail under the original common law doctrine of impossibility, he had to show that no one else could have performed the contract.[5] However, this harsh rule has gradually been eroded, and the Restatement of Contracts [6] has departed from the early common law rule by recognizing the principle of "commerical impracticability". Under this doctrine, a party is discharged from his contract obligations, even if it is technically possible to perform them, if the costs of performance would be so disproportionate to that reasonably contemplated by the parties as to make the contract totally impractical in a commercial sense.[7] This principle was explicated in Natus Corp. v. United States,[8] where the Court of Claims, although holding that the defense was not justified on the facts of that case, went on to explain:

> In taking this position, we readily concede that the doctrine of legal impossibility does not demand a showing of actual or literal impossibility.

> Removed from the strictures of the common law, "impossibility" in its modern context has become a coat of many colors, including among its hues the point argued here—namely, impossibility predicated upon "commercial impracticability." This concept—which finds expression both in case law . . . and in other authorities . . . is grounded upon the assumption that in legal contemplation something is impracticable when it

3. The initial contract price was $63,655. Performing by the alternative method (barging) would have cost an additional $59,520.

4. Restatement of Contracts § 460 (1932) provides in pertinent part:

> Where the existence of a specific thing . . . is, either by the terms of a bargain or in the contemplation of both parties, necessary for the performance of a promise in the bargain, a duty to perform the promise . . . is discharged if the thing . . . subsequently is not in existence in time for seasonable performance. . . .

In accord with this rule is Texas Co. v. Hogarth Shipping Co., 256 U.S. 619, 629–630, 41 S.Ct. 612, 65 L.Ed. 1123, 1130 (1921); Parrish v. Stratton Cripple Creek Min. & Development Co., 116 F.2d 207 (10th Cir. 1940), cert. denied, 312 U.S. 698, 61 S.Ct. 738, 85 L.Ed. 1132 (1941); see especially Kansas, Oklahoma & Gulf Railway Co. v. Grand Lake Grain Co., 434 P.2d 153 (Okl.1967).

Discharge of a party for impossibility of performance abates the severity of the old common law doctrine that not even objective impossibility excused performance; see Annot., 84 A.L.R.2d 12, 22 (1962).

5. See generally 84 A.L.R.2d at 35–36.

6. Restatement of Contracts § 454 (1932) states:

> Definition of Impossibility.

> In the Restatement of this Subject impossibility means not only strict impossibility but impracticability because of extreme and unreasonable difficulty, expense, injury or loss involved.

7. For example, one California case applied this result where it was about ten times as expensive to perform as was contemplated by the parties. Mineral Park Land Co. v. Howard, 172 Cal. 289, 156 P. 458 (1916).

8. 371 F.2d 450, 178 Ct.Cl. 1 (1967).

can only be done at an excessive and unreasonable cost. As stated in Transatlantic Financing Corp. v. United States . . .:

> . . . The doctrine ultimately represents the ever-shifting line, drawn by courts hopefully responsive to commercial practices and mores, at which the community's interest in having contracts enforced according to their terms is outweighed by the commercial senselessness of requiring performance . . . [citations omitted].[9]

Sec. 465 of the Restatement also provides that a serious risk to life or health will excuse nonperformance.[10]

Alaska has adopted the Restatement doctrine whereby commercial impracticability may under certain circumstances justify regarding a contract as impossible to perform. In Merl F. Thomas Sons, Inc. v. State,[11] this court was confronted with an appeal from a grant of summary judgment against a contractor who alleged in defense of nonperformance that the contemplated means of performing a clearing contract was to move equipment across the ice on the Susitna River from Talkeetna to the job site. Due to thin ice, this means of performance was impossible. Despite the state's contention that the equipment could be transported across the ice at Hurricane, some 70 miles to the north, we reversed the grant of summary judgment, holding that the contractor's allegation that all parties contemplated that equipment would be moved across the ice at Talkeetna raised a question of fact material to the defense of impossibility of performance. We quoted with approval Professor Williston's analysis of the concept of impossibility:

> The true distinction is not between difficulty and impossibility. As has been seen, a man may contract to do what is impossible, as well as what is difficult. The important question is whether an unanticipated circumstance, the risk of which should not fairly be thrown upon the promisor,

---

9. *Id.* at 456. See also Transatlantic Financing Corp. v. United States, 124 U.S.App.D.C. 183, 363 F.2d 312 (1966).

10. Restatement of Contracts § 465 states:

When Apprehension of Impossibility Excuses Beginning or Continuing Performance.

(1) Where a promisor apprehends before or during the time for performance of a promise in a bargain that there will be such impossibility of performance as would discharge or suspend a duty under the promise or that performance will seriously jeopardize his own life or health or that of others, he is not liable, unless a contrary intention is manifested or he is guilty of contributing fault, for failing to begin or to continue performance, while such apprehension exists, if the failure to begin or to continue performance is reasonable.

(2) In determining whether a promisor's failure to begin or to continue performance is reasonable under the rule stated in Subsection (1), consideration is given to

(a) the degree of probability, apparent from what he knows or has reason to know, not only of such impossibility but of physical or pecuniary harm or loss to himself or to others if he begins or continues performance, and

(b) the extent of physical or pecuniary harm or loss to himself or to others likely to be incurred by attempting performance as compared with the amount of harmful consequences likely to be caused to the promisee by non-performance.

11. 396 P.2d 76 (Alaska 1964).

has made performance of the promise vitally different from what was reasonably to be expected (footnote omitted).[12]

In the case before us the detailed opinion of the trial court clearly indicates that the appropriate standard was followed. There is ample evidence to support its findings that "[t]he ice haul method of transporting riprap ultimately selected was within the contemplation of the parties and was part of the basis of the agreement which ultimately resulted in amendment No. 1 in October 1966," and that that method was not commercially feasible within the financial parameters of the contract. We affirm the court's conclusion that the contract was impossible of performance.[13]

DAMAGES

The court below found that the decision to utilize the alternate riprap source and the ice haul method of transporting it "was the joint decision of the parties reached in arm's length bargaining and was mutually agreed." Because adequate evidence supports that finding, the cases appellant cites permitting a contractor to recover under an implied warranty of specifications theory are not applicable. Since Chugach did not unilaterally specify the ice haul method, it no more warranted that method than did Northern.

Commencing in February 1967, Northern both orally and by letter began to question the feasibility of the ice haul method. On March 16, it advised of the loss of its Euclid loader, and suggested that an alternate method of hauling the rock be considered and the contract modified. Northern requested authority to demobilize its equipment so as to reduce continuing rental costs. On March 21, 1967, Northern asked to be released from responsibility for loss of life or equipment if an attempt was to be made to haul rock across the lake. On March 22, 1967, it stated:

> We cannot morally require any employee of ours or of our subcontractor's [sic] to operate equipment on the ice any longer this spring. We feel extremely fortunate that we did not lose a life when we lost the L–30 Loader. . . . We are ready to negotiate an alternate method of hauling the rock
> . . . .

Subsequently, an additional letter was sent, emphasizing in detail the impossibility of hauling rock across the ice.

Despite Northern's verbal and written protestations, Chugach implacably insisted on performance of the contract as agreed upon. Repeated demands by Chugach culminated in a January 1968 letter threatening to declare Northern in default, and to take such further steps against its surety as might be necessary, unless all rock was hauled by April 1. As a result, the final and ultimately fatal, effort was undertaken in February.

---

12. Id. at 79, quoting from 6 Williston, Contracts § 1963 at 5511 (rev. ed. 1938).

13. Affirmance of this holding disposes of Chugach's contention that it was entitled to liquidated damages for delay. Only if the contract were held to be possible to perform could a right to damages for delay arise, for otherwise the legal duty to perform would be discharged.

It is Northern's contention that if it is not entitled to recover under an implied warranty theory, it should be awarded compensation under the so-called "changes" clause of the contract. Under that clause, Chugach reserved the right to make changes in the contract plans and specifications; but if the cost of the project to Northern was increased as a result of the modification, the contract price would be increased by an amount equal to the reasonable cost thereof.[14]

Under comparable clauses in government contracts, contractors have been awarded their additional costs in endeavoring to meet faulty specifications that were impossible to comply with, even when such costs were incurred prior to a negotiated modification. For example, in Hol-Gar Mfg. Corp. v. United States [15] the Government solicited proposals for the manufacture and delivery of electric generator sets in accordance with an elaborate set of specifications drafted by the Air Force Air Research and Development Command. On the basis of Hol-Gar's proposal, a fixed-price contract was negotiated. Upon testing, pre-production samples were found not to comply with the Government specifications. At subsequent meetings, Hol-Gar's representative stated that they did not believe that the engine which they had selected could meet the Government's performance requirements, and that the specifications should be changed to permit a substituted engine. The contract was then amended, relaxing the size and weight limitations in the existing specifications. Hol-Gar submitted a claim for costs incurred in trying to perform within the requirements of the original specifications. It had initially been agreed that if, as a result of testing, changes in the specifications were required, such changes

14. Art. I, sec. 2, of the Chugach-Northern contract specifies:

Changes in Construction. The Owner, acting through the Engineer and with the approval of the Administrator, may from time to time during the progress of the construction of the Project, make such changes, additions to or subtractions from the Plans and Specifications which are part of the Proposal as conditions may warrant; provided, however, that if substantial change in the construction to be done shall require an extension of time, a reasonable extension will be granted if the Bidder shall make a written request therefor to the Owner within ten days after any such change is made. If the cost of the Project to the Bidder to make the change shall be increased or decreased, the contract price shall be amended by an amount equal to the reasonable cost thereof in accordance with a construction contract amendment signed by the Owner and the Bidder and approved by the Administrator, but no claim for additional compensation for any such change or addition will be considered unless the Bidder shall have made a written request therefor to the Owner prior to the commencement of work in connection with such change or addition. The reasonable cost of any increase or decrease in the contract price covered by contract amendment as outlined above, in the absence of other mutual agreement, shall be computed on the basis of the direct cost of materials, f. o. b. the site of the Project, plus the direct cost of labor necessary to incorporate such materials into the Project (including actual cost of payroll taxes and insurance, not to exceed ten percent of payroll cost of labor), plus fifteen percent of the direct cost of materials and labor. Labor cost shall be limited to the direct costs for workmen and foremen. Costs for Bidder's main office overhead, job office overhead and superintendence shall not be included.

15. 360 F.2d 634, 175 Ct.Cl. 518 (1966).

were to be processed in accordance with the "changes" clause of the contract (which was very similar to the "changes" clause of the Chugach contract). The court held:

> Since the necessity for the change was not due to plaintiff's fault, but to faulty specifications, an equitable adjustment requires that plaintiff be paid the increase in its costs over what they would have been had no change been required.

The Armed Services Board of Contract Appeals has recognized the correctness of the allowance of costs incident to an attempt to comply with defective specifications. See, e.g., J. W. Hurst & Son Awnings, Inc., 59–1 BCA ¶ 2095 at 8965 (1959), where the Board stated:

> . . . Where, as here, the change is necessitated by defective specifications and drawings, the equitable adjustment to which a contractor is entitled must, if it is to be equitable, i.e., fair and just, include the costs which it incurred in attempting to perform in accordance with the defective specifications and drawings. Under these circumstances the equitable adjustment may not be limited to costs incurred subsequent to the issuance of the change orders [citations omitted].[16]

In Maxwell Dynamometer Co. v. United States,[17] the Court of Claims relying on *Hol-Gar*, also found that the plaintiff was entitled to recover increased costs and expenses which were incurred in attempting to comply with a specification requirement that was impossible to meet.[18]

Closely analogous to the Chugach situation is the decision of the Armed Services Board of Contract Appeals in *Landsverk Electrometer Co.*[19] A manufacturer of dosimeters entered into a contract, thinking that an electrical leakage requirement could be met; but recognizing that it would be necessary for him to "stretch the state of the art" to comply. When, after vain attempts, the contractor advised the Government that it could not meet the specification, the Government relaxed the specification. Although it was held that the contractor was not entitled to extra compensation for the work performed in attempting to meet the specifications before notification to the Government, because the parties had contemplated the necessity of substantial research efforts to meet the required specifications and the contractor had not expended substantially more effort to that end than it was reasonable to anticipate, the Board went on to state:

> There was here no insistence by the Government that the contractor perform, or continue to try to perform, in the face of the contractor's protests

16. Id. at 638. The court additionally based its decision on a finding of breach of implied warranty of the specifications. Judge Davis in concurring, however, evaluated the record as indicating that neither party warranted the specifications, a situation analogous to that of Chugach and Northern.

17. 386 F.2d 855, 181 Ct.Cl. 607 (1967).

18. See also Bell v. United States, 404 F.2d 975, 186 Ct.Cl. 189 (1968); Jack Heller, Inc., 72–1 BCA ¶ 9341 (ASBCA 1972).

19. 67–2 BCA ¶ 6649 (ASBCA 1967).

that performance was impossible and it should be relieved of its obligation to meet that portion of the specification. On the contrary, within two hours of the appellant's telling the Government that it had become convinced that it simply was unable to perform to the upgraded specification, the Government relaxed the specification and permitted performance at the old, lower level. Had the Government, after it had, or should have, become aware that performance could not be achieved, continued to direct further efforts by a contractor, that direction would certainly constitute a compensable change in the contract, the understanding of the parties [sic].[20]

Unlike the Government in the *Landsverk* case, Chugach continued to demand performance, and we hold that its insistence after it was, or should have been, aware that performance could not be accomplished by the ice haul method constituted, in effect, a compensable change in the contract. Notions of equity and fairness compel this result. If liability for increased costs under the "changes" clause of Government contracts has been predicated on the defectiveness of Government specifications, of which the Government has no actual knowledge, then surely one must hold Chugach liable here, for it had been informed not once but repeatedly that the contract was impossible of performance by the ice haul method.

If Chugach, on being advised of the unfeasibility of the ice haul method, and of its hazards to life and property, had issued a change order prior to the fatal accident of February 1968 but at some time after it knew or should have known that performance was impossible, Northern would have been entitled to the extra costs incurred by it in seeking to perform by the impossible method after Chugach had, or should have, become aware of this impossibility. In fact, Chugach apparently recognized this principle of law, for it had agreed earlier to pay Northern an additional sum for its abortive efforts to obtain rock from the initially-designated quarry. Once alerted to the impossibility of performance by the agreed-upon ice haul method, Chugach's adamant insistence on such performance and its refusal to issue a change order should not be permitted to bar Northern's claim under the "changes" clause. It would indeed be anomalous to hold Chugach liable for such extra costs previously incurred if it belatedly provided for a change order after ascertaining the impossibility of utilizing an ice road, while absolving it from such liability when it continued to insist on an impossible and highly hazardous performance. Despite the fact that no change order was actually issued by Chugach, we hold that it should be held liable for Northern's increased costs incurred after such time as Chugach was reasonably placed on notice that it was not feasible to perform the contract by means of the ice haul method. At that time, it should either have agreed to a termination of the contract or issued a change order providing for some other method of hauling the rock. Those costs incurred by Northern thereafter in its vain attempts to perform the impossible in accordance with Chugach's demands should have been recompensed.

20. Id. at p. 30,823.

The case is remanded for further proceedings in accordance with this opinion. Upon remand, the court should determine when Chugach knew or should have known of the impossibility of performance by the ice haul method; and if that date is ascertained to be prior to the actual termination of the contract, Northern should be awarded its costs incurred thereafter, the amount to be determined in accordance with the "changes" clause of the contract.[21]

Affirmed in part, reversed in part and remanded.

ERWIN and FITZGERALD, JJ., not participating.

Case Brief

1. Parties/their relationship/how matter reached this court: Northern Corporation, Appellant/Contractor v. Chugach Electric Association, Appellee/Owner. The Superior Court, Third Judicial District, Anchorage, discharged parties from contract on ground of impossibility of performance, but denied both parties' claims for damages and attorney's fees. Contractor appeals and owner cross-appeals.

2. Cause of action: Appellant seeks recovery for costs incurred in attempted completion of the contract less revenues received.

3. Facts: Appellant and appellee entered into a contract for the procurement and hauling of rock from a designated area within a quarry, the rock to be transported across a specified lake to a certain dam site when the lake had frozen enough to permit heavy vehicle traffic. When suitable rock was not found at the originally-designated site, the agreement was reformed to permit a new site and the contract price was increased by $42,000. All the required rock was procured and prepared for transporting. Although both parties had agreed that the rock was to be transported across the lake, appellant soon discovered that the ice was too thin to permit this arrangement, appellant losing a loader and a tractor through the ice. Nevertheless, appellee insisted upon performance, threatening, in January 1968, to hold appellant in default of contract unless the rock was transported by April 1, 1968. On February 1, 1968, appellant began hauling rock with half-loaded trucks; nevertheless two trucks and their drivers broke through the ice, resulting in the death of the drivers and the loss of the trucks. Appellant then ceased operations, informing appellee that it would make no more attempts to haul rock and that it considered the contract terminated for impossibility of performance.

4. Relief requested: Recovery by appellant for costs incurred in the attempted completion of the contract, less revenues received. Appellee counter-claimed, contending that it had overpaid appellant for work performed under the contract and thus was entitled to liquidated dam-

---

21. Our decision makes it unnecessary to consider Chugach's contention on its cross-appeal that because it was the prevailing party, it was entitled to costs and attorney's fees.

ages for the period between the date of completion specified in the amended contract and the date of its termination by appellant. (Appellee's claim of overpayment was abandoned on appeal.)

5. Legal theories relied upon:

(Appellant) (1) Express and implied warranties that the designated quarry contained enough rock for the job; thus breach of warranties entitles appellant to damages.

(Appellant) (2) (Alternatively) the modified contract was impossible to perform, justifying an award to appellant of reasonable costs incurred in attempted performance.

(Appellant) (3) The increase in costs to appellant constitutes a compensable change in contract under the changes clause of the contract.

(Appellee) (1) Appellee is entitled to liquidated damages for delays in performance of the contract and for costs and attorney's fees.

6. Issues:

(1) Is appellant entitled to damages for breach of alleged express and implied warranties contained in the original contract pertaining to available quantities of rock?

(2) (Alternatively) was the contract as modified impossible of performance? [a]

(3) If the modified contract was impossible of performance, is appellant entitled to reasonable costs incurred in attempting to perform it?

(4) Is appellee entitled to liquidated damages for delays in performance of the contract and for costs incurred by attempting performance, and for attorney's fees?

7. Holding:

(1) No;

(2) Yes;

(3) Yes;

(4) Previous holdings make it unnecessary to consider this issue.

Disposition of Case: Lower court decision affirmed in part (Issues 1 and 2), reversed in part (Issue 3), and remanded.

8. Reasoning of the court:

(Issue 1) Since the original agreement was superseded by an amendment executed by both parties to the contract and since the amendment provided for additional costs incurred by the appellant, the court need not be concerned with whether warranties were breached with reference to the quantity of rock available at the originally-desig-

---

a. Court calls this the "focal issue."

nated quarry. Appellant does not contend that the amended contract did not designate quarries containing suitable quantities of rock.

(Issue 2) Since both parties' expectation was that the rock be hauled across the ice by truck, and since the expectation presupposed ice frozen deeply enough to support such passage (which expectation was not fulfilled), and since this presupposition was material to performance, appellant's duty to perform was discharged by reason of impossibility. Additionally, appellant is excused under the principle of commercial impracticability, which has superseded the original harsh rule of impossibility. (Citation to Restatement of Contracts § 454(132): a party is excused from his contract obligation, if it is so disproportionate to that reasonably contemplated by the parties as to make the contract impractical in a commercial sense. (Restatement of Contracts § 465 excuses non-performance if life or health would be at risk by performer.) **b**

(Issue 3) Upon remand, the Court should determine when appellee knew or should have known performance was impossible and if that date preceded actual termination of the contract, appellant should be awarded costs incurred thereafter. Notions of equity and fairness entitle appellant to its extra costs incurred in seeking to perform by the required but impossible method after such time as appellee was reasonably placed on notice that it was not feasible to perform the contract by the means required.

(Issue 4) See Holding, above.

9. Resulting legal rules (existing rules cited by court):

   (1) The doctrine of impossibility has been expanded to include the principle of commercial impracticability.

   (2) A party to a contract is entitled to recover increased costs incurred in attempting to comply with a specification requirement in the contract that is impossible to meet, if such requirement is insisted upon by the other party to the contract.

10. Dicta: None

B. ANALOGIZING

Your case briefs will be useful as the basis for analogizing, the process of reasoning from case to case. Analogizing, pointing out the similarities and differences among cases, is the primary form of legal reasoning.[4] It is of great importance to legal argument because of the doctrine of precedent (*stare decisis*),[5] which rests upon the presumption that justice requires the law to treat

---

b. Transatlantic Financing Corporation and other cases are cited.

4. Analogizing is often used more narrowly to mean "showing similarities" as opposed to "distinguishing."

The legal meaning of "analogy"—like its non-legal meaning—is "comparison made possible by similarities."

5. Precedent and *stare decisis* are usually used interchangeably by legal

persons in similar circumstances similarly. The use of precedent helps prevent court decisions based upon influence, bias, or sentimentalism, and to avoid the whimsical or random application of law. The use of precedent therefore promotes the uniform application of the law to all persons.

Reliance upon precedent also provides legal adjudication consistent in time. It helps assure that the law will be applied today as it was applied yesterday and will be applied tomorrow. Thus precedent provides a guide for conduct, assuring that conduct legal today will not be illegal tomorrow.

You will rely on precedent when you compare your case or fact situation to earlier cases or fact situations. You cannot apply precedent to the facts of your case, however, unless:

(1) Your case is analogous in significant respects to the case you are comparing it with, and

(2) the opinion in the earlier case is either binding upon your case or persuasive to it.

Regarding condition (1), a case is considered analogous to a previous case if its key facts [6] and the rule of law to be applied are similar. Conversely, if either the key facts or the applicable rule of law is different, the case can be "distinguished" from the preceding case and the doctrine of precedent will not apply.

With regard to condition (2), analogous previous court decisions may be either binding, persuasive, or not binding upon the court deciding the instant case. Only when the previous court decision is binding is it mandatory for *your* court to follow it. Analogous decisions of superior courts in each judicial system are binding upon inferior courts in that system. Analogous decisions of the United States Supreme Court are binding on all other courts. Analogous decisions of the highest state court are binding upon a trial court in the same state. But higher courts in a jurisdiction are not bound by analogous lower court decisions in that jurisdiction, though they may consider those decisions persuasive. And although analogous decisions of a court in one judicial system are generally not binding upon a court in another system, they also may be adopted as persuasive.[7] Dictum is never binding, but may be persuasive when it appears in the opinion of a higher court of the same jurisdiction. Dicta in decisions of the United States Supreme Court are often accorded great weight by lower courts.

writers. (*Stare decisis* is Latin for "to stand as decided.")

6. For the definition of "key facts" see p. 84.

7. The legal doctrines of *res judicata* and "full faith and credit" are ex-

ceptions. Statsky and Wernet, *Case Analysis and Fundamentals of Legal Writing* (1977), have a comprehensive treatment of analogization (281–322).

After ensuring that key facts of the previous cases are similar to those of the case under consideration and that the legal rule applied in the previous case is either binding or persuasive, you can apply analogy. To do so:

(1) Compare and contrast the key facts of the earlier cases with *your* facts.

(2) If the key facts are similar, extract from the earlier cases the legal principle(s) upon which those cases were decided.

(3) Apply those principles to your *case*.

These three steps may seem mechanical, but the results of analogizing are far from cut-and-dried because the decision of whether facts are similar or different is a subjective one. Only if the facts of your case are "on all fours" can you assume that a court will find your case exactly like the previous one. Hardly ever are facts of one case exactly like those of another; that situation is about as rare as a final examination question containing exactly the facts of a case studied in your casebook! Similarity is a matter of degree: other relationships between cases may be expressed as "applicable," "analogous," "dissimilar," or "inapposite."

Because opinion-forming is a subjective process, courts may variously interpret prior decisions. What an earlier case really *means* can thus only be found in subsequent court opinions. An illustration of this assertion is the ancient case that established the "insanity defense," which provides that insanity is a total defense to behavior that would otherwise be criminal. More than 400 years ago, the court in *Beverley's Case* [8] held that no felony or murder could be committed without felonious intent and that a person deprived of reason could not possess such intent. Later courts might well have interpreted this rule to require a determination about whether the accused person did or did not have the requisite intent. Instead, later courts asked *what degree* of incapacity would excuse the accused person from criminal conduct. As a result of that interpretation, today a person is not guilty of a crime he committed with specfic intent to do so if his mental capacity is judged to preclude his forming general intent. [9] Had courts interpreted the legal principle in *Beverley's Case* differently, the modern insanity defense would not exist in its present form.

The case of *Laird v. State,* which follows, illustrates the subjective quality of judicial analogizing. Note how, in the majority opinion, earlier cases are used to justify the decision, while the same cases are cited in the dissent as justification for a different conclusion.

8. 76 Eng.Rep. 1118, 1121 (K.B.).

(See discussion in G. Block, "The Semantic Delusion of the Insanity Defense," *University of Pittsburgh Law Review*, Vol. 44, Issue 3.)

9. The trial of the attempted assassin of President Reagan illustrates this point.

LAIRD v. STATE

Supreme Court of Florida, 1977.
342 So.2d 962.

SUNDBERG, JUSTICE.

This is an appeal from a judgment entered in the Circuit Court of the Seventeenth Judicial Circuit, in and for Broward County. We have jurisdiction under Article V, Section 3(b)(1), Florida Constitution.

Appellants John Laird and Lorraine Coffey were charged by information with one count of possession of cannabis in excess of five grams and one count of possessing paraphernalia. After pleading not guilty, appellants filed a motion to dismiss the information on the grounds that Section 893.13(1)(e), Florida Statutes, and related portions of Chapter 893, proscribing possession of marijuana, are unconstitutional as violative of the right to privacy. Appellants urged that the statutory provision, by including the private, noncommercial possession and/or use of marijuana in a private home, did not bear a substantial relationship to a proper governmental purpose.

After denial of their motion to dismiss, appellants moved to withdraw their pleas of not guilty and enter pleas of *nolo contendere* to the possession count, while reserving the right to appeal the denial of the motion to dismiss. Appellant Laird admitted having the marijuana in his apartment on the day in question, and appellant Coffey admitted being present at the apartment. The trial court accepted appellants' pleas, withheld adjudication, and placed Laird and Coffey on two and one-half years' probation. The State entered a *nolle prosequi* as to the paraphernalia possession charge.

Notice of appeal to the District Court of Appeal, Fourth District, was timely filed, but on appellants' motion, the cause was transferred to this Court by order of the District Court dated February 4, 1976.

Appellants see this case—which raises the narrow issue of whether the State can prohibit private possession of marijuana in the home—as a clash between a basic constitutional right to privacy and the State's police power. It is urged upon us that appellants enjoy the constitutional right to smoke marijuana in the privacy of Laird's domicile. The reasoning of cases such as Griswold v. Connecticut, 381 U.S. 479, 85 S.Ct. 1678, 14 L.Ed.2d 510 (1965), and Eisenstadt v. Baird, 405 U.S. 438, 92 S.Ct. 1029, 31 L.Ed.2d 349 (1972), is said to be applicable to the instant controversy. Appellants argue that a decision of the Supreme Court of Alaska, Ravin v. State, 537 P.2d 494 (Alaska 1975), provides persuasive authority for the position which they advance.

For the reasons discussed herein we are unable to accept appellants' contention. We reject the notion that smoking marijuana at home is the type of conduct protected by the constitutional right to privacy and, on this record, affirm the trial court.

In *Griswold v. Connecticut,* supra, the United States Supreme Court determined that a Connecticut statute which made the use of contraceptives a criminal offense was invalid as an unconstitutional invasion of the right to privacy of married persons. Mr. Justice Douglas, writing for the majority, found "that specific guarantees in the Bill of Rights have penumbras, formed by emanations from those guarantees that help give them life and substance." 381 U.S. at 484, 85 S.Ct. at 1681. The marital relationship was held to lie "within the zone of privacy created by several fundamental guarantees." Id. at 485, 85 S.Ct. at 1682. Justice Douglas placed heavy emphasis upon the marital relationship of the *Griswold* parties:

> "We deal with a right of privacy older than the Bill of Rights—older than our political parties, older than our school systems. Marriage is a coming together for better or for worse, hopefully enduring, and intimate to the degree of being sacred." Id. at 486, 85 S.Ct. at 1682.

Griswold's protection of the privacy of the marital relationship was extended to certain intimate aspects of the lives of single persons as well in Eisenstadt v. Baird, supra, and Roe v. Wade, 410 U.S. 113, 93 S.Ct. 705, 35 L.Ed. 2d 147 (1973). *Eisenstadt* invalidated a Massachusetts statute which made it a crime to sell, lend, or give away any contraceptive drug, medicine, instrument, or article. The statute permitted physicians to administer or prescribe contraceptive drugs or articles for married persons and allowed pharmacists to fill prescriptions for such items for married persons. The Court determined that the Massachusetts law could be upheld neither as a deterrent to fornication nor as a health measure nor as a prohibition on contraception. The third justification was dismissed on privacy grounds:

> If under *Griswold* the distribution of contraceptives to married persons cannot be prohibited, a ban on distribution to unmarried persons would be equally impermissible. It is true that in *Griswold* the right of privacy in question inhered in the marital relationship. Yet the marital couple is not an independent entity with a mind and heart of its own, but an association of two individuals each with a separate intellectual and emotional makeup. If the right of privacy means anything, it is the right of the *individual,* married or single, to be free from unwarranted governmental intrusion into matters so fundamentally affecting a person as the decision whether to bear or beget a child. . . . . 405 U.S. at 453, 92 S.Ct. at 1038.

In *Roe v. Wade,* supra, an unmarried pregnant woman who wished to undergo an abortion sought a declaratory judgment that the Texas criminal abortion statutes, which proscribed all abortions except those procured or attempted by medical advice for the purpose of saving the life of the mother, were unconstitutional. The Supreme Court held, inter alia, that the right to privacy encompasses a woman's decision whether or not to terminate her pregnancy, but that a woman's right to an abortion is not absolute and may to some extent be limited by the State's interest in safeguarding her health, in maintaining proper medical standards, and protecting potential human life. After listing some decisions in which the Court or individual justices had discerned the existence of the constitutional right to privacy, Mr. Justice Blackmun, writing for the majority, declared:

". . . These decisions make it clear that only personal rights that can be deemed 'fundamental' or 'implicit in the concept of ordered liberty,' Palko v. Connecticut, 302 U.S. 319, 325, 58 S.Ct. 149, 82 L.Ed. 288 (1937), are included in this guarantee of personal privacy. They also make it clear that the right has some extension to activities relating to marriage [citation omitted]; procreation [citation omitted]; contraception [citation omitted]; family relationships [citation omitted]; and child rearing and education [citations omitted]."   410 U.S. at 152–153, 93 S.Ct. at 726.

This statement of the scope of the constitutional right to privacy remains the definitive statement of the law in this area.

Appellants argue that another United States Supreme Court decision, Stanley v. Georgia, 394 U.S. 557, 89 S.Ct. 1243, 22 L.Ed.2d 542 (1969), controls the instant controversy. In *Stanley,* the Court reversed a conviction for possession of obscene matter in violation of a Georgia statute. The appellant in *Stanley* merely owned certain allegedly obscene films for showing in his own home; these films were seized from his residence incident to a search undertaken to find evidence of bookmaking activities. It is true that, in reversing the defendant's conviction, the Court found the right to privacy to exist in a context outside of the intimate personal relationships at issue in *Griswold, Eisenstadt,* and *Roe v. Wade, supra.* But in so doing the Court, speaking through Justice Marshall, laid special emphasis on Stanley's First Amendment rights:

". . . [Appellant] is asserting the right to read or observe what he pleases—the right to satisfy his intellectual and emotional needs in the privacy of his own home. He is asserting the right to be free from state inquiry into the contents of his library. Georgia contends that appellant does not have these rights, that there are certain types of materials that the individual may not read or even possess. Georgia justifies this assertion by arguing that the films in the present case are obscene. But we think that mere categorization of these films as 'obscene' is insufficient justification for such a drastic invasion of personal liberties guaranteed by the First and Fourteenth Amendments. Whatever may be the justifications for other statutes regulating obscenity, we do not think they reach into the privacy of one's own home. If the First Amendment means anything, it means that a State has no business telling a man, sitting alone in his own house, what books he may read or what films he may watch. Our whole constitutional heritage rebels at the thought of giving government the power to control men's minds."   394 U.S. at 565, 89 S.Ct. at 1248.

And in a footnote concerning contraband articles, the Court carefully limited its holding:

"What we have said in no way infringes upon the power of the State or Federal Government to make possession of other items, such as narcotics, firearms, or stolen goods, a crime. Our holding in the present case turns upon the Georgia statute's infringement of fundamental liberties protected by the First and Fourteenth Amendments. No First Amendment rights are involved in most statutes making mere possession criminal." 394 U.S. at 567, n. 11, 89 S.Ct. at 1249.

In two recent cases the United States Supreme Court has declined to extend further the scope of the constitutional right to privacy. The Court recently affirmed the constitutionality of Virginia's anti-sodomy statute even as applied to two consenting adult male homosexuals. Doe v. Commonwealth's Attorney, 425 U.S. 901, 96 S.Ct. 1489, 47 L.Ed.2d 751 (1976), aff'g, 403 F.Supp. 1199 (E.D.Va.1975). In Paul v. Davis, 424 U.S. 693, 96 S.Ct. 1155, 47 L.Ed.2d 405 (1976), respondent's name and photograph were included in a flier of "active shoplifters," after he had been arrested on a shoplifting charge in Louisville, Kentucky. After that charge had been dismissed, Davis brought an action against petitioner police chiefs, who had distributed the flier to area merchants, alleging that petitioners' action under color of law deprived him of his constitutional rights. The Supreme Court, in denying Davis relief held, inter alia, that his contention that the defamatory flier deprived him of his constitutional right to privacy was meritless. Mr. Justice Rehnquist, writing for the majority, suggested:

". . . [O]ur other [1] 'right of privacy' cases, while defying categorical description, deal generally with substantive aspects of the Fourteenth Amendment. In *Roe* the Court pointed out that the personal rights found in this guarantee of personal privacy must be limited to those which are 'fundamental' or 'implicit in the concept of ordered liberty' as described in Palko v. Connecticut, 301 U.S. 319, 325, 58 S.Ct. 149, 82 L.Ed. 288 (1937). The activities detailed as being within this definition were ones very different from that for which respondent claims constitutional protection—matters relating to marriage, procreation, contraception, family relationships, and child rearing and education. In these areas it has been held that there are limitations on the States' power to substantively regulate conduct." 424 U.S. at 713, 96 S.Ct. at 1166.

Thus, as indicated ante pp. 963–964, Justice Blackmun's articulation in *Roe v. Wade* of the limited scope of the right to privacy remains the current state of the law.

The foregoing discussion should suggest the inappositeness of the leading Supreme Court cases on the right to privacy and the case we decide today. Here we do not face the intimacies of the marital relationship or of procreation. There is no clear First Amendment issue posed by the question of whether appellant may legally smoke marijuana in his own home. Thus, we are not persuaded by the Alaska Supreme Court's resolution of this issue in *Ravin v. State,* supra. We note further that the *Ravin* court in part based its

1. The Court had just distinguished Roe v. Wade, supra; Terry v. Ohio, 392 U.S. 1, 88 S.Ct. 1868, 20 L.Ed.2d 889 (1968); and Katz v. United States, 389 U.S. 347, 88 S.Ct. 507, 19 L.Ed.2d 576 (1967).

decision on state constitutional provisions which have no analogue in Florida.[2] 537 P.2d at 500–504.

Appellant has presented to this Court a sampling of scientific authority to the effect that marijuana poses no significant public health problem. The State, recognizing the limitations of the procedural posture in which this cause reaches us, has made no effort to counter this material. In a proper case appellate courts may take judicial notice of such expert opinions, and, as noted by appellants, scientific authority on the subject of marijuana's harmfulness has been discussed in several such decisions. See, e.g., *Ravin,* supra; State v. Kantner, 53 Haw. 327, 493 P.2d 306 (1972); People v. Sinclair, 387 Mich. 91, 194 N.W.2d 878 (1972).

This Court is ill-suited to make such a *de novo* judgment in a case, such as this one, which comes to us on a denial of a motion to dismiss. The record before us is simply inadequate to support a determination of whether the health hazards of smoking marijuana justify its proscription to the general public. None of the parties really argued whether the legislature lacks a "rational basis" for its decision to ban private possession of cannabis.[3] (Since we have determined that there is no fundamental right to smoke marijuana, the test becomes whether there is a "rational basis" for outlawing such an activity as opposed to a "compelling state interest" in the subject matter of the legislation.)[4] Thus in affirming the trial court, we do not foreclose the possibility of making such a determination on a properly-developed record wherein both sides have had an opportunity to present evidence of competing expert authorities before an impartial tribunal.

The judgments are affirmed.

ENGLAND, HATCHETT and DREW (Retired), JJ., concur.

OVERTON, C. J., and BOYD, J., concur in result only.

ADKINS, J., dissenting with an opinion.

ADKINS, JUSTICE, dissenting.

I respectfully dissent.

A constitutional right to privacy has been clearly established by the United States Supreme Court in Griswold v. Connecticut, 381 U.S. 479, 85 S.Ct. 1678, 14 L.Ed.2d 510 (1965); Eisenstadt v. Baird, 405 U.S. 438, 92 S.Ct. 1029, 31 L.Ed.2d 349 (1972); Roe v. Wade, 410 U.S. 113, 93 S.Ct. 705, 35

2. Art. I, § 22, Alas.Const., reads:

"The right of the people to privacy is recognized and shall not be infringed. The legislature shall implement this section."

See also Justice Boochever's concurring opinion in *Ravin,* supra, at 513–516.

3. "Left to another day is the question of regulation or prohibition of marijuana possession or sale in public and

the issue of denial of equal protection, as more harmful recreational drugs [alcohol and tobacco] are not similarly prohibited." Brief of Appellant, pp. 7–8.

4. For a critical discussion of this two-tier model, see Massachusetts Bd. of Retirement v. Murgia, —— U.S. ——, 96 S.Ct. 2562, 2568, 2573, 49 L.Ed.2d 520 (Marshall, J., dissenting).

L.Ed.2d 147 (1973), and Stanley v. Georgia, 394 U.S. 557, 89 S.Ct. 1243, 22 L.Ed.2d 542 (1969). In *Stanley v. Georgia,* supra, this right was one basis on which the court allowed private possession of materials which the State could properly prohibit an individual from selling. The basis of the regulation considered by the court in *Stanley* was the exercise of the State's police power to protect the public morals and public decency. The court held that, although exercising the police power to these ends was proper, such power could not be validly extended to punishing private possession of obscene materials. The First Amendment rights of the individual were a second basis for the decision in *Stanley;* however, allowing regulation of these rights in public while condemning such regulation in private indicates that the right to privacy was the paramount justification for the decision.

No other constitutional rights were coupled with the right to privacy in the other cases cited above. They are clearly applicable to this case since they establish the individual's right to privacy with regard to birth control and abortion, which directly affect the individual's control over his or her bodily functions.

Brown v. Board of Education, 347 U.S. 483, 74 S.Ct. 686, 98 L.Ed. 873 (1954), establishes that the court may determine and take judicial notice of the facts which form the basis for legislation. The scientific information provided by appellant and discussed in Ravin v. State, 537 P.2d 494 (Alaska 1975); State v. Kantner, 53 Haw. 327, 493 P.2d 306 (1972); and People v. Sinclair, 387 Mich. 91, 194 N.W.2d 878 (1972), shows that the existence of the alleged harmful effects of marijuana have not been scientifically proven. It is questionable whether marijuana causes physical or moral damage, while the harmful effects of legal recreational drugs—alcohol and tobacco—have been well documented.

As in *Stanley,* however, the private possession of an object may be acceptable while the sale or use in public of the same object may not. The right to privacy is the only fundamental right which can reasonably be seen as infringed by the marijuana laws. No justification is shown for invalidating the statutes as they relate to sale. The regulation of this substance other than in the home is clearly a proper exercise of the State's police power.

Note, in the *Laird* opinion, the reference to binding (controlling) and to persuasive cases. Since *Griswold* and *Eisenstadt* are United States Supreme Court decisions, they would be binding if the key facts and the rule of law to be applied were similar. Therefore, the Florida court carefully distinguishes those cases from *Laird,* by arguing that the rights protected in *Griswold* and *Eisenstadt* are "fundamental" and the right sought to be protected in the instant case is not such a right. The court also distinguishes *Roe v. Wade,* another Supreme Court opinion, for the same reason.

In distinguishing *Stanley,* another Supreme Court case, the Florida court reasons that the rights protected there are First Amendment rights, unlike those sought to be protected here. But *Ravin v. State* is an Alaska case, in another jurisdiction not binding upon Florida, so the Florida court need only note that it is not "persuaded" by the Alaska Supreme Court's resolution of the issue in *Ravin.*

As you read the dissent in *Laird,* you get a clear picture of the manner in which courts utilize the process of analogizing and distinguishing. What the majority opinion has distinguished, the minority considers binding or persuasive, by a different interpretation of the facts and applicable rules of law. And whereas the majority opinion leaves for a later decision the subject of the harmfulness of marijuana, the minority finds these due "judicial notice" and cites *Brown v. Board of Education,* a Supreme Court case, as precedent.

Study the process of analogization carefully. You will be using it as the chief method of case analysis throughout law school and during your professional career.

C. SYNTHESIZING

As well as learning how to brief and analogize cases, you need to know how to synthesize cases, in order to predict the outcome of actual and hypothetical fact situations. A synthesis is a summary of the key facts and legal rules of two or more court opinions. Synthesizing is important in thoroughly understanding each case. By viewing the case as one of a group of similar cases, you can see how each case fits into the "line" of cases or remains outside.

If you have briefed the opinions in your casebook, the job of synthesis is half done. All that remains is to list the significant data about each case in appropriate categories, so as to highlight the material similarities and differences that accounted for similar or different court decisions. An illustration of this procedure follows; cases used are those which were briefed above (pp. 86–114).

	Transatlantic Financing Corp.	American Trading and Production Corp.	Northern Corp. v. Chugach El. Ass'n.
Facts	Contract for shipment of oil to Mideast via alternative route, intended route being unavailable through no fault of either party.	Contract for shipment of oil to Mideast via alternative route, intended route being unavailable throuh no fault of either party.	Contract to procure and haul rock. Appellant paid additional costs in futile effort to fulfill contract, on demand of appellee.
Relief Requested	Payment for additional expenses incurred.	Payment for additional expenses incurred.	Payment for additional expenses incurred, less revenue already received.
Legal Theories	Benefit conferred upon appellee payable in *quantum meruit*, contracted route being unavailable through no fault of either party.	(1) In *quantum meruit* benefit conferred upon appellee for performance, since contract was legally impossible to perform through no fault of either party. (2) Commercial impracticability, which excused appellant from performance. (3) Contract (Liberties Clause) provides expressly for compensation in these circumstances.	(1) Impossibility of contract (2) Compensable change of contract. (3) (Other theories not relevant.)
Issues	Did closing of Suez Canal render performance by appellant legally impossible?	(1) Was contract legally impossible to perform, so as to confer benefit upon appellee for performance, payable in *quantum meruit?* (2) Was performance by appellant excused due to commercial impracticability? (3) Does Liberties Clause of contract expressly require compensation under these circumstances?	(1) Was contract legally impossible of performance? (2) If so, is appellant entitled to reasonable costs incurred in attempting performance on demand of appellee?
Holding	No.	(1) No. (2) No. (3) No.	(1) Yes. (2) Yes.
Reasoning	Only one of three conditions necessary for legal impossibility was met here (unforeseen contingency).	(1) Performance of contract did not require route through Suez Canal; thus no in *quantum meruit* liability. (2) No extreme or unreasonable difficulty proved by appellant; thus no excuse due to commercial impracticability. (3) Liberties Clause inapplicable since appellant did reach designated port.	(1) Contract was legally impossible to perform since conditions necessary to performance were not present. (2) If, on remand, appellee is found to have insisted on performance, when it knew or should have known of impossibility, appellant is entitled to costs incurred in attempting performance.

The chart above indicates that cases with seemingly different fact situations are nonetheless comparable. Although the particular facts in *Northern Corporation* do not appear to resemble those of *Transatlantic Financing Corporation* and *American Trading and Production Corporation,* they are comparable because they fit into the same general fact-categories. That is, contracts to ship oil to the Mideast are analogous to a contract to procure and haul rock in that both are contracted-for services. The difference in the court decisions are *despite* that similarity. The same legal theories are applicable and the same issues are raised. Using the chart as a guide, you might write the following case synthesis:

The application of the doctrine of impossibility and its offshoot, commercial impracticability, is demonstrated in the opinions of two federal circuit courts and a state supreme court. The cases are *Transatlantic Financing Corporation* (1966), *American Trading and Production Corporation* (1972), and *Northern Corporation* (1974). The first two cases involve contracts to ship oil from the United States to the Mideast. Through the fault of neither party to the contracts, the customary route via the Suez Canal was closed after the ships were en route to their destination, forcing the carriers to take an alternative longer route around the Cape of Good Hope. In *Transatlantic,* the relief requested by the carrier owner was for additional delivery costs (about 15% over the contract price) and in *American Trading,* the relief requested was for additional compensation (about 33% over the contract price) for the additional costs resulting.

In *Transatlantic,* the federal court rejected the carrier's argument that the contract was legally impossible to perform under the prevailing circumstances, and listed three requirements for the doctrine of impossibility, only the first of which was present in *Transatlantic:* (1) a contingency; (2) allocation of the contingency by agreement or custom; and (3) occurrence of the contingency, rendering performance commercially impracticable. The court held that the risk of the contingency had not been allocated to the defendant, and in fact might more properly be allocated to the plaintiff, who might have purchased insurance to cover the contingency. Nor was the commercial impracticability doctrine applicable, since neither the crew nor cargo were harmed by the longer route. The court added that to justify relief under the doctrine of impossibility there must be more variation than is present here between expected and actual cost of contract performance.

In *American Trading,* the federal court also held that the contract to deliver oil to the Mideast was not rendered legally impossible despite the contract specification of transit through the Suez Canal, for this specification was the "expected" not "required" route. The court considered separately the issue of commercial impracticability, holding that it was not applicable because it resulted only from extreme or unreasonable losses, not present in this case, in which the extra expense was less than one-third more than the contract price; the fact that the voyage via the Cape was twice as long as the contemplated Suez route was insufficient to constitute commercial impracticability. Both the *Transatlantic* and *American Trading* decisions stated that mere increase in cost was not enough to trigger the impossibility or commercial impracticability doctrines.

However, in *Northern,* a state court held that a contract was impossible of performance when the party attempting performance suffered the loss of two employees' lives and two trucks in the effort to haul gravel as specified in its contract. The court cited the doctrine of commercial impracticability, derived from the doctrine of impossibility, in which a party is discharged from contract obligations if the costs of performance are so disproportionate to those contemplated by the contracting parties as to make performance "totally impractical in a commercial sense." *Northern* differs from both *Transatlantic* and *American Trading* in that in *Northern,* the attempted performance was demanded by one party to the contract and caused unreasonable and excessive losses to the other party.

Now, having synthesized these three cases, you are in a good position to apply your insights to the facts of another case. Consider this hypothetical:

John Doe v. Frendly Protective Company [10]

This is an action by John Doe, plaintiff, based upon an accident policy which provided for payment of all medical bills to the subscriber upon notice of the accident, accompanied by a medical report signed by subscriber's attending physician. John Doe, subscriber, was injured by a tree branch that fell, hitting him on the head as he was walking in his yard. He became comatose for a period of 30 days, after which he filed a claim for medical expenses with his insurer, Frendly Protective Company. Insuror refused payment, citing the following paragraph in his accident policy:

Unless notice of any injury or of the beginning of any sickness is received in writing at the home office of this company in Boston, Massachusetts, on or before the expiration of fourteen days from the commencement of such disability together with particulars of the injury or sickness, including a statement of the time, place and cause of injury, or date of beginning and an accurate description of the sickness, signed by the claimant or attending physician, the claim shall be invalid.

Using the legal principles extracted from the three cases you have just synthesized (above), can you make a prediction about the outcome of this hypothetical case? Here is a response written by a law student:

A provision in an accident policy requiring insured to give notice of injury to insuror within a specified period of time will probably not be construed as requiring performance of that provision when performance by the insured is impossible through no fault of either party. In this case, John Doe was made comatose for 30 days as a result of his injury, making it impossible for him to provide notice of his injury within the required four-

10. This hypothetical case was modified from an actual case, Reed v. Loyal Protective Association, 154 Mich. 161, 117 N.W. 600 (1908).

teen days from the commencement of his disability. He should not suffer a forfeiture of his rights due to a requirement in the insurance policy to do that which was impossible for him to do.

One final caveat: even in cases that have similar facts, unless the same issues apply (that is, the legal theory applied to the facts of the case), the cases cannot be analogized and synthesized.

For example, assume that you have read an opinion in which the owner of a private residence swimming pool was held liable for the injuries sustained by a neighbor's three-year-old child when she wandered into the unfenced area of his pool, fell into the pool, and nearly drowned. You now read another case in which a three-year-old child wandered into a neighbor's unfenced yard and climbed upon his large trampoline. The neighbor, seeing the child, dashed out of his house and administered a beating so severe that the child required medical care.

The facts of the two cases are similar, but the legal theories to be applied differ, so you can come to no conclusions about the second case based upon the results of the first case. In the first case the cause of action is based upon the theory of negligence; in the second, the theory would be based upon an intentional tort, probably battery. Thus the cases cannot be usefully compared or synthesized.

CHAPTER FIVE
Expository Techniques

A. EXAMSMANSHIP

The skills of case briefing, analogization, and synthesis are of far-reaching importance to attorneys, but for most law students, the critical exercise of those skills is provided in law school final examinations. These examinations, upon which the entire grade for the course depends, are approached with dread and foreboding by all neophyte law students. For this reason, suggestions for preparing for and taking final examinations seem in order.

1. Preparing for the Final Examination

The process of preparing for the final examination begins with the very first day of class. The groundwork is laid by day-by-day reading of the assigned material, note-taking in class, and briefing of the court opinions in your casebooks. For in order to succeed in law school, you must (1) know the subject matter, (2) be able to communicate your knowledge within a stipulated time (that never seems long enough), and (3) express your ideas in appropriate legal language (including the favorite legal terms your instructor has used in class).

This kind of preparation would surely have guaranteed an "A" in your undergraduate courses. But, alas, not in law school. Here you are all "A" students, all determined to continue making "A's." And since the quantity of material to be learned—though formidable—is finite, all highly-motivated law students will obtain a thorough grasp of it. Therefore, writing skill becomes disproportionately important in grade-determination.

Besides containing correct and complete information, the "A" examination must be clearly stated, well-organized, and succinct. Writing that rambles, discussions that begin somewhere out in left field and never quite make it back to home base, and arguments so unfocused that they seem to miss the point leave the instructor with the impression of ineptitude, no matter how salient the (badly expressed) ideas may be.[1] So a student may be as knowledgeable as his friend and get a "C" while his friend gets an "A."

---

1. When I first began to read law students' final examinations, I innocently assumed that if "missing" material was actually present in the examination—though hidden by ineffective writing—and if the student, in a post-examination interview, pointed it out to the professor, the professor would then change the student's grade. I was soon set straight by students who reported to me that the professor's reaction was invariably something like, "Oh, yes, well, that's a shame." No grade change.

But cheer up! Once you have mastered the amenities of grammar, the skills of organization, and the techniques of case analysis—discussed in previous chapters—all you will need is practice. Practice by writing course outlines in standard English, using complete sentences and appropriate legal language. Practice by analogizing and synthesizing lines of cases from your casebooks. Practice by tracing the development of the legal doctrines learned in the course, indicating their change during the years and their current status in various jurisdictions. And practice by writing essay answers to questions of the sort that you will be asked in final examinations. This last writing practice helps to put you at ease when you reach the moment of truth in the form of final examinations. Familiar with the answering of similar test questions, you will be able to relax and give them your best effort.

That is the reason that essay questions and answers are included in this book.[2] You can model your own answers after the sample answers provided—or perhaps write even better answers. Some law professors place their previous examinations on file in the law library. Ask about them at the Reserve Desk, and practice writing answers to those questions. The more writing you do, the better you will write.

2. Taking the Final Examination

The fateful day arrives. You have, by studying and writing, avoided panic so stultifying it prevents adequate performance. The test is before you. What should you do first? The obvious answer is also the wrong one. Do *not* immediately begin to write, assuming that your ideas will fall into orderly succession. Instead, read quickly the entire test, orienting yourself to the job at hand and deciding how much time to spend on each question. Often the professor has done that for you. If not, apportion your time in accordance with the number of points he has assigned to each question. If he has given no indication of the value of each question, assume all to be of equal weight and allot equal time to each question.

If the first question seems inordinately difficult and a subsequent one easier to deal with, don't waste valuable time wrestling with the first question; go on to the first one you find that seems easier. After you have "warmed up" on the less difficult questions, you will probably find the previously intractable one more manageable. Furthermore, you may, in the midst of answering another question, suddenly gain an insight that will make the previous one more comprehensible. If so, stop just long enough to write down that insight, lest it disappear as suddenly as it arrived.

Having selected the question you will answer first, read it once more, slowly. Underline all language that seems unusually significant. Look carefully at the final directions so that you will be sure to comply with them.[3] Then list on your scratch pad the **major issues** that must be resolved before the question

---

2. Chapter Six, pp. 140–168.

3. See "Some Caveats," Chapter Five, Section A(3).

can be answered.   Leave room between major issues for **subissues, legal doctrines,** and **analysis.**   Arrange the issues in the order in which you will discuss them.   Several arrangements are possible.   Perhaps the most natural is chronological, as in a hypothetical problem, like the following, in which a single individual is beset by a series of difficulties.   Significant words and phrases have been italicized: [4]

A, an *adult,* rented a boat from a small business at the side of a lake, and was happily fishing when a *heavy tropical rainstorm* occurred. As A hurriedly began to row toward shore, *one of the two oars broke,* slowing his progress substantially.   He finally reached land, soaked and shivering, pulled the boat onto the beach and dashed toward a house, owned by H, which was *unoccupied and unlocked.* As he went inside to get out of the rain, the floor boards, which were *rotten,* gave way, and A fell and twisted his ankle.

A remained in the house, in pain, until the rain subsided, then he managed to row back to the *rental shop.   Entering the shop,* A fell on a *broken step* and *banged his head.*   The *shopowner,* B, sympathized with A about his fall and A told him that his ankle was very painful.   B thereupon told A that he had had *much experience with broken ankles,* and that A's ankle was clearly broken and should be splinted and strapped.   Luckily, said B, he had some ace bandage for sale, so A bought the bandage, and B *strapped and splinted* A's *ankle.*

Several days later, since the ankle continued to be *painful* and *turned blue,* A consulted a physician who found that A had a *sprained ankle, worsened by* B's *ministrations,* a mild *concussion,* resulting from having *struck his head,* and *bronchial pneumonia,* probably from *exposure* to the *rain and cold weather.*   Discuss A's possible *claims* against H and B.

Probably the most efficient way to deal with A's several claims is chronologically.   At issue, first, is A's status with regard to H, and H's consequent rights and duties vis-a-vis A.   The answer to this question will depend on the key language that you have underlined in your reading.   After you have thoroughly discussed A versus H and reached a conclusion, you will move on to A versus B.

In some fact situations, on the other hand, one issue is the "**threshold issue**"—a decision about which may obviate any further discussion.   When this is the case, you will certainly want to discuss the threshold issue first.   For example, consider a dispute between A and B for the ownership of a substance found under property to which A has title, but which B occupies.   The substance had been buried by A under his own, adjacent property, but as time passed, seeped into the property B occupies.   A is unaware of B's occupancy, A having moved his homestead to another state some years before.   The first issue to be resolved is obviously whether B now has, by adverse possession,

4. From these phrases you can extract the key facts, discussed in Chapter Four, p. 84.

title superior to A's to the property on which B lives and under which the disputed substance was found. This issue is a threshold issue because if . . . A is found to have superior title to the land, the question of ownership of the substance can be resolved without further consideration.[5]

A third method of organization can best be used when one event occasions a number of possible actions by one victim. The action most likely to succeed should probably be discussed first, then the others, in order of diminishing likelihood of success. Similarly, if one victim has possible claims against a number of individuals, the individual against whom the victim has the strongest claim should be dealt with first. Other factors being equal, priority should be given to the claim against the individual with the "deepest pocket." Another procedure is to use reverse order, dispensing first (briefly) with the claims least likely to succeed, and so labeling them.

Whatever your decision about the order of the major issues, you will use the space you have left under each issue to list the legal principles and precedents that must be considered in order to answer the issues. If enacted laws apply, show whether they govern the facts of your case.[6] If cases provide precedents, show that the facts in your case resemble (or differ from) the facts in the cases you are discussing.[7] It is unlikely that your case will precisely fit either principles or precedents. Your job will be to decide whether the hypothetical problem fits closely enough for the principles and precedents to apply.

Beginning law students tend to think that their decisions should always be unequivocal: a firm "yes" or "no." In fact, professors seldom present in final examinations hypothetical problems that require such conclusions. So a cautious "perhaps" may turn out to be the proper response—or "probably yes" or "probably no." Your final decision, moreover, whatever it is, will be less important than the thoroughness of your analysis.

What you have jotted down on your scratch pad should not have taken you more than one-fifth of the time you have allotted to the question you are answering. If your efforts have been effective, the result of your jottings will resemble the results of the well-known formula for examination-taking, called IRAC. More law students can repeat the formula than can successfully use it, so I have described how the formula works before naming it. IRAC stands for "issue," "rule," "analysis," and "conclusion." You should check your outline against these steps.

- Have you included all relevant issues and none that are irrelevant?

---

5. But even if the legal issue is resolved once the claim of the adverse possessor is held invalid, you should not close your discussion of the question at this point. Instead, go on to consider the other issues that must be decided in the unlikely event that the threshold issue is decided in favor of the adverse possessor. In all hypothetical problems, explore all possibilities, the most likely first.

6. Enacted laws include constitutions and charters, statutes and ordinances, and court rules that govern procedures to be followed in litigation.

7. This procedure involves analogizing and distinguishing, discussed, supra, in Chapter Four, pp. 114–123.

- Have you arranged them in the best order for discussion?
- Have you utilized all applicable legal authority ("rules")?
- Is your analysis of that authority, as it applies to your facts, complete and objective?
- Have you satisfactorily analogized and distinguished your facts and those of the cases which are most similar to yours?
- Does your conclusion follow logically from these steps?

If so, your answer should be logical, well-structured, and complete.

Consider the following hypothetical fact situation:

A, a college professor, carrying his briefcase in his rear bicycle basket, was bicycling carefully along the bike path parallel to B's house. A loudly barking dog leaning out of a passing car startled A causing him to veer and hit the curb, catapulting A into B's flower garden, bending A's bicycle frame and ruining B's flowers. B observed the incident from his front window, and while A went back to pick up his eyeglasses from the bike path where they had fallen, B snatched A's briefcase. Carrying the briefcase toward his house, B yelled, "When you pay for the damage, you'll get this back." A dashed after B and grabbed back his briefcase so roughly that B fell down, angry but unhurt. A left, carrying his briefcase and dragging his bent bicycle. Discuss possible tort actions of B against A and A against B.

Using a chronological approach, you may decide that the first issue to be resolved is whether B has a cause of action in trespass against A for A's first entry onto B's property. The applicable rule is that a non-volitional entry upon property is no trespass unless the entry is preceded by negligence. A's entry can be characterized as non-volitional by reference to the given facts. You will probably recall similar cases in your casebook that may provide precedent and indicate how the legal rule was interpreted by the courts.

Now you must decide whether to continue with the claims of B against A or to switch to the possible claims of A against B, thus maintaining the chronological approach. Either procedure is acceptable, as long as you are consistent in your development and clearly indicate your procedure.

When you begin to discuss the conduct of A as he grabbed his briefcase from B, you may decide to state the rule that reasonable force necessary to recover possession of chattel after wrongful taking is permissible after fresh pursuit. You should then follow immediately with the issues of whether the degree of force used to retrieve his briefcase was reasonable and whether A's pursuit will be considered "fresh." Reversal of the order of issue and rule will not change the sequence of the other steps, analysis and conclusion.

The IRAC formula may be modified to suit your purpose. You may choose, for example, to begin with the conclusion. If you do, you will be using the deductive method of reasoning.[8] You may choose to reverse the

8. For a discussion of deduction, see Chapter Three, pp. 68–71.

issue and rule in an entire question or in part of the question. If you do, the formula you use will be RIAC. And in questions in which the legal rule is supplied, you will extract the issues from the fact situation and apply the rule.

Although you can thus re-arrange the IRAC formula to suit your needs in each situation, be sure to clothe IRAC in appropriate attire. That is, the IRAC skeleton should not be apparent, for IRAC is a structure on which to build, not a final product. Without complete documentation, adequate development, and clear transition, the IRAC formula will be ineffective.

3. Some Caveats

During my tenure at this law school, I have read many essay examinations on numerous legal topics. One would assume that the errors made on these examinations would be of "infinite variety." Not so: the same types of errors are committed over and over, regardless of the subject matter. Those errors have prompted the following caveats:

(1) You have read the question and outlined your answer. Now, one last time before you begin to write, re-read the question. The reason? Too many clever answers have been provided to questions that were not asked. That last glance at the question will avoid this error, which is usually heavily penalized by the professor. His assumption is that you have chosen to answer a different question because you could not answer his. However, some students tell me that this is not the case. They have answered the "wrong" question unwittingly; they could have answered the professor's question had they only looked at it that final time before starting to write.

(2) In your answer, be sure to adopt the stipulated point of view. For example, if your role is that of a junior partner advising a senior partner about a prospective client's chances of bringing suit or defending against a suit, be objective and exhaustive in your analysis. Avoid polemic and rhetorical flourishes.

　　Even if you are asked to be partisan (e.g., as attorney for the defense), do not emulate Perry Mason addressing a jury. You are dealing with an appellate court (which is actually your law professor), not a jury. So do not minimize or ignore opposing arguments. Acknowledge weaknesses in your client's case and attempt to deal with them. When possible, show that deficiencies in one area are offset by strengths in another. Make your points by careful analysis, not by omitting, twisting, or exaggerating the given facts. If you are making a presumption that is not in the fact situation, say so.

(3) Do not be misled by a question that seems obvious to you. Professors are too devious to select problems whose solutions are obvious. Look carefully for points on both sides of all issues; the more one-sided the question seems, the more you should suspect that your analysis—not the question—is simplistic.

(4) Therefore, avoid dogmatic assertions. Never begin your analysis with words like "obviously," "clearly," or "certainly." These are almost sure to irritate your professor, who has carefully fashioned questions whose answers, he believes, are neither obvious, clear, nor certain. Even in the final paragraph, it is unwise to use such absolutes; after all, you could be wrong!

(5) Use unslanted language. Avoid what are sometimes called "purr" and "growl" words, used in persuasive writing to induce readers to adopt desired views. The professor will not be duped by slanted words. You can best impress him by clear thinking and logical reasoning.

(6) Avoid hyperbole. One student wrote, "This was a bald, unmitigated lie." She would have been better advised to write, "This was a lie," or, even better, "This was not true." For hyperbole, although it is intended to make the writing more forceful, actually has the opposite effect. The more it is used, the more deadening it is to the reader's sensibilities. Worse, hyperbole creates a gushy, schoolgirl effect, damaging to legal writing.

(7) For the same reason avoid using intensifiers, adverbials to support weak adjectives. Choose the proper adjective instead, and it will stand alone. For example, for "excessively often," substitute "excessive"; for "extremely important," "important"; for "very grave," "grave." In fact, "very" can be edited out of any sentence, to advantage, as can "perfectly" (as in "perfectly clear"), and "absolutely" (as in "absolutely certain"). The same holds true for "clearly," "certainly," and "definitely." And the ubiquitous "rather," which has little meaning and is used mostly as an affectation, should almost always be omitted.[9]

(8) Unless otherwise requested, base your argument only on legal grounds. The layman is entitled to approach a fact situation intuitively, emotionally, morally, ethically: as a neophyte attorney, you must approach it legally. The layman can ask, is this right, fair, moral? You must ask, is this legal? Your concern is with what the law *can* do, not what it *ought* to do.

(9) Be sure to complete your analysis: do not state the law and fail to relate it to your facts; do not state law and facts and forget to analyze and conclude from them; and do not state your conclusion without showing how you reached it.

(10) Avoid postures of arrogance or humility in your writing. A note of condescension is implicit in locutions like "it is evident that," "without question" and "obviously." On the other hand self-deprecation is unwise, as in, "I am not sure I have included everything . . ." or

---

9. "Rather," currently a fad word, was at one time used to reduce the effect of the following adjective, as in "rather warm." Now, however, it is tossed into a sentence, without any such reason. A television celebrity, in one sentence, admitted that he was "rather horrified" and "rather amazed" at a "rather unique" occurrence.

"(sp?)" after legal terms you think you may have misspelled. A good maxim might be, Don't assert your superiority; your instructor may not agree. Don't advertise your shortcomings; he may not notice them.

(11) Properly highlight and subordinate. Nondiscriminating treatment of facts and issues may not be enough to get you the grade you want. Remember too that too much emphasis on minor issues takes precious time and space and may prevent you from properly emphasizing major issues. Even if space and time are not limited, your instructor wants to see major issues dealt with first and most extensively.

(12) Say what you mean, exactly and only once. Do not adopt the oral rhetorical device of saying what you intend to say, saying it, then saying you have said it. (Your professor may have been prolix orally, but he will expect you to be succinct in writing.)

(13) To achieve style, affect none. Try instead for orderly, logical presentation. Treat even complex ideas with clarity, succinctness, and simplicity of statement. Affectation, elegance, and the appearance of profundity will not mask a paucity of ideas; call attention to what you are saying, not to how you say it.

(14) In general, avoid levity. Use formal, standard English. Your professor may have adopted a fraternal attitude in class. He may have made jokes at which you dutifully laughed and he may even have laughed at your jokes. But sitting in his lamplit, lonely study, grading tests, he is a different person. His only interest is to get through the stack of examinations, and to assess the knowledge of each student and be reasonably certain he has not erred in his judgment. Jokes are the last things he is interested in, and your efforts at levity may even be punished. The same goes for folksiness, slang, colloquialisms. At best, these waste your space, his time.

(15) Keep your own personality out of your writing. Write with ideas instead. Therefore avoid the first person approach, as in "I think," "I believe," "I would suggest." Worst of all is "I feel," an expression anathema to many law professors, who expect a cerebral rather than a visceral response to their examination questions. Almost as annoying is the palsy "we" approach, as in "we must consider carefully," or "we will next discuss."

Instead of the first person use third person, as in "the defendant is probably liable" (not "I think the defendant is liable"). The effect of your writing will be less biased, the writing more succinct with the third person approach.[10] Some examples follow:

---

10. But avoid referring to yourself in the third person (as, "The writer believes. . . ."). If you find it necessary to refer to yourself, use the first person.

This	**Not This**
The facts indicate	I have found that the facts indicate
The courts concur	In my research, I find that courts concur
The next issue	Let us consider the next issue

(16) Finally, a few general suggestions about the writing itself, some new, some appearing elsewhere, but worth reiterating. There may be exceptions, but the following advice is usually reliable:

(a) Choose a framework: deal with the events in your problem chronologically, or with one party at a time. Your decision will vary with the facts.[11]

(b) Use a separate paragraph for each issue. The first sentence of each paragraph is usually the topic sentence. Deal with subordinate issues immediately following the main issues from which they arise.

(c) Place arguments in their most effective order, with those most likely to succeed up front. Or dispense with less cogent arguments first, but briefly, and so label them.

(d) Write in paragraphs of about four to six sentences. Fewer sentences indicate incomplete development of ideas. More sentences than six probably result from the inclusion of unrelated ideas—or redundancy. Proper paragraphing makes your writing appear well organized.

(e) Separate and clearly label pro and contra arguments, e.g., liabilities and defenses to liabilities.

(f) If space is no problem, leave some room after each answer for possible later inspiration. In allocating time, leave a few minutes at the end for editing.

(g) Be sure there are no gaps in your reasoning. Have consideration for the professor if you expect consideration from him: don't force him to make leaps of faith. (He may not like to leap, and have little faith.) The difference between a "B" student and a "D" student may only be that the former is a "putter-inner" and the latter a "leaver-outer."

(h) Finally, bear in mind the theory of the Greek Anaxagoras, teacher of Socrates, about the origin of the universe: "All things were in chaos when mind arose and created order." Socrates, hearing this, reasoned that man, thinking for himself, could bring similar order to human affairs. Your job is to bring order to the mass of unorganized data presented in your essay examinations—and awaiting you in your legal practice.

---

11. For a further discussion of methods of development, see Chapter Three, Sections B and C, and pages 130–133, supra.

B. LOGICAL FALLACIES

A marvelous short story by Max Shulman, called "Love is a Fallacy," should be on the reading list of every law student. It deals with the sad denouement of a love affair between a clever, logical law student and a beautiful-but-dumb coed whom he decides to transform, by the discipline of logic, into an intellectual giant worthy of himself. To avoid revealing the ending of the tale, I shall add only that along the way the author defines and illustrates the logical fallacies that law students—and others—often fall into.[12]

In writing final examinations and as practicing attorneys, you should recognize and avoid logical fallacies, some of the most common of which are discussed below:

a. The *Post Hoc Fallacy,* more accurately, *Post Hoc Ergo Propter Hoc,* means, "After this, therefore on account of this." This form of fallacious reasoning assumes that because an event or action occurs after another event or action, the second is caused by the first. A homely example is "Every time I do my wash, it rains." Or, "Every time I brag about my child's good health, he gets sick." (Therefore to avoid rain, do not wash clothes; to ensure your child's good health, do not brag about it.) This fallacy should be recognized and exposed when it is utilized by shrewd attorneys in litigation. And it goes without saying that the Post Hoc fallacy should be avoided in one's own legal arguments for, as the Sahakians point out, "[R]easoning without committing error is an obvious asset for all persons, regardless of their walk in life." [13]

b. *Dicto Simpliciter* involves the application of a general rule to cases that are actually exceptions to the rule. For example, "Murder is punishable by imprisonment. Therefore all United States military personnel who participated in killing during the Vietnamese War should be imprisoned." "My Webster's Dictionary does not list the word 'inumbrate.' Therefore you should not use it in your brief." ("My" Webster's may be a *circa* 1900 edition!)

c. *Hasty Generalization,* the converse fallacy, involves jumping to a conclusion without adequate sampling; e.g. "Professor Brown frequently forgets to call roll; college professors certainly are absent-minded." (The conclusion may be correct, but it cannot be deduced without much broader and more representative sampling.)

d. *Non Sequitur* (literally, "it does not follow") consists of a conclusion which does not logically follow from its supposed proof. The "proof" may have no relationship to the "conclusion" which depends upon it: "The use of marijuana is widespread; therefore immigration laws should be more strictly

---

12. For a more serious discussion of these and other fallacies, see William S. and Mabel Lewis Sahakian, *Ideas of Great Philosophers,* 1966, 11–23.

13. Id., p. 12.

enforced." Unproven, of course, is that immigration has any effect upon or connection with the use of marijuana.[14]

e. In the *Ad Hominem* fallacy, the speaker or writer attacks the person of his opponent rather than his opponent's ideas or arguments. Al Smith, when he was candidate for president, was opposed by some, not because of his experience, ideology, or actions, but because of his religion. President Ford's political detractors joked about his supposed physical clumsiness, hoping thereby to imply mental ineptness too. And recently, a vegetarian food bar in the local airport was declared unsuitable by some local residents because its manager "looked like a hippie."

f. Closely allied to the *Ad Hominem* attack is a fallacy called "poisoning the well," the question "When did you stop beating your wife?" being the classic example. By basing his question upon the presumed guilt of his adversary the speaker puts him in the untenable position of acknowledging guilt no matter how he answers the question. Unethical attorneys have been known to use such questions in order to trap a witness into making incriminating statements.

g. The rhetorical question also becomes a logical fallacy when it is used as an indirect attack. "Is our do-nothing President ever going to take a firm stand on inflation?" is an example. As in "poisoning the well," the rhetorical question is a form of question begging: it fails to prove the presumption on which it rests.

h. Another form of question begging is the use of circular reasoning: "What is a sentence?" "A sentence begins with a capital letter, ends with a period and expresses a complete idea." "How do you know whether the idea expressed is complete?" "Because it begins with a capital letter and ends with a period." The problem with circular reasoning it that it seems to provide an answer but actually does not.

i. Perhaps because our language and manner of looking at reality impose an "either/or" attitude, the Either/Or fallacy is sometimes successfully utilized in law by a clever attorney who hopes that his opponent will feel compelled to choose between two offered alternatives. The English language seems to suggest polar choices by setting up dichotomies like "right/wrong," "good/bad," "black/white," instead of considering the various possibilities in between. A foreign student in one of my English classes fell into such a trap. In order to obtain a scholarship, he was required to answer the following question (among others): "Have you ever plotted to overthrow the U.S. government or engaged in any subversive activity against the U.S. government?" The unfortunate foreigner thought he had to choose between the two alternatives, and after much soul-searching, selected one. (Needless to say, he did not get the scholarship.)

j. *Argumentum ad Populum* (Appeal to the Masses), is handy to unscrupulous politicians. Perpetrators of this fallacy appeal to the prejudices of the masses instead of discussing the issues. Their appeal might be to racial bias,

---

14. This statement is also an enthymeme. For a discussion of the enthymeme, see Chapter Three, pp. 70–71.

to religious prejudice, to patriotism, or to their listeners' perception of superiority or inferiority—whatever can be expected to cause in the audience an immediate, unthinking, emotional reaction. During the Florida senatorial election campaign of 1950, George Smathers was running against the incumbent Claude Pepper, a liberal who had held the Senate seat for many years. Smathers was widely quoted as telling rural audiences consisting largely of ultra-conservative voters, that Pepper was a believer in Pragmatism and that Pepper's sister was a well-known Thespian. These revelations, made to voters innately suspicious of "-isms" and who perhaps confused "thespian" with "lesbian," may have helped achieve Smathers' resounding victory over Pepper at the polls.

k. In the *Tu Quoque* (You Do It Yourself) fallacy, the argument is that if one group or individual has the right to do something, all other similar groups of individuals should also have that right. But this argument is fallacious if (1) the groups are not identical, (2) the situations involved are not alike, or (3) the "right" is inappropriately held by the first party. For example, university students argue that they should have the right, as does the university faculty, to choose curricula and appoint new deans. But does the fact that students are invariably transient dwellers in the university while faculty are relatively permanent affect this argument? If so exceptions (1) and (2) should be applied, and the argument is fallacious.

l. Finally, the *Fallacy of Misplaced Authority* depends upon the assumption that because a person excels in one area, he also holds credentials in other, unrelated matters. Thus, film stars like Jane Fonda are considered expert in political matters, writers of best-selling books on baby care are authorities in the anti-war movement, and winners of Olympic medals are thereby knowledgeable about breakfast cereals. Of course, the opinions of celebrities about subjects outside their fields of competence are no more valuable than the opinions of the average man in the street. Suspect also should be the opinion of a bona fide authority, with credentials in the field being discussed, whose objectivity is in question. Thus the president of an oil company can hardly be expected to discuss without bias the taxation of excess profits of oil companies; nor can a food scientist who is a paid consultant to a hamburger chain be expected to be unbiased on the subject of fast foods.

The Appendix provides illustrations of logical fallacies for you to identify.

CHAPTER SIX

Problems and Answers for Writing Practice

Thus far this book has largely been composed of rules and guidelines for writing, along with exercises to help you follow the rules. But rules and guidelines, though useful, cannot be applied without real writing practice, and unfortunately law school provides no writing for practice. Your only writing in law school is done in dead earnest, usually in the setting of a final examination, in competition with your colleagues for grades. With each such writing, your academic career hangs in the balance. And, as everyone knows, the good positions go to those who do well in law school.

So writing practice is not only helpful; it is vital. This chapter provides the opportunity for that practice. The rules and strategies of the first five chapters should be used in writing well-organized, cogent essay answers to each problem in this chapter. So that you will not have to review the law in order to write your answers, the relevant legal rules are provided at the beginning of each set of problems. Thus even non-law students, after carefully reading the legal rules, should be able to write competent answers to the legal problems presented.

An important caveat: the legal rules provided are not necessarily operative in your jurisdiction, nor are they complete. They are for use only—and specifically—for these exercises and are therefore intentionally simplified for this purpose. Using them you can by-pass research and concentrate on writing, that otherwise neglected area of legal education.

Be aware, too, that the legal fact situations presented here are generally less complex than those you will meet in your law school final examinations, although a few of the problems approach that level of complexity. I have intentionally made the problems simple because I find that beginning law students can develop their writing and analytical skills more easily by dealing with simple problems and are then able to apply these skills in handling more complicated problems in final examinations. The strategies are the same; the only difference is in the degree of complexity.

The time limitations suggested for answering the problems should not be taken too seriously. But if it takes you much longer than the suggested time to write answers, you will be aware that you need to speed up. Conversely, if you finish much before the suggested time, but have missed vital issues, you should know that you need to spend more time on analysis.

The answers provided are not offered as "model answers" in the sense that they are necessarily complete or perfect solutions, perfectly written. They are

merely well-written answers, produced by students like yourself. Perhaps you can do better!

Finally, after writing answers to the problems provided here, you should proceed to your own law library where "real" final examinations are often placed on reserve by your own law professors for your use. Write answers to those questions too; if you know the subject matter, you should now be well prepared to cope with them.

Using only the following legal principles, write answers to the hypothetical legal problems below. You should take about 40 minutes to read the facts and write your answer. These legal rules should not be considered complete or for use in problems other than those presented here. You may not need to use all the rules for each problem. A good answer, written by a student, follows each problem.

WRITING PROBLEMS, SET I

Legal Rule

Burglary: Breaking and entering into the dwelling of another in the night-time with the intent of committing larceny.

Definitions

1. "Dwelling": Someone must live therein or have lived there and intend to return.

2. "Nighttime": Between an hour after sunset and an hour before sunrise.

3. "Breaking": Force, however slight, must be used in entering, and the entry be without the consent of the occupant. Some part of the body must enter, or an implement which is then used to effect the crime.

4. "Larceny": The taking and carrying away, with the intent to steal, of the personal property of another.

Problem I

The E. Z. Marks had bought a new home. They moved all their possessions into it, but left the premises at 6 P.M. to stay overnight at a motel because their electricity had not yet been connected. Atilla Z. Hun entered the house through an open window. He carried out silver and china, leaving through the back door, which he had unlocked from the inside. Is Hun guilty of burglary?

Answer to Problem I

A. Z. Hun's conduct fulfills one of the elements of burglary: by taking silver and china from the Marks' house with the intent to steal, he has committed larceny. The intent to steal can probably be imputed to Hun since he entered without the consent of the owners and through an open window.

Three questions remain, however. The first is whether Hun's action occurred at night. Since the facts indicate that the Marks ceased moving their possessions into the house because of darkness, Hun probably entered the house after dark, and thus an hour or more after sunset, thus satisfying the definition of "nighttime." Even if that requirement is satisfied, however, there is a second question of whether Hun's entry was into a dwelling. The rule states that in order to be a dwelling, someone must live there. Since the Marks had not yet moved in, the house may not qualify under this definition. The court must decide whether a house, prepared for next-day occupancy, qualifies as a dwelling.

The third issue is whether Hun's action meets the definition of "breaking." Since his entry was through an open window, it does not, for some force must be used to achieve the entry, and Hun used no force. The unlocking of the door might meet the definition of "force, however slight," but Hun unlocked the door to leave, not to enter.

Hun will therefore probably not be found guilty of burglary, since his behavior fails to satisfy at least one of the required elements.

Problem II

At 10 P.M., while Ben Zene was at the movies, Ken Twin climbed the high fence surrounding Zene's house and entered the porch through the unlocked porch door. He then loaded all of the porch furniture onto the back of his pickup truck. Although the living room windows which opened onto the porch were locked, Ken was able to maneuver one open by using a long wire. He climbed through that window, intending to take items from the house, but, hearing a noise, decided to leave hurriedly instead. Discuss.

Answer to Problem II

Ken Twin is probably guilty of burglary for his first act of removing the porch furniture and putting it into his truck. He had the requisite intent to commit larceny, and his entry through the unlocked porch door will probably constitute "force, however slight." Whether the porch will be considered a dwelling under the given rules is a second issue. If it is so defined, Twin has committed burglary even before he entered Zene's house itself.

Twin is also guilty of burglary for his second act, entry into Zene's house. (1) He had, as he entered, the intent to commit larceny; (2) he used force (the wire) in gaining entry; and (3) he entered without the occupant's consent. The actual absence of the owner does not change his occupant status, nor the status of his home as a dwelling. Twin's change of mind about the burglary does not nullify the "intent" requirement; the intent must only be present at the time of the entry.

Problem III

At 2 A.M., M. I. Tired, intoxicated and seeing a house that appeared empty, broke a window, climbed through it into the house, and went to sleep on the livingroom rug. The house is unoccupied, since its owner, Fig Nuton, is away on reserve military service. When M. I. awakens four hours later, he notices—with the first rays of daylight—Nuton's valuable coin collection and decides to take it. He leaves with the coins through the back door. Has M. I. Tired committed burglary?

Answer to Problem III

M. I.'s conduct satisfies some of the elements of burglary. He has committed larceny after breaking and entering a dwelling. The absence of the owner does not change the status of the house as a dwelling, if the owner intends to return, and the facts indicate that he does. M. I.'s breaking of the window satisfies the breaking requirement, and the owner has not consented to the entry. The nighttime requirement is satisfied despite the actual occurrence of the larceny during the daytime, since M. I. entered at night, and intent on entry is relevant under the rule.

However, the "intent" requirement for burglary is absent here. M. I. broke into Nuton's house only to sleep, not to commit larceny. The requirement of intent is not met when he later changed his mind. The jury may, however, infer intent from M. I.'s behavior, disbelieving M. I.'s claim that he did not intend to take the coin collection at the moment he entered the house. If so, M. I. will probably be found guilty of burglary.

Problem IV

Ima Thief worked as a cleaning woman for the D. Zasters. They regularly provided her with a key by which she could enter to clean during their absence. She had secretly taken that key to the L. Icit Key Company and had a duplicate key made.

Since she knew that the Zasters were away on vacation, Ima entered the house with her duplicate key, broke the lock on a wall safe, and exited with the contents. The time at which this occurred is uncertain. Ima says that the incident occurred at 3 P.M., but a neighbor of the Zasters says she saw Ima in the yard of the Zaster house at 9 P.M., although she did not see Ima entering or leaving the Zaster house. Is Ima guilty of burglary?

Answer to Problem IV

In this crime the requisite intent was present and the larceny was carried out. The Zasters' house, though empty at the time, was a dwelling according to the legal definition. Ima's entry was without the consent of the Zasters.

The crucial issues to be determined are (1) whether entry by a duplicate key, achieved illegally, constitutes a "breaking" and (2) whether the jury will believe Ima's statement that the incident occurred at 3 P.M.

Entry by an illegally-gained key will almost certainly constitute "breaking," the slight force being Ima's using the key to open the lock and her pushing the door (or pulling it) open. With regard to the second issue, the trier of fact will have to decide whether the neighbor really saw Ima in the Zasters' yard at 9 P.M. If they believe the neighbor, they may well conclude that the incident occurred at night and not, as Ima asserts, at 3 P.M. and Ima will be found guilty of burglary.

Before answering the next two problems, add the following legal rules:

I. Burglary is a felony of the second degree if, in the course of committing the offense, the actor

    A. purposely, knowingly, or recklessly inflicts or attempts to inflict bodily injury upon another, or

    B. is armed with explosives or a deadly weapon.

(An act is defined as "in the course of committing the offense" if it occurs in an attempt to commit the offense or in flight after the attempt or commission.)

II. Otherwise, burglary is a felony of the third degree.

Problem V

A. Felon was in the habit of stealing from houses while the people who lived there were away. He never carried a gun while comitting his crimes.

For some time, Felon had carefully been observing the home of the Victims and had seen the Victim family leaving the premises after loading their station wagon with suitcases and gift-wrapped packages. It was the day before Christmas, and Felon assumed that the Victims had gone away for the holiday. The Victim family had indeed left for the holiday, but their eldest son John had, on the day of their departure, returned from college to study for his final examinations.

That night, while John was sleeping in his bedroom upstairs, Felon pried open the front door lock of the Victims' house, intending to enter and steal whatever valuables he could find. John, hearing Felon, jumped out of bed and found Felon standing in the livingroom. Felon turned to flee. John yelled "Stop!" He then descended the stairs and ran toward Felon. When Felon saw John approaching, he grabbed a poker from the fireplace, and brandishing it threateningly at John, he made good his escape, without taking anything from the Victims' house. What is Felon guilty of, if anything?

Answer to Problem V

Felon is guilty of burglary, either in the second or third degree. All of the elements of the crime are present: (1) Felon has forcefully entered the house of another; (2) the house is a "dwelling" because the Victims' son is occupying it (and even if he were not, they intend to return); (3) the entry was at night; and (4) Felon intended to commit larceny. These are the elements of third degree burglary.

Whether Felon is guilty of burglary in the second degree will depend upon two issues: whether the poker he has armed himself with is considered a "deadly weapon"; and whether, when he brandished the poker he intended to inflict bodily injury upon John or just to scare John enough to insure Felon's escape.

If the poker is considered a deadly weapon, Felon is guilty of second degree burglary whether or not he intended to use it to harm John. Irrelevant also is the fact that Felon was unarmed when he entered the Victims' house;

he has armed himself while committing the crime. Since a poker is made of iron and is heavy enough to cause substantial injury, it may well be considered to be a deadly weapon, especially since pokers have been used to kill during the commission of crimes.

Even though the poker is not judged to be a deadly weapon, Felon may still be charged with second degree burglary if the jury believes that he attempted to use it to inflict bodily harm upon John Victim, although Felon did not actually do so. Felon may argue, in his defense, that he has never carried a gun in the commission of a burglary and that his intent, in brandishing the poker, was only to escape, not to harm John. He may also be able to show that he was too far away from John in the room to make such an attempt possible. If the jury believes him, Felon will be found guilty of third degree burglary.

Problem VI

John and Mary Proprietor live in quarters above their store. After Mary had retired for the night, John Proprietor went down to the store to take inventory. He unintentionally left open the door to the stairs leading to the Proprietors' apartment.

Ken Robb, passing by, sees John at work; he also notices that the door leading up to the apartment is ajar. Thinking that he might pick up some useful or valuable items, he walks up the stairs and into the apartment livingroom.

Mary hears Ken and calls out, "John, is that you?" Receiving no answer, she gets out of bed and goes into the livingroom. Ken has hidden behind the livingroom door and when Mary comes past, he grabs her in a karate hold and throws her on the floor. Then he dashes down the stairs and out through the door. Ignoring any other crimes that Robb may be guilty of, discuss whether he has committed burglary and if so, of what degree.

Answer to Problem VI

In order for Robb to be guilty of burglary in either degree, he must have, using some force, entered a *dwelling, without* the occupant's *consent,* at *night,* with the *intent* to commit larceny.

All the requisites of burglary are present except one. The Proprietors' apartment meets the definition of a dwelling, despite its being situated above their store. Robb entered at night, without Mary Proprietor's consent, and, on entering, had the intent to commit larceny. (That he subsequently changed his mind is no defense.)

If Robb were guilty of burglary, and if his karate attack upon Mary Proprietor caused her any bodily injury, he would be guilty of burglary in the second degree, because he attacked Mary intentionally. That he was not engaged in burglary but was trying to escape when he attacked Mary would be no defense, because the attempt to escape is held to be a part of the commission of the crime.

However, one requisite of burglary is that the entry to the dwelling be accomplished with some force, however slight. John Proprietor had left the door ajar. The question is therefore whether the door was open sufficiently that Robb was able to enter without pushing it open farther or making any physical contact with the door that would be definable as "slight force." If the trier of fact believes that Robb was able to enter the house using no force whatsoever, he is not guilty of burglary.

WRITING PROBLEMS, SET II

Using only the following legal principles, write answers to the hypothetical legal problems below. You should take about 30 minutes to read the facts and write your answer. The legal rules should not be considered complete or accurate. All the rules may not be needed in answering each problem. A good answer, written by a student, follows each problem.

Legal Rules

1. Because there is a duty to conduct oneself with the care for others that a "reasonable man" would take, negligent conduct is that which imposes an unreasonable risk upon others.

II. A causal link must exist between a negligent act and the harm suffered by the victim of it (the act is the cause-in-fact, "but for" which no harm would have occurred).

III. If customary practice is dangerous, conforming to that practice may not prevent one's conduct from being negligent.

IV. If a person contributes proximately to his own injuries, he is barred from recovery (contributory negligence); if a person, voluntarily, with knowledge of the hazard, places himself in a position of danger, he assumes the risk and is barred from recovery (assumption of risk).

V. If a person fails to exercise a "last clear chance" to prevent injury to another, he is liable despite contributory negligence by the other person.

VI. Violation of a state statute constitutes negligence per se.

Problem I

Spectators at college football games held in Rah-Rah Stadium customarily use their programs to make small paper airplanes which they sail through the air toward the playing field. Abel attended the Paluka U. versus Rah-Rah U. game, and after a Rah-Rah touchdown he and other fans hurled these airplanes, with some vigor, downward through the air. At that moment Baker stood up, turned around, and waved to friends in the stands above. Abel's airplane struck Baker's eye, causing considerable damage to the cornea and necessitating surgery.

Discuss Baker's claims and his chance for success against Abel.

Answer to Problem I

Baker (B) may have a cause of action in negligence against Abel (A) because the tossing of paper airplanes in a crowded football stadium may be considered to impose unreasonable risk upon other persons. If so, the argument that A was engaging in a customary activity along with others will not succeed. Courts have held that, even when the custom, dangerous activity may be considered negligent.

B would not have suffered harm except for A's act; thus there is a causal link between B's injury and A's tossing of the airplane. A may argue, however, that B assumed the risk of injury from flying paper planes when he attended the football game. Unless A was an out-of-town visitor who did not know of the Rah-Rah custom, this argument may succeed.

A may have another argument under the theory of contributory negligence. "But for" B's standing up and looking up into the stands, the airplane may have struck him on the back of his head, without harm. The question, then, is whether B's act contributed to his injury when, aware of the airplanes floating through the air all around him, he stood up and looked upward. If so, B will be barred from recovering.

B's chance for success in his claim will depend on (1) whether A's conduct in tossing paper airplanes violated the duty of care for others, (2) and if so, whether B assumed the risk of injury by attending the game, (3) or whether B negligently contributed to the accident by looking back and upwards while airplanes were being tossed. The court may well find that B's contributory acts bar him from recovering from A's behavior.

Problem II

I. Ken Duit drove his car to his eye doctor's office for an eye examination. The doctor put drops in Ken's eyes, blurring Ken's vision, and suggested that Ken wait for two hours before driving home in order for his eyes to return to normal. After half an hour Ken grew bored and decided to leave, although his vision was still somewhat blurred. As he drove along slowly and carefully, he came to a section of the road where construction was taking place and crews of workers were working, having parked their trucks in the bicycle path along the side of the road.

At this time I. Mae Student was bicycling home from classes. Seeing the construction trucks parked on the bicycle path and the crews at work next to them on the edge of the roadway, she decided she would be safer biking on the left side of the road facing oncoming cars than on the right side of the road in the stream of traffic. (A state statute requires that bicyclists either use bicycle paths or ride in the stream of automobile traffic.)

Ken, driving as far as possible to his right in order to leave plenty of room for oncoming vehicles on his left, failed to see Mae and hit her bicycle, causing injuries to Mae. Discuss Mae's negligence claim against Ken.

Answer to Problem II

Ken has the duty to conduct himself with the care that a reasonable person would have for others. In driving with blurred vision despite his doctor's advice, Ken fails in this duty. If his action is the cause-in-fact of Mae's injury Ken will be liable for negligence, according to the given legal rules.

In addition, although the facts do not so indicate, if a statute prohibits persons with impaired vision from driving, Ken may be in violation of it and therefore negligent per se.

Otherwise, Mae's negligence claim may fail because the "but for" link between Ken's behavior and Mae's injury is not established. Mae's own actions may have contributed to her injury. By bicycling on the left side of the road she was, in fact, negligent per se because she was in violation of a state statute. However, Mae can defend against that charge by arguing that it was necessary for her own safety to ignore the statute. In this case, with trucks parked on the bikeway, Mae may have been within her rights to choose what seemed to be a safer alternative.

Her choice may bar her from recovery, however. By riding her bicycle facing traffic, Mae placed herself in a position of danger. She thus "assumed the risk" and contributed toward the harm that she received. She could have instead dismounted from the bicycle and walked it along in whatever paths were provided for pedestrians. If, in so doing, she had been forced to use the roadway and had been struck by Ken, her claim against him would have been much stronger, for vehicle drivers should expect pedestrians to walk on the left and drivers have a duty of care to avoid hitting them.

As it is, Mae's likelihood of success is small. Even if Ken is held negligent for driving with blurred vision, Mae will probably be barred from recovery because of assumption of risk and contributory negligence.

Problem III

Rae C. Driver is driving south in a 35-mile-an-hour zone at 35 miles an hour. The traffic light at the intersection is red as she approaches it, but it suddenly turns green and she continues through it without slowing down. Meanwhile, D. E. Termind is approaching the same intersection, driving east at 35 miles an hour. He sees Rae coming toward him at his left, but the traffic light is yellow, so he continues through, because it is legal to continue through a yellow traffic light. He assumes Rae will apply her brakes because the light is still red in her direction. D. E.'s assumption is wrong, and Mae's car hits his. Discuss liability.

Answer to Problem III

Both parties are liable for negligence. By not slowing down as she approached a red traffic signal, Rae C. Driver imposed an unreasonable risk upon others. Her conduct was the cause-in-fact of the harm that she and D. E. Termind suffered; "but for" her negligence, the collision would not have occurred.

On the other hand, "but for" D. E. Termind's attempt to beat Driver's approaching car by proceeding through the intersection on a yellow light, the collision would not have occurred. D. E. Termind's conduct may therefore be considered to be the cause-in-fact of the accident.

His conduct will also be considered negligent because of the "last clear chance" rule. Seeing Driver approaching, he had the final opportunity to slow down and stop on the yellow light, thus averting the collision. Even if Termind is not held negligent for failing to take advantage of the last clear chance to avoid the accident, he will probably be barred from recovery because of contributory negligence or assumption of risk. His behavior contributed to the accident, and he chose to assume the risk of crossing the intersection in front of an oncoming car.

WRITING PROBLEMS, SET III

Assume that the following legal rules are in effect. Then write an essay answer to each question posed at the end of the hypothetical fact situation. Use only the rules provided; all of the rules may not be required for each question. These rules come from the Restatement (Second) of Torts, but they are not to be considered complete and should therefore not be relied upon to answer any but the problems presented here.

Legal Rules

I. A person is liable to another for battery if he acts intending to cause a harmful or offensive contact with another and such contact results.

   A. If a person intends a harmful contact with another, or intends to cause apprehension of a harmful or offensive contact with another, and harmful contact with a third person results instead, the one causing that harm is liable to the third person.

   B. In order for a person to be harmed or offended, he need not himself be touched; anything so closely connected with his body as to be customarily regarded as part of his person is considered to be part of himself.

II. A person is liable to another for assault if he acts intending to cause a harmful or offensive contact or apprehension of an imminent contact to another person and he thereby causes the other person to be apprehensive of an imminent contact.

   A. Assault lies even though the person gives the other person the opportunity to avoid the result by obeying a command, unless the first person is privileged to enforce the command.

   B. Mere words do not constitute assault.

III. A person is not liable for otherwise actionable conduct in assault or battery if the receiver of the conduct has consented to it or if public interest in the conduct is great enough to justify the harm caused or threatened to the receiver.

   A. Anyone subjected to assault or battery has the privilege of using reasonable force to protect himself, but exceeding this privilege will make him the aggressor.

   B. Consent to conduct is terminated if the person to whom the consent was given exceeds the bounds of the consent.

Problem I

Alfred and Betty are friends who enjoy practical jokes and often play them on each other. Without any ill will and entirely as a joke, Albert hangs a bucketful of cornmeal over a closed door in such a way that when Betty opens the door the cornmeal will fall on her. The trick works; Betty is covered with cornmeal. Being a good sport Betty laughs at first. Later, however, she develops an eye infection from the cornmeal and requires extensive medical treatment. Betty is now considering legal action. What likelihood has she of success?

Answer to Problem I

Betty (B) may have a cause of action against Alfred (A) in battery. A intended to place the cornmeal so that it would fall on B. The resulting contact may well be considered enough to constitute the "offensive contact" required for battery. That A did not intend to cause the eye infection that occurred does not reduce his liability for his action, since he did intend the conduct that resulted in the eye infection. The question is whether A intended an offensive or harmful contact. The facts state that A had no "ill will" and intended his prank "entirely as a joke." Without the intent to cause offense or harm, there can be no battery.

Also crucial in deciding A's liability for battery is whether B had consented to his conduct. If B's consent to their practical joking relationship is held to constitute her implicit consent to his cornmeal prank, A will not be held liable for battery, even if he did intend an offensive contact, unless the bounds of B's consent are judged to have been exceeded in this case.

A may argue that B, by her initial reaction of laughter following the incident, signified that she did not consider the bounds of her consent to have been exceeded. However, B's interest in pursuing a claim against A indicates that, at least after her initial laughter, she did consider her consent to their practical joking relationship to have been exceeded by A's conduct in this incident.

B's delay in taking action will not preclude her recovery of damages. There is no requirement that the victim of harmful or offensive conduct bring suit without delay. If the court is convinced that A intended an offensive or harmful contact that was not impliedly consented to by B, or if it believes A's conduct exceeded the bounds of B's consent, B will succeed in her action against A for battery.

Problem II

A. Player is playing tennis with a friend, B. Tsim, a much better player. A does not like to lose, and as the game progresses he becomes more and more irritable. Finally when B wins the set, A runs to the net brandishing his racquet and yells, "Duck, or I'll hit this ball right into your face!" He then hits the ball wildly. B ducks. A intended to miss B even if B did not duck, and the ball does not come close to B. However it does strike C. Knott, who is behind a bush out of A's vision, searching for a lost ball. C suffers a concussion. What is A liable for, if anything?

Answer to Problem II

Both B and C may bring suit against A. A is liable to B for assault. A drove the tennis ball toward B, intended to cause B apprehension of an imminent offensive or harmful contact. Although A provided B with an option by which B could escape harm, A is still liable, for A is not privileged to enforce his command ("Duck!"). Since B did duck, he clearly expected that otherwise the ball was likely to hit him, and feared injury as a result. Although "mere words" do not constitute assault, the words here were reinforced by conduct that is actionable.

Although A may argue that he was only joking and thus lacked the requisite intent to offend or harm B, the context indicates that this is not true. The further argument by A that B's consent to play tennis encompassed consent to A's final action will probably fail because A's conduct exceeds the bounds of what is normal in a game of tennis.

C has no claim against A in assault, for he did not see the tennis ball propelled by A toward him and therefore did not suffer apprehension of imminent contact. He does have a claim against A in battery although A did not intend to strike C with the ball and in fact was not even aware of C's presence behind the bush.

All of the elements requisite for battery are present. A intended by his act to cause apprehension of imminent contact. That this apprehension occurred in B, not C, does not remove A's liability. The liability extends to C as the injured third person. As to the argument that A struck C only by mistake, that fact does not eliminate A's liability to C. When intent to commit battery is present, and an unintended victim receives the action, the doer of the act is liable to that person just as if he were the intended victim. C therefore has a cause of action in battery against A.

––––––––––

In order to answer the next set of problems, you will need to add the following legal rules to those you have been using. Remember that all rules do not necessarily apply to all the problems.

Legal Rules

IV. If a person intends to confine another within fixed boundaries or if his action results in such a confinement and if the other person is conscious of or harmed by the confinement, the first person is liable for false imprisonment.

    A. If the person confining another person does not intend to do so, and

    B. If the confinement is transitory or otherwise harmless, the first person is not liable.

V. A person is privileged to retake property that another person has wrongfully taken from him, after first asking the taker to return it. If the first person is mistaken in his belief that the property was taken, the privilege is nullified.

VI. A person who recklessly or intentionally causes severe emotional distress to another is subject to liability for that distress and, if bodily harm results to the second person, is liable for that harm as well.

   A. In order for language to be reckless it must be so outrageous as to exceed the bounds of decency.

   B. A person is liable to a third person for emotional distress for conduct described in V (above) if that person is a member of the immediate family of the person at whom the conduct was directed, whether or not the third person suffers bodily harm, and to any other person present who suffers bodily harm from the conduct of the actor.

Problem III

While shopping at a grocery store, Ms. K. Smart (K) saw a five-pound bag of sugar with one price sticker placed over another. The top sticker read "$3.00," but K peeled it off and found another reading "$2.50." When she attempted to pay for the sugar at the checkout counter, the Checker (C) noticed that the top sticker had been removed and said to K, "What a cheat! What a gyp! It's cheats like you that make food prices go up!" K had already placed $2.50 on the counter, and, very upset at C's words, she picked up the sugar and headed for the door.

The store manager (M), hearing the checker's words, assumed that K had not paid for the sugar, and he stopped in front of K as she was about to leave the store. K pushed M to one side in order to get to the door, saying, "Get out of my way, you Jerk!" M attempted to take the sugar out of K's hand, but instead knocked her pocketbook to the floor, causing it to open and the contents to spill out. M then stepped aside, and K picked up her belongings and left the store, carrying the sugar. What liability, if any arises from this incident?

Answer to Problem III

K has no claim in assault against C because "mere words" do not suffice for an action in assault. As to a claim of intentional infliction of emotional distress by K against C, two elements of the tort are present: (1) C's words were uttered intentionally and (2) for the purpose of causing K distress. However, mere insults are not enough to activate this tort and C's words, though unfair and unkind, fall within the description of mere insults. To be actionable, the language would have to be describable as "outrageous" by a reasonable person.

M, in attempting to bar K's exit, may be liable for false imprisonment. His act seems intended to keep K inside the store. She was aware of her confinement, as evidenced by her pushing M aside in order to depart. However, the fact that she was able to push him out of her way will probably nullify her claim of false confinement.

With regard to K's liability to M in battery, this action will also probably fail. Although K's words were accompanied by an action offensive to M (pushing him) she is privileged to free herself from her confinement, and her effort to do so does not seem excessive.

M's conduct, in trying to grab the sugar from K, is unprivileged whether he was reacting to K's shove or attempting to regain possession of merchandise he believed had not been paid for. He is privileged to use reasonable force in protecting himself against K's shove, but his grabbing of the sugar was not in self-protection, but an attempt to regain possession of the sugar. His effort in this respect is not privileged, for (1) he must request that K give him the sugar before trying to re-take it, and (2) the privilege to regain possession is nullified because he is mistaken in his belief that K has not paid for it. (Even if K owes an additional 50 cents for the sugar, the first reason nullifies any privilege of M.)

Whether M is liable for battery against K for knocking her pocketbook to the floor will depend upon whether his offensive intent was directed at some item closely related to K's person. If he had intended contact with K's pocketbook, he would be probably liable for battery, because a woman's pocketbook is so closely associated with her body as to be considered a part of her person. But although M's offensive contact was with K's pocketbook, he intended contact with the sugar. Unless the bag of sugar is considered so closely associated with K that an intended offensive contact with it is equivalent to an intended offensive contact with K herself, M will not be liable for battery.

The likelihood is therefore that none of the behavior described in the fact situation is actionable in torts: neither C's conduct toward K, nor K's conduct toward M, nor M's conduct toward K.

Problem IV

Two 12-year-old boys, Cain (C) and Abel (A), are playing a game of throwing stones at each other on the sidewalk in front of their house. A stone thrown by A hits C on the head, causing C considerable pain. In retaliation, C hurls a stone at A, which misses A and knocks off the hat of a pedestrian (P) who is walking past.

Thinking that A had thrown the stone, P angrily grabs A and shakes him, saying, "I'm going to knock your block off." A kicks and hits P until P frees A and leaves, threatening to have A arrested. Discuss tort liability.

Answer to Problem IV

Regarding A's liability to C: C was harmed by a stone that A threw at him intentionally. In order to satisfy the requirements of battery, A must have intended to cause the harmful or offensive contact. The element of assault may be present if C saw the stone approaching and was apprehensive of imminent, offensive contact.

However, A will probably not be held liable to C because C has consented to A's conduct by agreeing to play the game—and in fact was also engaging in throwing stones. C's consent will eliminate liability for an act for which A would otherwise be liable.

Regarding C's liability to P: C is liable to P for battery because C acted intending to cause a harmful or offensive contact (throwing the stone) and did so when the stone struck P's hat. The hat that was knocked from P's head is so closely connected with P that it will probably be considered part of P's person. If P saw the stone before it reached him, C may also be liable to P in assault, for placing P in apprehension of an imminent contact. However, since P did not know who had thrown the stone, he may not have seen it before he was struck, removing C's assault liability.

If A was placed in reasonable apprehension of imminent physical harm by P's threat, accompanied by P's act of shaking A, P is liable for assault. Whether P actually intended to "knock [A's] block off" is not relevant if A was apprehensive that P would do so. Even if P did not harm A by shaking him, if A was offended by that act, P is liable to A for battery since P's behavior was intentional and without privilege.

P may also be liable to A for false imprisonment. By holding his arm, P briefly prevented A from getting away. A was aware that he was confined, as indicated by his struggle to free himself. However, P may argue that he did not intend to confine A, only to retaliate for A's supposed act of striking P's hat with a stone. Since A's confinement was only transitory and since A was not harmed by it, P's defense against the charge of false imprisonment may succeed.

Finally, regarding A's kicking and hitting of P: Since A acted in order to escape from P, who had mistakenly confined A, A will probably not be held liable to P for battery. One is permitted to defend himself against another unless one's reaction is excessive, which it does not seem to have been in this case.

Problem V

Ima Customer went to A. Dolt's jewelry store with her six-year-old daughter Jean and Monte, another child the same age. Ima intended to buy a watch for Jean's birthday, but after Jean had chosen the watch and tried it on, Ima discovered she did not have enough money to pay for the watch. She therefore asked A to allow her to charge the watch, although she had no charge account with the store. A responded that Ima could instead pay for the watch by sexual favors to him.

When Ima indignantly refused, A yelled at her: "Don't be so high and mighty; I know you are a whore!" He then reached across the counter as if to grab Ima, but did not do so.

By this time Ima had removed the watch from Jean's wrist and the three persons left the store, Ima yelling, "You'll be sorry for this!" Both Jean and her little friend Monte have had frequent nightmares as a result of this incident. Ima would like to bring suit against A. Dolt. What are her chances of success?

Answer to Problem V

Because of A. Dolt's conduct, Ima may have a cause of action for assault against him on her own behalf and for the intentional infliction of emotional distress on behalf of herself and Jean.

When A reached across the counter to grab Ima, he intended to cause an offensive contact with her. If she was indeed offended by his act, as seems certain by her interest in taking legal action, the only remaining issue is whether Ima was apprehensive of *imminent* contact. If A's proximity was such that a reasonable person could apprehend immediate contact by his reaching across the counter, or if he were close enought to come quickly around the counter to make contact with Ima, all elements of assault exist and A will be held liable to Ima for assault.

In order for A to be liable for the intentional infliction of emotional distress, the words he used must have been beyond the bounds of decency, such that a reasonable person would, on hearing them, exclaim, "Outrageous!" If Ima is not a prostitute, A's words may certainly meet this criterion. If, as well, Ima can prove that she has suffered mental or physical distress resulting from his language, A will be liable to Ima for this tort. The facts do not indicate that she suffered such distress, although she was angry enough to consider legal action.

Ima's daughter Jean has suffered demonstrable mental distress resulting from A's conduct toward her mother. Her nightmares are traceable to this incident. That A did not address his comments to the child, and may even have been unaware of her presence is no defense. Jean's presence and her status of close relationship with her mother make A liable to her for any emotional distress she suffers from the incident.

This close relationship does not exist between Ima and Jean's little friend Monte. A therefore will not be liable to Monte for the emotional distress (nightmares) he suffered from the encounter. But if Monte suffers "bodily harm," such as loss of weight or other physical effects resulting from A's conduct toward Ima, A will also be liable to Monte for the intentional infliction of emotional distress.

Problem VI

Arline (A) is a telephone operator in a small town. Bainsby (B) asks her help in finding the address of a client in another town. A refuses to give B the information he wants, but does not explain why she will not give him the information. (In fact, the telephone company prohibits such information to callers.)

B is irritated. He tells A that he is a very important executive in B's Automotive Agency, and he demands to speak to A's employer. A refuses to connect B. B then calls A a worthless critter, a loser, and a god-damned female. He further states that he will teach her a lesson the next time he sees her.

Late that night as she is leaving work A sees B, about ten yards away, leaning against the lamppost at the corner of the street, with his hands in his pockets. Much upset, A nevertheless walks past B, who does not change his position, but stares at A, unblinkingly. A suffers from nervousness and sleeplessness for several weeks afterwards. What liability?

Answer to Problem VI

B's language on the telephone to A is rude and insulting, but will probably not meet the standard of "outrageousness" required for the intentional infliction of emotional distress. His telephone threat to teach her a lesson the next time he sees her is offensive and places A in fear of attack, but two elements of assault are lacking: words alone do not constitute assault, and B did not threaten immediate contact. Nor is B liable for assault when A sees him staring at her as she leaves work, since he makes no attempt at a harmful or offensive contact at that time.

B may, however, be liable to A for the infliction of emotional distress because by the combination of threatening language (by telephone) and his subsequent appearance, seemingly to carry out his threat, he has caused A emotional and physical distress. B's defense against this charge may be that he did not intend his presence to cause A emotional distress and that his position at the lamppost as B approached was entirely coincidental. If the jury believes him, B will not be found liable to A. The key issue is whether B's action is outrageous and beyond the bounds of reasonable behavior. If so, B will be liable to A.

Problem VII

Aikins (A) and Baldy (B) are clients of a large private gymnasium. After working out with barbells and other weights, A and B, as is their custom, undress and enjoy a long soak in the gym's Turkish bath.

While they are soaking, through an error, the gymnasium owner locks the door leading from the bath to the room where they have left their clothes. When they attempt to leave the room they discover that the only exit from the bath is through a large room, lined with mirrors, in which about 50 teenaged girls are practising ballet.

They discuss their dilemma and A decides to leave. Wrapping his towel around himself he traverses the room, ignoring as well as he can the stares of the ballet dancers. A subsequently informs the owner about B's plight and the owner unlocks the door to the room holding B's clothes. B contracts a heavy cold from his long stay in the Turkish bath, and the cold turns into pneumonia. What liability results?

Answer to Problem VII

The confinement of both A and B by the gymnasium owner was unintentional. Therefore if the confinement was transitory or otherwise harmless, the owner will not be liable. The men were both aware of and annoyed by their confinement. A, however, was confined for only a brief time and was not harmed in any other way by it. A therefore has no claim against the owner.

The question to be decided before the owner's liability to B can be determined is whether the only means of exit that was available was one that a reasonable person would choose over confinement. A did choose that exit and suffered only minor embarrassment and no physical harm, but A's sensitivity to indignity might be less than that of a normal reasonable person. If the court decides that B was justified in remaining in the Turkish bath rather than exiting in front of the ballerinas, the gymnasium owner will be liable to B for false confinement, since B's subsequent illness satisfies the requisite harmful result.

WRITING PROBLEMS, SET IV

Only the legal rules given below are to be used in answering the problems that follow. All rules may not be applicable to each problem, and the usual caution applies: the rules are not complete and should not be relied upon in answering problems other than those posed here.

Legal Rules

(Possession of Personal Property) [1]

I. Possession of property consists of physical possession plus the intent to possess and exclude others from possession.

II. Possession is a basic property interest carrying certain rights such as:

A. the right to continue peaceful possession against everyone except those who have a better right;

B. the right to recover possession when the property is wrongfully taken.

III. The finder of property has certain rights:

A. the finder of lost property on the land of another acquires title against all but the true owner, especially when the finder is not a trespasser;

B. the finder of "treasure trove"—coins or money secreted by an unknown owner—has the same rights as the finder of lost property;

C. the finder of abandoned property (property voluntarily relinquished by its owner) is entitled to possession and title of the property;

D. the finder of misplaced property, however, does not obtain title, but the owner of the property on which it was found is considered to be the holder of the goods for the true owner.

Problem I

One A. Hunter was engaged, with his hounds, in the hot pursuit of a fox in a wild, unpossessed area. N. Termeddler, happening upon the scene and seeing that the fox was tiring, killed the fox and carried it away. A. Hunter sued for the value of the fox and received a judgment in his favor; N. Termeddler

---

[1]. From C. H. Smith and R. E. Boyer, *Survey of the Law of Property*, 2nd Ed., 1971, pp. 456–457.

now appeals. You are a judge in the court of appeals; write an opinion for the court.[2]

Answer to Problem I

Wild animals living in their natural state are owned by no one. Therefore he who (1) has the intent to possess the animal and exclude others from possession and (2) gains physical possession of the animal is the rightful owner.

A. Hunter (A) intended to possess the fox and was engaged in the effort to capture it. However he had not yet mortally wounded the fox or in any other way brought it under certain control. Mere pursuit of a wild animal, although accompanied by the intent to capture it, does not convey the right of possession.

N. Termeddler's (N's) interception of A's pursuit of the fox and his subsequent gaining of physical possession of the animal satisfied the two requirements of possession: intent to possess exclusively and physical possession. N's conduct may have been unkind and discourteous, but A has no legal remedy available to him. Therefore the judgment of the court in awarding ownership of the fox to A was erroneous and should be reversed. This court finds in favor of the plaintiff, N. Termeddler.

Problem II

A group of four boys were playing, as was their custom, in a vacant lot. One of the boys found what looked like a large ball of used twine that had been re-wound for later use and then either lost or thrown away. The boys played with the ball of twine for some time, throwing it from one to the other until it finally began to unravel, revealing that the center was composed of old paper currency in the amount of $10,000. The boy who found the ball now claims the money. Is his claim likely to be upheld by a court?

Answer to Problem II

The boy's entitlement to the money inside the ball of twine depends first of all upon whether it was lost, abandoned, or misplaced. If the ball of twine was abandoned the finder has title superior to that of any other person. If the twine was lost, or is classified as treasure trove, the finder has rights superior to all but the right of the true owner. If the twine is classified as misplaced, the lot owner may hold it for its true owner.

In this fact situation the true owner of the twine is making no claim for it and is, in fact, unknown. The twine may well be considered to be lost property. Then the only claim to the money other than that of the finder would be that of the owner of the vacant lot, if the boys were trespassers upon the lot when they found the twine. Since they were in the habit of playing on the lot, they will probably not be considered trespassers. If they are not trespassers, the boy who found the twine may be held to be the rightful owner.

---

2. These facts are adapted from a famous early legal decision which you may wish to read. See Pierson v. Post, 3 Caines 175 (Supreme Court of N. Y. 1805).

The question now becomes whether the boy who found the twine can be said to have found the money enclosed within the ball of twine. It is arguable that he did not, but that the money was not found until it was revealed by the unravelling twine. If so, then all the boys, by their tossing the ball of twine back and forth, participated in "finding" the money and all will be considered co-finders and entitled to a pro rata share of the money.

If the true owner of the money should appear and demand the money back, his claim will prevail unless the boys were able to prove that the ball of twine had been abandoned by the true owner.

Problem III

A maid in a motel, while cleaning the room of a departed guest, found a bundle of dollars, secured by a rubber band, between the mattress and box springs of the bed. She took the money to the motel owner and gave it to him for keeping until the original owner claimed it. She made the provision, however, that should the original owner not claim the money within a year, she would return for it. The motel owner attempted to locate the owner of the bills, but did not succeed. At the end of the year, the maid returned and demanded that the money be turned over to her. Does she have the right to it?

Answer to Problem III

The maid's right to the money, if she has the right, is only against all others except the rightful owner. The question of whether she has even that right depends upon whether the money is considered to have been lost, abandoned, or misplaced.

In this situation, the final category seems to be the appropriate one. The money was probably not abandoned, since it was carefully secured by a rubber band and placed in a spot from which the owner intended to remove it. For the same reason, it will probably not be classified as lost. The owner probably knew where it was; he merely forgot to retrieve it when he left the motel.

If the money was misplaced by the owner, the owner of the property where the money was left is entitled to retain possession of it, as against the right of the maid, for two reasons: (1) the original owner may still remember where he left the money and return to claim it; and (2) the duty of the maid is to turn over to her employer any property left in the rooms and found in the course of her employment.

The maid therefore has no legal right to enforce her provision that the money be turned over to her by the motel owner at the expiration of a year unless the original owner was found. The motel owner will continue to hold the money for the true owner.

Problem IV

A. Bird is a birdwatcher who enjoys early morning walks in the country. One weekend, intent on such a walk, she parked her car on the highway adjacent to property that Farmer Clark owns but does not cultivate and that is not visible from his farmhouse. Bird went onto Clark's property looking for birds, and while walking along discovered a mound of dirt. Curious, she dug into the dirt and found a rusty tin box, which, when opened, revealed numerous gold coins.

Bird carried the box to her car and placed it in the trunk, then headed home. En route she had a flat tire. A passing motorist, B. Helpful, stopped to aid her in changing the tire, and Bird told him of her find and showed him the coins. Aware that they were very valuable, Helpful helped himself to as many coins as he could stuff into his pockets while Bird was not watching.

Helpful has now come to you to find out what rights he, Bird, and Clark have with regard to the coins. Answer his question, using only the rules provided for this group of problems.

Answer to Problem IV

Since the coins were on the property of Farmer Clark, he had physical possession of them. However, if he was unaware of their presence on his property, he cannot be said to have the intent to possess them or to exclude others from possessing them. In order to decide whether Clark has a right to the coins, therefore, the first question to be answered is whether he knew of the presence of the coins on his property.

If Clark himself placed the coins where A. Bird found them, he is their rightful owner, having met the two requirements for possession: physical possession and the intent to possess and to exclude others from possession. Clark then has the right to peaceful possession against all other persons and to recover possession of the coins if they were wrongfully taken.

It seems unlikely, however, that Clark had placed the coins in the place where Bird found them. If he had had the intent to exclude others from possession, he would probably not have buried the coins so near the highway and so far from his home as not to be visible from there.

If Clark had not placed the coins where Bird found them, but knew they were there, he may still have the requisite intent to possess them, and would then have the right to maintain peaceful possession against all except the true owner of the coins. However, this also seems unlikely. If Clark had found the coins, he would probably have moved them to a spot where he could better maintain exclusive possession of them. Thus his intent to possess the coins may be negated by his failure to move them, even if he claims awareness of their presence.

If the coins are defined as misplaced property, Clark would still retain possession of them, as against both Bird and Helpful, despite his unawareness of their existence. With respect to misplaced property (goods left by error), the owner of the property on which it is found retains it until the return of the true owner. Thus, although Bird found the coins, Clark's right to them would be superior to hers.

That the coins will be designated as misplaced property, however, seems unlikely. They have more the characteristics of "treasure trove" (valuable coins secreted in the earth by an unknown owner). Since whoever left them covered them with a mound of dirt, they do not seem to have been left inadvertently.

As finder of treasure trove, Bird has the same rights as the finder of lost property. Generally the finder of lost property acquires title to it against all except the true owner (in this case the unknown person who buried it). But to clarify Bird's rights, her status on Clark's property must be decided. She may have permission to walk on Clark's farm. If so, she is not a trespasser and had rights to the coins superior to Clark's. But if, as the facts suggest, Bird has come onto Clark's land without his knowledge, she may be classified as a trespasser. Her rights to the coins are then less certain and may be a question for the court to decide, since the legal rule is not clear on this point.

Less questionable is Helpful's status with regard to the coins. In removing the coins from Bird's car trunk without her permission, Helpful is a wrongdoer and, although he has the intent to possess the coins as well as physical possession of them, both Bird and Clark have a better right to the coins than Helpful and may recover peaceful possession of them from him.

Problem V [3]

N. Owner bought an unoccupied house in 1938, which he never lived in. About two years later, during World War II, the house was requisitioned by the armed forces, and soldiers were stationed there. During this period, A. Soldier lived in the house.

One day, while he was in the bedroom that was used as sick bay, Soldier found a brooch wedged into the upper frame of a window of the room. The brooch was covered with cobwebs and dust, as if it had been there for years. Soldier took it home to his wife during his next leave, and she told him that it looked very valuable. He then consulted his commissioned officer, who advised him to take it to the police, which he did. The police gave Soldier a receipt for the brooch and held it for two years. When no one claimed it, the police turned the brooch over to Owner, who sold it. Owner offered Soldier a reward for finding the brooch, but Soldier refused, claiming that he, not Owner, was the rightful owner.

In 1945, Soldier sued Owner for the value of the brooch. What would you believe the reasoning of the Court will be and what the decision?

Answer to Problem V

First to be decided is how the brooch is to be classified. It will probably not be considered abandoned property because a person intending to abandon property would probably not take the trouble to place it carefully into a crevice out of sight of the average observer. The brooch will therefore probably be considered either misplaced or lost property.

The owner of the brooch may (like the owner of the billfold found under the mattress in a motel) have removed the brooch and put it into the crevice for safekeeping, then forgotten it was there. If so, the brooch would be con-

---

3. This problem is an adaptation of a famous English case which you may wish to read. See Hannah v. Peel, 1 K.B. (1945).

sidered misplaced property. Or the owner, while cleaning the window, may have lost the brooch. It may have dropped into the crevice without the owner's knowledge and remained there despite a search for it. If so, the brooch would be classified as lost property.

If the brooch is considered misplaced, Owner will have rights to it superior to the right of Soldier, presumably because the true owner of the brooch would be more likely to return for the brooch to the house where it was lost. But this reasoning does not really apply to the present facts because the house was never occupied by Owner, and at least 7 years have passed since he purchased the house, which was then already vacant. The brooch almost certainly was left in the crevice during the occupancy of previous owners. Owner never knew of its existence and therefore had no intent to possess it until it was given to him by the police, some two years after Soldier found it.

If, on the other hand, the brooch is classified as lost, Soldier will have title to the brooch superior to all others except that of the true owner. Since Soldier was living in the house in which he found the brooch, Soldier was not a trespasser. Soldier did not find the brooch in the process of carrying out his duties as an employee of Owner (as did the maid in the motel who found the money under the mattress while changing the bed).

Soldier's conduct, with regard to the brooch was exemplary. Though he might have kept the brooch for himself without being discovered, he turned it over to the police and waited for the true owner to appear. Equity seems to require that the brooch be designated as lost rather than misplaced, since Soldier, by the facts, seems to have a superior right to possession of the brooch, or the value thereof, than Owner.

The Court will therefore probably find that the brooch was lost and that Soldier is entitled to recover its full value.

WRITING PROBLEMS, SET V

The following set of problems deals with contracts. The same caveats apply here as to the previous problems. The rules provided are not necessarily in effect in your jurisdiction and are certainly not complete. They should be used only in the problems provided here. All of the rules are not applicable to every problem, but you will need no other rules to deal with the problems. Allow about one hour to read and answer each question.

Legal Rules

I. Parties are free to make whatever contracts they please as long as the contracts involve no fraud or illegality.

II. Minors (persons under 21) and mentally incompetent persons have no legal capacity to incur contractual duties.

    A. Thus contracts entered into by minors are voidable by them.

    B. But contracts entered into by minors for the necessities of life are not voidable.

C. If a minor represents himself as an adult and thereby receives and retains benefits from a contract, he can not avoid the contract by pleading his minority.

III. The mental illness or defect of one party to a contract makes the contract voidable by that party or his successor in interest, unless the party's mental disability has not affected the making of the contract.

IV. Courts will not permit the enforcement of shockingly unfair (unconscionable) contracts.

Problem I [4]

A, a public school teacher for more than 40 years, became mentally ill at age 60 and took a one-year leave of absence from her teaching. Her psychiatrist subsequently diagnosed her illness as involutional psychosis, complicated by cerebral arteriosclerosis.

Some years before her illness, she had elected Option One of the Teachers Retirement System in which she was enrolled, this option allotting small periodic money payments to her after her retirement, with her husband as beneficiary of the unexhausted reserve after her death. However, when her leave of absence expired at the end of the year, and while she was still under psychiatric treatment, A executed an application of retirement revoking her previous assignment of her husband as beneficiary and requested instead the maximum payment of benefits during her lifetime, with nothing payable after death. At the same time she borrowed $8760, the maximum cash withdrawal possible, from the retirement system.

Three days before she changed her retirement option she had written the Retirement Board a lucid letter stating her intention to retire and requesting the answers to eight specific questions about the various alternatives available to her. The chief clerk of the Board testified that he responded to A's questions both in writing, and orally when she appeared before him. She did not receive the written statement, however, until after she had changed her retirement plan during her personal visit. Two months after retiring, A died.

A and her husband, B, had been married happily for 38 years at the time of her death. After she took leave of absence from her teaching, B quit his job to care for her, because she had, according to both B and the psychiatrist, become very depressed. The couple were in very modest circumstances. On the day she changed her retirement plan, B drove her to the Retirement Board, but he said that he did not know why she was going and did not ask for fear she would "begin crying hysterically."

B now brings suit against the Retirement Board to revoke his deceased wife's actions in changing her retirement benefits so as to exclude him from benefits as her beneficiary. What result?

---

4. These facts are similar to those of a famous case, Ortelere v. Teachers Retirement Bd., 25 N.Y.2d 196, 303 N.Y.S.2d 362, 250 N.E.2d 460 (1969). You may wish to read the actual decision and dissent.

Answer to Problem I

Since there was no evidence of fraud or illegality in the final contract between A and the retirement system only two issues must be considered in deciding whether contract signed by her is voidable.

The first issue is whether A was mentally ill and thus without legal capacity to incur contractual duties. Since A had been diagnosed as mentally ill by the psychiatrist who took care of her, and had been forced by that illness to take a leave of absence from her teaching, there seems no doubt that she comes under this classification. Furthermore, her very action of changing her retirement plan two months before her death so as to cut her husband, B, off from benefits as her beneficiary may be considered additional proof of her mental illness. She and her husband had been happily married for many years, he had quit his own job so as to care for her during her final illness, and she was well aware of their "modest" financial condition. The conclusion may therefore be that had she been mentally competent, she would hardly have elected to change her retirement plan so as to greatly reduce the amount paid from the funds she had contributed to for 40 years and at the same time deprive her husband of all beneficiary rights on her death. If A is found to have been mentally ill when she signed the final contract with the retirement system, the contract will be held void and her earlier option will prevail, reinstating her husband as beneficiary.

But it is at least arguable that despite the diagnosis of involutional psychosis, A was mentally competent at the time she entered into her final transaction with the board. One indication that she was mentally competent is that at the same time she wrote a letter to the board, lucidly listing eight specific questions about alternatives available to her. Her letter reflected substantial understanding of the retirement system.

A second indication that A was mentally competent during her final transaction with the board is that her choice of the new option is rationally explicable in view of the new circumstances in which A found herself. Her decision to receive the maximum payments seems reasonable, based upon the greater needs of support for herself and her husband, since he had quit his job to take care of her. There is no evidence in the facts that A had any premonition of impending death, so her election of the maximum retirement benefits may well have been made to provide the greatest possible returns during her lifetime. Her borrowing of the maximum amount from the retirement fund ($8760) also seems reasonable in this context.

If the court finds that A's acts in her final transaction with the retirement system were unaffected by her mental illness, despite her physician's diagnosis of involutional psychosis, the final contract will be held enforceable and B's claim that A's previous contract be enforced instead will probably be denied.

There is, however, one other issue that may result in a decision favorable to B. If the transaction between A and the retirement board two months before A's death resulted in an unconscionable contract, the court may refuse to enforce it. The court may consider it unconscionable to enforce a contract made by a person mentally ill, two months before her death, effectively nullifying 40 years of participation in a system established for the protection of its participating teachers and their heirs.

Problem II [5]

A married couple, who were Spanish immigrants and spoke no English, visited an appliance store in New York City. While they were looking at a refrigerator-freezer, they were approached by a Spanish-speaking salesman, who attempted to sell them the appliance. The husband explained that they could not buy the refrigerator-freezer because he was about to lose his job the following week. In response, the salesman explained that the appliance would actually be free; they would be paid $25.00 in commission for each similar appliance that they sold friends and neighbors.

Following this salestalk, the husband signed a contract, written in English, for $1,145.88: $900.00, the cash price of the refrigerator-freezer, and $245.88 in credit charges. The cost of the refrigerator-freezer to the dealer was $348.00.

The refrigerator-freezer is now in the possession of the purchasers. The only payment made by them was in the amount of $32.00. The appliance store owner (plaintiff) brings action for a total of $1,364.10: $1,145.88, for the original purchase price; $227.35 for attorney fees; and $22.87 for late charges. What result?

Answer to Problem II

In order to determine the probable result, two issues need to be resolved: (1) whether the contract between the seller and the purchaser was fraudulent; and (2) if not, whether the contract was unconscionable. An affirmative answer to either question would make the contract avoidable.

With regard to possible fraud on the seller's part, since the buyers could understand no English, they were completely dependent upon the Spanish-speaking salesman, who seems to have improperly influenced them by convincing them that they would not need to pay for the appliance. Since their "friends and neighbors" were poor like themselves, there was almost no possibility that the purchasers could sell enough similar appliances to avoid paying for the appliance they purchased. If the salesman knew that such a possibility was so remote as hardly to exist, the seller may be deemed to have committed fraud.

Fraud might also have existed in the signing of the sales contract. Had the contract been written in Spanish, the defendants might have detected the exorbitant credit cost of the purchase. Since it was not, and the plaintiffs knew the defendants understood no English, fraud by the seller may be suggested. If the court finds that the defendant was fraudulently induced to sign the contract, it will refuse to enforce it.

---

5. This is a paraphrase of an actual court case. For the decision, see Frost-ifresh Corp. v. Reynoso, N.Y.Dist.Ct., 52 Misc.2d 26, 274 N.Y.S.2d 757 (1966).

If the court finds no fraud, however, it may still consider the contract unconscionable. The credit charge of $245.88 was almost equal to the plaintiff's cost of the appliance. There is no indication that defendants were told of these exorbitant credit costs, and they were unable to discover this fact for themselves because the contract was printed in a language they could not read. If the court finds that the contract was unconscionable, it may refuse to enforce it and to elect one of the following options: (1) Defendant might be required to reimburse plaintiff only for plaintiff's cost of the appliance ($348.00); (2) defendant might be required to pay for plaintiff's cost of the appliance, plus a reasonable markup and installment cost; or (3) defendant may be offered the alternative of returning the appliance to the seller at no cost to plaintiff or at a charge covering the amount of use he has had of the appliance.

Problem III [6]

A, who is sixteen years old, purchased from B, an automobile dealer, a used car. B was aware that A was a minor. A at first put $50.00 down toward the price of the car, then returned two days later accompanied by his grandmother and aunt. During this second visit, A's aunt drove the car around the lot several times. Then A paid the remaining $90.00 due on the car, with money his aunt had lent him for this purpose. The dealer gave A a receipt, naming A as the purchaser.

A kept the car for a week. The car then broke down and he took it back to the dealer and was told by the dealer's mechanic that the main bearing was burned out and repairs would cost from $45.00 to $95.00. He refused to pay this amount and left the car on the dealer's lot. Then he wrote a letter to the dealer disaffirming the sales contract and demanding the return of his purchase price.

The dealer states that he "understood" that A needed the car for transportation to and from his summer job at a restaurant eight miles from his home. A said, however, that he never drove it to work, and used it only for recreational purposes. A stated that his usual method of getting to work was with the restaurant cook, and that sometimes he "bummed" rides. The dealer further stated that an inference could be drawn from the evidence that the burned-out bearing was caused by A's operation of the car without putting oil in the crankcase.

Is A legally entitled to a refund?

Answer to Problem III

Since A paid for the car in cash and received a receipt from B, the dealer, and since there seems no evidence of fraud or other illegality in the sale, a legal sales contract exists. It is not relevant that A borrowed money from his aunt for part of the purchase price of the car or that his aunt apparently ap-

---

6. These facts are substantially the same as those of Bowling v. Sperry, 133 Ind.App. 692, 184 N.E.2d 901 (1962). You may wish to read the decision of the court in its entirety.

proved the purchase after driving the car around the dealer's lot. The contract, signed by the dealer, contained A's name as purchaser.

As a minor, however, A has no legal capacity to incur contractual duties, and he may therefore choose to disaffirm any contract signed by himself unless the article purchased was for a necessity of life. The dealer says he understood that A needed the car to drive back and forth to his employment. Even if A did make such a statement, the car was in fact not used for that purpose, but only for recreational purposes, during the week that A owned it. Thus, although to a teenager, a car might seem a necessity, the dealer has no ground for claiming "necessity" as a means of holding A to the contract.

The question of whether the burned-out bearing was due to an inherent defect in the car or to A's failure to put oil in the crankcase need not be considered. Whichever the case, A is legally within his rights as a minor to disaffirm the contract.

The court will probably force the dealer to refund A's purchase price of $140.00, minus a charge to A for whatever benefit he received from the use of the car for one week.

Problem IV

A, a student at Podunk University law school, is 20 years old, but looks older. Because his handwriting is almost illegible, he buys an electric typewriter costing $1,000.00 from B, owner of a local office supply company. A pays cash for the typewriter and receives a receipt from B. At the bottom of the receipt is printed the following statement: "The buyer hereby warrants that he is 21 years old or older." A line follows the statement, and at B's suggestion, A signs his name on the line without reading the statement.

A uses the typewriter for a few months, but then he decides that law school requires too much effort and time. He also discovers that his use of the typewriter has not brought him success in his final examinations. Therefore, one month after his twenty-first birthday, he returns to the office supply store, places the typewriter on the counter, and informs B that he no longer has any use for the typewriter and wants his $1,000.00 back. B promises to think about A's request and give him an answer in a few days.

B now consults you, knowing that you are in law school. He explains that he cannot sell the used typewriter at anything like its "new" price. For one thing, the machine, while not abused, has had considerable use, and for another, the new models have just come out, reducing the value of this earlier model. Advise B of his probable rights.

Answer to Problem IV

The sales contract entered into by A and B seems valid, involving no fraud or illegality. B had no reason to doubt that he was dealing with an adult, and cannot be said to have used fraud to persuade A to sign the contract. Nor does there seem to have been any fraudulent intent on A's part in signing the contract signifying that he was an adult.

Since A was in fact a minor when he bought the typewriter, he would ordinarily not be held to a contract he wished to disaffirm. In this case, however, A represented himself as an adult and received certain benefits from the contract, namely the use of the typewriter for several months. On the other hand, A's return of the typewriter is evidence that he no longer wishes to retain these benefits. The legal rule states that in order for A to be held to a contract he signed while a minor, claiming to be an adult, he must both *receive* and *retain* the benefits of the contract. The court must decide whether A has done so.

If the court decides he has, A will not be aided by the defense that he erred in signing the statement that he was at least 21 years old. Courts generally consider that persons should be held to promises made in writing and not be permitted to waive such promises on the ground that they did not read what they signed.

If the court decides that A's return of the typewriter permits him to avoid the contract, B may argue that A should nevertheless be held to it because the typewriter was a necessity, and minors cannot void contracts for necessities. This argument is likely to fail. Courts generally consider that only items like food, clothing, and shelter, are definable as necessities. An electric typewriter for a law student would not come under this classification.

The court may choose a middle path between holding A to his contract and permitting him to avoid it. It may instead require B to accept the returned typewriter and refund to A the amount of money it can be sold for in its used condition.

APPENDIX

Chapter One, Section 1

Punctuate restrictive and non-restrictive clauses

1. *Maria and 3 other girls are in a room:* Maria spoke to the girl who was washing grapes.

2. *Maria, one girl, and 3 boys are in the room:* Maria spoke to the girl who was washing grapes.

3. *There are 3 dogs in a yard:* The dog which had been barking ran toward us.

4. *There is one dog and three cats in the yard:* The dog which had been barking ran toward us.

5. *There are 3 dogs and a cat in the yard:* The cat which had been sitting in the tree jumped onto Joe's shoulder.

6. *There is just one river in the vicinity:* The river which was still and deep bordered our land.

7. *There are several houses on the block:* Gordon bought the house which had green shutters.

8. *A pear, an apple, an orange, and a banana are in a bowl:* Mack chose the fruit which was ripest.

9. *A pear, an apple, an orange, and a banana are in a bowl:* Mack chose the apple which was ripest.

10. *The restaurant had only one waiter:* The diner questioned the waiter who was conciliatory.

11. *There are 3 dentists in town:* Mrs. Brown goes to the dentist who uses laughing gas.

12. *There is only one dentist in town:* Mrs. Brown goes to the dentist who uses laughing gas.

13. People who crossed the country in those days suffered many hardships.

14. Al Wilson who used to coach football coached the boys' team.

15. Our new car which we were so proud of was badly dented in the collision.

16. He talked to anyone who would listen.

17. The moon which was at the full gave enough light to read by.

18. Walker River which flowed by our house was too cold to swim in.

169

General Rules for the Use of Commas in Restrictive and Non-Restrictive Relative Clauses:

When a relative clause identifies the noun it modifies, it is called "restrictive"; no commas are used to separate it from the rest of the sentence.

When a relative clause is not needed to identify the noun it modifies, it is called "non-restrictive" and must be separated from the remainder of the sentences by commas.

"Who" and "which" may introduce either restrictive or non-restrictive clauses, but "that" introduces only restrictive clauses. In sentences 3, 7, and 8, "that" would be used more frequently than "which" (the noun modified being a "non-person"), but either "that" or "which" is correct.

Answers to Chapter One, Section 1

1. Maria spoke to the girl who was washing grapes.
2. Maria spoke to the girl, who was washing grapes.
3. The dog which had been barking ran toward us.
4. The dog, which had been barking, ran toward us.
5. The cat, which had been sitting in the tree, jumped onto Joe's shoulder.
6. The river, which was still and deep, bordered our land.
7. Gordon bought the house which had green shutters.
8. Mack chose the fruit which was ripest.
9. Mack chose the apple, which was ripest.
10. The diner questioned the waiter, who was conciliatory.
11. Mrs. Brown goes to the dentist who uses laughing gas.
12. Mrs. Brown goes to the dentist, who uses laughing gas.
13. People who crossed the country in those days suffered many hardships.
14. Al Wilson, who used to coach football, coached the boys' team.
15. Our new car, which we were so proud of, was badly dented in the collision.
16. He talked to anyone who would listen.
17. The moon, which was at the full, gave enough light to read by.
18. Walker River, which flowed by our house, was too cold to swim in.

Chapter One, Section 2

Case of the Relative Pronoun (Who/Whom)
Correct errors when necessary:

1. Who did you go out with last night?
2. Who did the coach choose to play first base?

3. Whom are you talking to?

4. If you can't trust John, who can you trust?

5. Now I know whom he laughed at.

6. He became enraged at whomever opposed him.

7. The man who they saw emerge from the car fired two shots.

8. The man who they say emerged from the car fired two shots.

9. The voters clearly indicated whom they wanted for mayor.

10. A suspect who the police said was John Jones was arrested.

11. A suspect who the police identified as John Jones was arrested.

12. I did not realize to who I was talking.

13. Whoever lived in the house opened the door.

14. A girl whom I knew last year returned to Gainesville to see me.

15. Whom was at the door?

16. I will go out with whoever I want.

17. I will borrow a pen from whomever has one.

18. Whoever is finished should leave.

Answers to Chapter One, Section 2

1. Whom did you go out with last night?

2. Whom did the coach choose to play first base?

3. Whom are you talking to?

4. If you can't trust John, whom can you trust?

5. Now I know whom he laughed at.

6. He became enraged at whoever opposed him.

7. The man whom they saw emerge from the car fired two shots.

8. The man who they say emerged from the car fired two shots.

9. The voters clearly indicated whom they wanted for mayor.

10. A suspect who the police said was John Jones was arrested.

11. A suspect whom the police identified as John Jones was arrested.

12. I did not realize to whom I was talking.

13. Whoever lived in the house opened the door.

14. A girl whom I knew last year returned to Gainesville to see me.

15. Who was at the door?

16. I will go out with whomever I want.

17. I will borrow a pen from whoever has one.

18. Whoever is finished should leave.

Chapter One, Section 3

(Case of Personal Pronouns)
Choose the correct form (in parentheses)

1. (We/us) women are still being discriminated against in some graduate programs.
2. Between you and (I/me) I am convinced the defendant is guilty as charged.
3. It is useless for John and (he/him) and for others with as little political clout as (they/them) to effect the changes they desire.
4. It is clear to (they/them) who study the problem that the old methods are inefficient.
5. Professors call on (we/us) students who are unprepared.
6. It is not for (we/us) to decide the legality of the act.
7. Uninhabited areas still exist where nature lovers like (we/us) can enjoy visiting.
8. The speaker's attitude surprised both (he/him) and (we/us).
9. John likes Ruth and Joan better than (we/us). [That is, John prefers Ruth and Joan.]
10. John likes Ruth and Joan better than (we/us). [That is, we do not like Ruth and Joan as well as John does.]
11. Neither (he/him) nor (she/her) has any writing problems.
12. After her attorney and (she/her) left, the office was closed.
13. The door closed after her attorney and (she/her).

———

Answers to Chapter One, Section 3

1. we
2. me
3. him . . . they
4. them
5. us
6. us
7. us
8. him . . . us
9. us
10. we
11. he . . . she
12. she
13. her

Chapter One, Sections 4, 5, 6, 7

(Dangling modifiers, squinting modifiers, split infinitives, sentence fragments, and run-on sentences)

1. Because of changing the hours for legal aid appointments, those who want assistance should visit the Legal Aid Clinic between 8 and 11 a. m. (Eliminate a dangling modifier.)

2. The deadline for completion of the brief had passed. Although there was hope that a time extension would be granted. (Eliminate a sentence fragment.)

3. Both defendants are guilty of assault since they were acting together. Although both will argue they were only joking and had no intention of harming the plaintiff. (Eliminate a sentence fragment.)

4. The depression in the ground was not readily apparent, it cannot be proved that the defendant was acting negligently since a reasonable person might not have seen the depression. (Eliminate a run-on sentence.)

5. The supreme court of Florida reversed the decision granting relief to an owner when a ceiling collapsed, however the courts are expanding the definition of what constitutes a reasonable inspection. (Eliminate a run-on sentence.)

6. We must also remember that Florida after the *Hoffman* decision becoming a comparative negligence state and as such plaintiff no longer being denied recovery if both plaintiff and defendant are negligent. (Eliminate a sentence fragment.)

7. Thus again the essential role of the factfinder in determining the amount of contribution for which each party will be held accountable. (Eliminate a sentence fragment.)

8. A response arrived in the mail probably in reply to the newspaper advertisement. (Eliminate a squinting modifier.)

9. The defendant seemed to never consider the wishes of the plaintiff in their business dealings. (Eliminate a split infinitive.)

10. On this point a judge should question the existence of an integrated writing, a question concerning the percentage bonus ultimately arises. (Eliminate a run-on sentence.)

11. Whether the defendant touched the person of the plaintiff. There seems no indication that he intended to do so. (Eliminate a sentence fragment.)

12. Petitioner claims denial of equal protection of the laws due to the affirmative action quota system, petitioner argues that classifications based on race are invidiously discriminatory. (Eliminate a run-on sentence.)

13. Several important circuit court cases that follow the Supreme Court's reasoning. (Eliminate a sentence fragment.)

14. Defendants were stopped by an inspector on I-75, he informed them that they were required to stop for inspection but if they would open the rear of their truck they could proceed. (Eliminate a run-on sentence.)

15. The defendants had a duty under Florida law to have their truck inspected, by not stopping they were in violation of the statute. (Eliminate a run-on sentence.)

16. The bar review meeting will take place probably in the auditorium at 3:00 P.M. (Eliminate a squinting modifier.)

17. His attorney had advised the defendant to not attend the pre-trial deposition. (Eliminate a split infinitive.)

18. Since the purpose of the inspection is to determine whether there is any unlawful offense being committed and is within the regulatory power of the Director of Agriculture. (Eliminate a sentence fragment.)

19. Having avoided prosecution by plea bargaining we now have a situation where criminals are free and repeating their crimes. (Eliminate a dangling modifier.)

20. Couched in ungrammatical English the writer risks his good legal reasoning being underestimated. (Eliminate a dangling modifier.)

21. Damaged by lightning the insurance policy did not cover the cost of repairs to the house. (Eliminate a dangling modifier.)

Answers to Chapter One, Sections 4, 5, 6, 7

1. Because of a change in the hours of legal aid appointments, those wanting assistance should visit the Legal Aid Clinic between 8 and 11 A.M.

2. The deadline for completion of the brief had passed, although there was hope that a time extension would be granted.

3. Both defendants are guilty of assault since they were acting together, although both will argue they were only joking and had no intention of harming the plaintiff.

4. Because the depression in the ground was not readily apparent, it cannot be proved that the defendant was acting negligently since a reasonable person might not have seen it.

5. The supreme court of Florida reversed the decision granting relief to an owner whose ceiling collapsed; however, the courts are expanding the definition of what constitutes a reasonable inspection.

6. Florida, after the *Hoffman* decision, became a comparative negligence state, and therefore plaintiff is no longer denied recovery if both plaintiff and defendant are negligent.

7. Thus again the essential role of the factfinder is in determining the amount of contribution for which each party will be held accountable.

8. (Two possibilities) A response, probably in reply to the newspaper advertisement, arrived in the mail.

   A response in reply to the newspaper advertisement arrived, probably in the mail.

9. The defendant seemed never to consider the wishes of the plaintiff in their business dealings. (Or ". . . never seemed to consider . . .")

10. On this point a judge should question the existence of an integrated writing; a question concerning the percentage bonus also ultimately arises.

11. The question is whether the defendant touched the person of the plaintiff. There seems no indication that he intended to do so.

12. Petitioner claims denial of equal protection of the laws due to the affirmative action quota system. Petitioner argues that the classifications based on race are invidiously discriminatory.

13. Several important circuit court cases follow the Supreme Court's reasoning.

14. Defendants were stopped by an inspector on I-75; he informed them that they were required to stop for inspection, but that if they would open the rear of their truck they could proceed.

15. The defendants had a duty under Florida law to have their truck inspected; by not stopping they were in violation of the statute.

16. (Two possibilities) The bar review meeting will probably take place in the auditorium at 3:00 P.M.

    The bar review meeting will take place in the auditorium, probably at 3:00 P.M.

17. His attorney had advised the defendant not to attend the pretrial deposition.

18. The purpose of the inspection is to determine whether there is any unlawful offense being committed, and the inspection is within the regulatory power of the Director of Agriculture.

19. Having avoided prosecution by plea bargaining, criminals now are free and repeating their crimes.

20. Couched in ungrammatical English, the writer's good legal reasoning may be underestimated.

21. The insurance policy did not cover the cost of repairs to the house damaged by lightning.

Chapter One, Sections 8, 9, 10

The Semi-colon/Comma Choice; the Colon; the Possessive Apostrophe
Supply the correct punctuation in the following unpunctuated sentences:

1. The committee gave as its reason for delaying action the absence of many of its members during the summer recess but it failed to take action on their return.

2. The witness for the defense failed to appear however the trial continued.

3. Three reasons were given for the cost overrun the general inflation the addition of features to the original plan and delay in construction due to bad weather.

4. During the recession the national debt increased the interest rate rose and the people lost buying power.

5. Banks are like siblings the more there are of them the more they compete.

6. Gary and Greta Browns will left everything to their children.

7. Ladies clubs have been known to be politically conservative.

8. Mr. Smiths and Mrs. Whites tax forms are in the file on the desk.

9. The noise of construction in the adjoining building was deafening nevertheless classes continued inside the law school.

10. The appropriated funds did not materialize however the school lunch program remained in effect.

————

Answers to Chapter One, Sections 8, 9, 10

1. The committee gave as its reason for delaying action the absence of many of its members during the summer recess, but it failed to take action on their return.   (Comma before a coordinating conjunction.)
   (or)
   The committee gave as its reason for delaying action the absence of many of its members during the summer recess; but it failed to take action on their return.   (Semi-colon before a coordinating conjunction.)

2. The witness for the defense failed to appear; however the trial continued.

3. Three reasons were given for the cost overrun: the general inflation; the addition of features to the original plan; and delay in construction due to bad weather.

4. During the recession the national debt increased, the interest rate rose, and the people lost buying power.

5. Banks are like siblings: the more there are of them the more they compete.

6. Gary and Greta Brown's will left everything to their children.

7. Ladies' clubs have been known to be politically conservative.

8. Mr. Smith's and Mrs. White's tax forms are in the file on the desk.

9. The noise of construction in the adjoining building was deafening; nevertheless, classes continued inside the law school.

10. The appropriated funds did not materialize; however, the school lunch program remained in effect.

Chapter One, Section 11

Number Errors

(Choose the proper form, within the parentheses in each sentence)

1. Mr. Jones is an outstanding (alumnus, alumna, alumni, alumnae) of the university.

2. Bretanie Women's College (alumnus, alumna, alumni, alumnae) of the class of 1944 were in attendance 75% strong at their 30th reunion.

3. The main (criterion/criteria) for high grades in law school (is/are) the ability to analyze and write effectively.

4. The broadcasting and newspaper (medium/media) (is/are) well represented, the former (medium/media) including both television and radio.

5. Included in the (dictum/dicta) of both the majority and minority opinions were the same legal points.

6. All of the (datum/data) collected by the research team (is/are) relevant to the case.

7. The plaintiff corporation changed (its/their) headquarters since instituting (its/their) suit.

8. The city of Dallas has added bicycle lanes to (its/their) road maps of the metropolitan area.

9. (Change the following sentence to avoid the masculine singular pronoun.) An attorney is expected to be on time for his appointments and to meet his deadlines.

10. (Change the following sentence to avoid the masculine singular pronoun.) When a person writes on legal subjects, he must seek to write accurately, clearly, and succinctly.

Answers to Chapter One, Section 11

1. alumnus

2. alumnae

3. criterion . . . is

4. media . . . are . . . medium

5. dicta

6. data . . . are

7. its . . . its

8. its

9. An attorney is expected to be on time for appointments and to meet deadlines.

(or)

Attorneys are expected to be on time for (their) appointments and to meet (their) deadlines.

10. A person who writes on legal subjects must seek to write accurately, clearly, and succinctly.

(or)

Persons writing on legal subjects must seek to write accurately, clearly, and succinctly.

Chapter One, Section 12

The Extra "That," Other Redundancies, and Some Deletions
(Correct all errors)

1. The question is is whether the porch of the victim's apartment is a "dwelling," according to the definition in the statute.

2. I recognize the valid national security reasons it was done.

3. Security Builders has filed a cross claim for any amount it is held liable in the original action.

4. It can and has been argued that if this reasoning were applied, all distributions of appreciated property would be subject to tax.

5. If the plaintiff would have slowed down at the intersection, the defendant would have been able to avoid the accident.

6. The appropriate forum for the trial to take place is now being decided.

7. A contract which one party is a minor is avoidable.

8. The case would have been settled out of court if the defendant would have agreed to the settlement.

Answers to Chapter One, Section 12

1. The question is whether the porch of the victim's apartment is a "dwelling," according to the definition in the statute.

2. I recognize the valid national security for which it was done.

3. Security Builders has filed a cross claim for any amount for which it is held liable in the original action. (Or, . . . for any amount it is held liable for . . .)

4. It can be and has been argued that if this reasoning were applied, all distributions of appreciated property would be subject to tax.

5. If the plaintiff had slowed down at the intersection, the defendant would have been able to avoid the accident.

6. The appropriate forum for the trial to take place in is now being decided.

7. A contract in which one party is a minor is avoidable.

8. The case would have been settled out of court if the defendant had agreed to the settlement.

Chapter One, Section 13

Count and Non-count Nouns

From the following list of words choose an appropriate one to fill each blank. Use each word at least once: much, many; little, few; less, fewer; amount, number.

1. _____ money is being spent to insure the most complete athletic facility available.

2. _____ tickets are available by mail than at the door.

3. A large _____ of information is being provided by research.

4. A large _____ of sharks were sighted yesterday in the Gulf.

5. According to many nutritionists, Americans eat too _____ salt.

6. A large _____ of studies have been done on the relationship of exercise to heart attack incidence.

7. _____ mail is undeliverable because the sender has omitted the zip code.

8. _____ expense was spared to provide enough data.

9. _____ statistics are available, however.

10. There is not _____ evidence that agreement is imminent.

11. On the other hand, there are _____ indications that the controversy has broadened.

———

Answers to Chapter One, Section 13

1. much,
2. fewer,
3. amount,
4. number,
5. much (or little),
6. number,
7. much (or little),
8. little,
9. few (or many),
10. much,
11. many (or few).

Chapter Two, Section A(1) and (2)

Word Placement for Emphasis and the Use of Lists:
Correct all errors

1. It was expressly decided in *Humbert v. Trinity Church* that the original owner must still bring action even if the tenant obtained or continued possession of land by fraud or if the tenant's claim is unfounded,

wrongful, and fraudulent in any respect. (Important idea: the orginal owner must bring action).

2. It could plausibly be inferred that public policy supports the formulation and institution of affirmative action programs, from the facts and reasoning of the *Allen* case. (Important idea: affirmative action programs are supported by public policy).

3. The key point here is that even if unknown to him, since he is the operator of a business, the owner will be held liable for what he should know and certain portions of his premises used by the public should thus be reasonably safe. (Important idea: the owner is liable for maintaining safe premises).

4. The court, in a later case, held that a storekeeper need exercise only reasonable care to keep his premises in a safe condition, where plaintiff was denied recovery when he slipped and fell on waxy paper in front of the storeowner's door, of uncertain origin. (Important idea: storekeepers need exercise only reasonable care).

5. The problem is the amount of time the condition existed; in one recent case where a customer slipped on trash on the floor of a business, the court found no liability where there had been no inspection for 3 hours, but in another case where a substance was on the floor of a store for 15 minutes, the court found liability, although both of these cases occurred inside the stores. (Important idea: courts differ on how long a condition must exist before a storeowner is liable for injury to customers caused by the condition).

6. Back in 1943, there was a news story in the Times about a returning war veteran with his wife and baby boy who could not find a place to live because they had a child; I was that baby and now 35 years later, with a wife and baby, I have not changed. (Important idea: persons refuse to rent to couples with children).

7. The dental surgeon testified, however, that football players whose mouths are injured can often be repaired with modern dental surgical techniques. (Important idea: modern surgery repairs gridiron dental injuries).

8. Since the bus driver raved and ranted at both passengers he could be liable for intentional infliction of emotional distress. (Important idea: both passengers have a cause of action for the intentional infliction of emotional distress.)

9. For the solar energy expert, a theme repeatedly occurs in his conversation: "Our energy is like a family with a savings account, we have to live within our income." (Important idea: available energy can be compared to a savings account.)

10. For an incorrect statement to be material and thus vitiate a policy it must have been made by the insured in response to a question that he understood or could reasonably be expected to understand or be ex-

pected to have sufficient information to answer. (Important idea: the insured person must understand the contract that he has signed.)

Answers to Chapter Two, Section A(1) and (2)
Answers to Word Placement for Emphasis and the Use of Lists

1. The court held, in *Humbert v. Trinity Church,* that even if (1) the tenant obtained the continued possession of land by fraud, or (2) the tenant's claim was unfounded, wrongful, or fraudulent, the original owner must still bring action to oust the tenant.

2. The holding of the *Allen* case implies that public policy supports the formulation and institution of affirmative action programs.

3. The owner must keep those portions of his premises used by the public reasonably safe since he will be held liable for all dangerous conditions about which he should have knowledge.

4. The plaintiff, in a later case, was denied recovery after he fell on waxy paper of uncertain origin in front of the storeowner's door, the court holding that the storeowner need exercise only reasonable care in maintaining safe premises.

5. Courts differ on how long a dangerous condition must exist inside a store before a storeowner is liable for customer injuries resulting from the condition. In one recent case in which a customer slipped on trash on the floor of a business when there had been no inspection for three hours, the court found the owner not liable; but in another case, when a substance had been on the floor only 15 minutes, the owner was found liable.

6. Times have not changed in the 35 years since a war veteran returing in 1943 with his wife and baby boy could not find a place to live; now, I, that baby grown up, still am unable to rent a place to live in with my wife and baby because persons refuse to rent to couples with children.

7. Modern surgical techniques can often repair the mouths of football players with gridiron injuries.

8. Both passengers at whom the bus driver raved and ranted have a cause of action for the intentional infliction of emotional distress.

9. The solar energy expert repeatedly asserts that energy is like the savings account of a family—the family must live within the income from the account and not use up the capital.

10. An insurance policy containing an incorrect answer by the insured person to a question asked on the policy will not be vitiated unless the insured person (1) understood the question asked, (2) could reasonably be expected to understand the question, or (3) could be expected to have sufficient information to answer the question.

Chapter Two, Section A(3)

Use Parallelism
Correct all errors:

1. It is assumed that because one should know what is in his possession, even though actual knowledge is absent, and therefore held strictly liable for that which he possesses.

2. The elements of intentional infliction of emotional distress are (1) extreme or outrageous conduct, (2) actual mental or physical harm and (3) it must be done intentionally or recklessly.

3. Battery is an unconsented to touching that harms or offends and there is no privilege to do so.

4. When deciding a forum for trial, one should weigh whether witnesses to the action can be brought to the forum, whether there will be great expense to bring the defendant to the forum, and whether the local nature of the controversy affects the jury's knowledge of it.

5. The lender may terminate this agreement at any time upon adverse re-evaluation of a maker's creditworthiness, if satisfaction is not provided by the maker regarding the terms of this agreement, or whenever the decision to terminate is made either by the lender or the maker.

6. The contract neither complies with the statute nor is there agreement between the contracting parties as to its terms.

7. An individual can assert four principal claims: claim to possession of tangible property; freely laboring and contracting; having the right to promised advantages (e.g., performance); and no interference in relationships.

8. The *Barwick* decision is unfair because the wrongdoer may profit from his wrong, and injuring of the present possessor occurs.

9. Bailment is established by agreed upon transfer of property when there is mutual benefit and the involved parties agree upon a period of time.

10. In Payne v. Payne, the court defined impotency as not only nonprocreation nor copulation but that it also must be incurable.

11. The owner reasonably has the responsibility to maintain the structure so that it is safe for the use of the lessee, that it is a sturdy structure, with proper wiring.

Answers to Chapter Two, Section A(3)

1. Since the assumption is that one should know what he possesses, he is held liable for his possessions even though he may not have that knowledge.

2. The intentional infliction of emotional distress is defined as intentional or reckless conduct that is extreme or outrageous and causes actual mental or physical harm to the victim.

3. Battery is touching that is harmful or offensive to the victim without privilege by the actor or consent by the victim. *

4. In choosing a forum for trial, the following must be considered: (1) whether witnesses to the action can be brought to the forum; (2) what the cost of bringing the defendant to the forum will be; and (3) whether the local nature of the controversy will affect the jury's knowledge of it.

5. The lender may terminate this agreement at any time: (1) if he receives adverse re-evaluation of a maker's credit; (2) if the maker does not provide satisfaction regarding the terms of the agreement; or (3) if either the lender or the maker decides to terminate the agreement. **

6. The contract does not comply with the statute, nor do the contracting parties agree on its terms.

7. An individual can assert four principal claims: (1) to possession of tangible property; (2) to freedom to labor and contract; (3) to the right to promised advantages (e.g., performance); and (4) to freedom from interference in relationships.

8. The *Barwick* decision is unfair because the present possessor may be injured and because the wrongdoer may profit from his wrong.

9. Bailment is established when property is transferred, if the parties involved benefit mutually and agree on a period of time.

10. In Payne v. Payne, the court defined impotence not only as non-procreation or non-copulation, but also as an incurable condition.†

11. The owner is responsible for maintaining a sturdy structure, safe for the lessee and with proper wiring.

Chapter Two, Section A(4)

Choose Connectors Carefully
Correct all errors:

1. When the plaintiff limps in, the jury will be inclined toward her favor because we must remember the old axiom that juries tend to be more favorable toward plaintiffs.

2. In this case, the depression was not readily apparent and it would be hard to prove the plaintiff was acting negligently, and if she was acting

---

* The redraft avoids confusing shifts in viewpoint. For a discussion of this point, see Chapter Two, Section B(8).

** The use of a list and parallel construction reveals that the third condition precludes the necessity for the other two.

† This change seems to be in accord with the intended meaning.

reasonably, as she claims she was, the same accident might have happened to anyone; it is possible a reasonable person might not have seen the depression.

3. The record discloses agreements between the attorneys and 170 of the parties owning land, and whose property was benefitted by the decree.

4. Four petitioners challenged their respective states' statutes as violative of *Furman* standards, and re-submitted the argument that the death penalty was unconstitutional, per se, in violation of the 8th and 14th amendment's prohibition of "cruel and unusual punishment."

5. If the instructors would put down a little pressure it could help, but it's hard for the instructor to stand in front of class and smoke and enforce this rule.

6. In the course of a busy life he built the Fitchburg Railroad, the Hoosac Tunnel, founded a great paper company, went to Congress and learned to write well.

7. There are 14 programs working with old folks, underprivileged, handicapped, foreign students and many more.

8. The criteria for receiving a license calls for qualified faculty members, organization and curriculum structure.

9. In view of the ease that the draft could be evaded, something good can be said about those who openly resisted.

10. Since the operation was unconsented, the patient has a cause of action.

––––––

Answers to Chapter Two, Section A(4)

1. Because juries tend to favor plaintiffs, and particularly plaintiffs who have obviously been injured, the jury will no doubt favor this plaintiff when she limps in.

2. The plaintiff claims she was acting reasonably, and to prove that she acted negligently would be difficult since the depression into which she fell was not readily apparent and a similar accident might therefore have happened to any reasonable person.

3. The record discloses agreements between the attorneys and 170 of the landowners whose property was benefited by the decree.

4. In challenging their respective states' statutes for violating *Furman* standards, four petitioners re-submitted the argument that the death penalty was unconstitutional because it violated the 8th and 14th amendments' prohibition of "cruel and unusual punishment."

5. If the instructors made a real effort they could enforce the "no smoking" rule, but not if they themselves smoke while teaching.

6. In the course of a busy life he built the Fitchburg Railroad and the Hoosac Tunnel, founded a great paper company, served in Congress, and learned to write well.

7. There are fourteen programs: for old, underprivileged, and handi-capped persons, and for foreign students. Many other programs exist in addition to these.

8. In order to receive a license, the school must provide qualified faculty members, adequate organization, and an appropriate curriculum.

9. In view of the ease with which the draft could be evaded, something good can be said for those who openly resisted it.

10. Since the patient did not consent to the operation, he has a cause of action.

Chapter Two, Section A(5)

Match Nouns and Verbs:

1. The union has a duty to support its members' grievances.

2. Treat the rapist like a person; treating him with contempt may only irritate his dislike for women.

3. The Senate reported progress; progress is certainly on the move.

4. By pricing middle and low income students out of an education, we have lost the perspective of the concept of public education.

5. Double bogeys on the last two holes frustrated her momentum.

6. Hearings examining the California supreme court's judicial perform-ance will add to the court's already damaged prestige.

7. If one momentarily forgets to pay attention to what he is doing, is no excuse for his failure to observe hazard.

8. Our distinguished panel will aid the staff by guiding and reacting to agendas and materials.

9. Many people would rather look at hearsay than listen to evidence.

10. Fellow legislator, Representative John Smith, rebuked the plan to re-duce the price of license plates for small cars.

11. Also, exhibiting certain control must have been made over a wild animal in order to determine possession.

Answers to Chapter Two, Section A(5)

1. The union has a duty to support its members in their grievances.

2. Treat the rapist like a person; treating him with contempt may only irritate him.

3. The Senate reported progress; the Senators are certainly on the move.

4. By pricing middle and low income students out of an education, we have lost the concept of public education.

5. Double bogeys on the last two holes frustrated her. (Or: halted her momentum.)

6. Hearings examining the California supreme court's judicial performance will further decrease the prestige of the court.

7. His momentary lapse in attention is no excuse for his failure to observe the hazard.

8. Our distinguished panel will aid the staff by preparing and reacting to agendas and materials.

9. Many people would rather listen to hearsay than to evidence.

10. Fellow legislator, Representative John Smith, rejected the plan to reduce the price of license plates for small cars. (The verb "rebuke" must have as object a sentient being. One can rebuke other persons, or even dogs, but not "plans.")

11. Possession of a wild animal is deemed to occur if one exhibits certain control over the animal.

Chapter Two, Section A(6)

Prefer the Active Voice

1. Many points are still to be considered by the jury.

2. The broadcast media should be included under the first amendment. It can be argued that the TV station was seeking to gather news when the trial was televised by the station. Thus, the judge's order can be viewed as prior restraint.

3. From the facts and reasoning of the *Allen* case, it could be plausibly inferred that the institution of affirmative action programs is supported by public opinion.

4. It was then illustrated in *Zell*, that there is almost universal acceptance of the concept of extrinsic parol or any other extrinsic evidence being admitted if the written agreement of the parties lacks legal efficacy.

5. It was feared by defendants that without a jury trial they would be disadvantaged.

6. If a defendant made a substantial preliminary showing that a false statement was made intentionally by an affiant in his affidavit for a search warrant, the search warrant should be voided and the products of the search excluded.

7. In *Hugendorf,* defendant was convicted of knowingly receiving, concealing and storing stolen furpieces which had been transported by him in interstate commerce.

8. The taxi driver's actions could be considered outrageous and intentional and harm was suffered by the passenger from the incident.

9. Persons serving the public are held to higher standards of conduct than other persons; therefore a strong case can be made by the defendant in assault. As soon as her purse was grabbed, there was battery.

10. When one's possessions are being held by another for the purpose of not allowing a person to leave a place, there is also false imprisonment.

11. It is assumed that actual knowledge of his possessions is held by everyone; therefore even without actual knowledge, the defendant is held liable for all that which he possesses.

Answers to Chapter Two, Section A(6)

1. The jury still has to consider many points.

2. The first amendment should apply to the broadcast media. The TV station can argue that it was seeking to gather news when it televised the trial. The judge's order would thus be prior restraint.

3. The inference of the facts and reasoning of the *Allen* case is that public opinion supports affirmative action programs.

4. *Zell* illustrates that extrinsic parol or any other extrinsic evidence is admissible if the written agreement of the parties lacks legal efficacy.

5. Defendants feared that they would be at a disadvantage without a jury trial.

6. If a defendant makes a substantial preliminary showing that an affiant intentionally made a false statement in his affidavit for a search warrant, the search warrant should be voided and the products of the search excluded. *

7. In *Hugendorf,* defendant was convicted of knowingly receiving, concealing, and storing stolen furpieces which he had transported in interstate commerce.

8. The taxi driver's actions, which can be considered outrageous and intentional, caused his passenger harm. **

9. Persons who serve the public are held to higher standards of conduct than other persons; therefore the defendant has a strong case in assault, because the grabbing of her purse constituted battery.

10. A person holding the possessions of another so that the second person is unable to leave is liable for false imprisonment.

11. The assumption is that everyone has actual knowledge of his possessions; therefore even if he does not have such knowledge, the defendant is liable for all his possessions.

---

* The last two passive forms are left intact because the doer of the action is not important.

** In the original sentence the causal relationship that seems to be an important factor was not expressed.

Chapter Two, Section A(7)

Use Concrete Language

1. The gravamen of this study is that it would appear from the relationship of the issues that all issues would be most expeditiously litigated in a single judicial proceeding.

2. While one can well appreciate an editorial policy which does not verify the contents of every letter to the editor or the identity of every signatory, it is clear that arguably scurrilous personal attacks ought not to be published anonymously with an editorial note explaining the exigency. (This sentence has an additional disadvantage of ambiguity because of the negative construction. Should such letters be published, then, *without* the editorial note explaining the exigency?)

3. When concepts are identified with the same cognomen, it is easy for the mind to slip into the assumption that the verbal identity is accompanied, in all its sequences, by identity of meaning.

4. There are a lot of loose ends to be finalized with the program, and its effectiveness will depend upon available personnel and the relationship developed between centers and various agencies.

5. A significant proportion of qualified persons are excluded from the judiciary because of the existing level of compensation.

6. This is in no way to be construed as a negative appraisal of the intellectual community nor of the current general condition of academia.

7. The peroration of a judicial tribunal must ultimately arrive at some point of finality.

8. In the interest of justice and elimination of continuous and protracted future litigation, it appears to be proper and dutiful to exercise the right of permutation in this matter even though it may tend to be hortative in the litigants involved.

9. The consumer affairs coordinator will have the following duties: to review existing mechanisms of consumer input, thruput and output, and seek ways of improving these linkages via the "consumer communications channel."

10. What I try to do is to orchestrate a series of people who put in inputs that eventually come out as a draft speech which I personally submit to the Secretary-General.

11. We should address the matter of how we can maximize the fact of our incumbency in dealing with persons known to be active in their opposition to our administration.

12. Precipitation entails negation of economy.

13. It is only human to make occasional errors.

14. The display of your entrance permit is mandatory.

15. A youth designated only as "Jack" sustained, incident to a loss of equilibrium, a fracture of the cranium.

16. Rodents, in the absence of their feline enemy, are prone to divert themselves.

17. The remittance of sums paid by customers purchasing articles in or of this establishment is hereby guaranteed in the event that such articles, or one or more thereof, shall be hereafter deemed unsatisfactory to or by the said customers.

18. There is a problem of judicial discretion as to whether to take cognizance of this case.

19. The Lord is my external-internal mechanism . . . He positions me in a non-decisional situation. He maximizes my adjustment.

Answers to Chapter Two, Section A(7)
Use concrete language

1. This study indicates that all issues are so closely related that they should be litigated in one judicial proceeding.

2. Although the editor understandably cannot verify either the identity of each letter writer or the contents of every letter, letters containing what might be considered scurrilous personal attacks should not be published, even with an editorial note of explanation.

3. Concepts with the same name are assumed to have the same meaning.

4. The program needs to be improved, and its effectiveness will depend upon how good its personnel is and how it gets along with other centers and agencies.

5. Present salaries are too low to attract qualified persons to the judiciary. (But what level of the judiciary does the writer mean?)

6. I am not criticizing the intellectual community nor the state of academics.

7. A judicial tribunal must eventually end its deliberations. (Since this was part of a written opinion, the word "peroration" is improper, and was probably an error.)

8. (This is only a guess, but the judge who wrote this opinion may have meant,) "In order to serve justice and eliminate litigation, this Court exercises its right to disagree with previous decisions, even though the present opinion is merely advisory."

9. (This sentence cannot be redrafted because it is couched so that there is no way to tell what the coordinator's actual duties are.)

10. I combine material written by staff experts into a draft speech for the [UN] Secretary-General.

11. (John Dean, who added,) "Stated more bluntly, how can we use available federal machinery to screw our enemies?"

12. Haste makes waste.

13. To err is human.

14. Show your pass.

15. Jack fell down, and broke his crown . . .

16. When the cat is away, the mice will play.

17. Satisfaction or your money back.

18. The court must decide whether to hear this case.

19. (The 23rd Psalm, written by a bureaucrat.)

Chapter Two, Section A(8)

Keep Your Sentences Clear

1. The primary problem area that will be encountered by the plaintiff's claim of transferred intent in intentional infliction of emotional distress is the fact that she is the grandmother of the victim and not an immediate family member.

2. In Merrit v. Reserve Insurance Company, a case which is not only factually similar to the present case, but it also shares with it the fact that no offer of settlement was ever made to the defendant, the court addresses the question of this duty of good faith.

3. Under a reasonable standard, for two young persons to torment an old man by grabbing his cane and running off with it, thereby causing the victim to stumble home, it may easily be concluded that an intentional infliction of emotional distress has occurred.

4. The imaginable distress that the old man suffered as he stumbled home, fearing injury or accident all the way is clearly an infliction of emotional distress by the defendants to which he is entitled just compensation.

5. As a result of our meetings with the House and Senate Education Committees, the House Appropriations Committee and the Senate Ways and Means Committee, which meetings have focused on our 1980 Budget Request and the related subject of contingency planning, I can report that legislative leaders appear to be understanding of our situation as described at the above meetings and supportive of our efforts thus far to deal with the situation.

6. In view of these supreme court and circuit court cases focusing on the issue of invalidated testing procedures, it would appear that the Petitioner does not have standing in the light the testing procedure utilized was not only unvalidated but it proved to disqualify minorities at a racially disproportionate rate, although it is not entirely known for sure that the Budgeting-Finance Aptitude Test of the state of Florida is or is not a validated testing procedure. But in the light of the presented facts, it can be inferred that the testing procedure has not been a validated one and it has been shown to disqualify minorities at a racially disproportionate rate.

7. Whether expert testimony should come from the same or similar communities or simply from any doctor with ordinary and reasonable skill in proving and disproving malpractice is unresolved in Florida, but the weight of authority seems to indicate that the rule to be applied is the same or similar community.

8. The defendant may attack the proceedings, claiming error in excluding contrary testimony of medical witnesses was improper, and may support this charge by pointing to Baldor v. Rogers where the supreme court of Florida declared that courts cannot hold a defendant in malpractice suits to the opinion of one physician and the exclusion of other contrary opinion.

Answers to Chapter Two, Section A(8)
Keep your sentences clear

1. The plaintiff may be unsuccessful in claiming transferred intent to the intentional infliction of emotional distress because this claim is usually restricted to immediate family members of the victim, and the plaintiff is the victim's grandmother.

2. In Merrit v. Reserve Insurance Company, the court considered the duty of good faith in a case factually similar to the instant case. In that case, as in this, no offer of settlement was ever made to the defendant.

3. The two young persons intentionally grabbed the old man's cane, forcing him to stumble home. Their action can reasonably be described as the intentional infliction of emotional distress.

4. The old man is entitled to just compensation from the defendants for the emotional distress he suffered as he stumbled home, fearing accident or injury all the way.

5. We have focused on our 1980 Budget Request and the related subject of contingency planning in our meetings with the House and Senate Education Committees, the House Appropriations Committee, and the Senate Ways and Means Committee. Legislative leaders who have met with us in these sessions appear, therefore, to understand our situation and to support our efforts to deal with it.

6. The supreme court and circuit courts have held that tests containing testing procedures similar to those used in Florida's Budgeting-Finance Aptitude Test were invalid because the procedures they utilized were unvalidated and the tests disqualified minorities at a racially-disproportionate rate. Although Florida's test has not been proved to utilize unvalidated testing procedures, the test has been shown to disqualify minorities at a racially disproportionate rate.

7. The issue of what kind of medical testimony is admissible in malpractice suits has not yet been decided by Florida courts. Whether to admit testimony from any physician of ordinary and reasonable skill or whether to restrict expert testimony to physicians from similar communities is the

question. Most other states accept expert testimony by physicians from communities similar to that in which the malpractice suit is brought.

8. The defendant may claim that excluding contrary testimony of other medical experts was improper, citing Baldor v. Rogers, in which the Florida supreme court held that courts may not exclude opinion of experts which contradict that of the physician acting as expert witness.

Chapter Two, Section B(1)

Jargon

(The following sentences were taken from students' writing.)

1. If she "ought to have known" that the floor was being repaired, her prior knowledge goes to the question of contributory negligence, but if her negligence did not go to the cause of her injury she may still recover in full.

2. The plaintiff has a case of intentional infliction of emotional distress in the case of the recent attack by the defendant because she suffered from a case of depression afterwards.

3. The defendant may raise consent but that defense will probably not be successful since the plaintiff was not fully informed before the incident of what would occur.

4. The plaintiff in no shape, manner or form expected the harassment to which she was subjected, nor did she by any manner or means consent to it.

5. The common law relating to larceny is now null and void, but it was in full force and effect in 1900.

6. John Brown, during his lifetime, to wit, on the day of January 20, 1932, was possessed of two acres of land and a dwelling thereon, and whereas the said John Brown sold one acre of that land, to wit, on the day of January 20, 1932, to one James Smith . . .

7. The deceased, in his last will and testament, did give, devise, and bequeath all rights, title and interest to all of his goods and chattel, free and clear, to his wife.

Answers to Chapter Two, Section B(1)

1. If she "ought to have known" that the floor was being repaired, her knowledge may be considered contributory negligence, but if her negligence did not contribute to her injury, she may still recover in full.

2. Because the plaintiff suffered from depression after the recent attack of the defendant, she has a cause of action in the intentional infliction of emotional distress.

3. The defendant may raise the defense that the plaintiff consented to his act, but he will probably be unsuccessful since the plaintiff was not fully informed before the incident of what would occur.

4. The plaintiff did not expect the harassment to which she was subjected, nor did she consent to it.

5. The common law relating to larceny is now void, but it was in force in 1900.

6. John Brown, on January 20, 1932, possessed two acres of land and on that day sold one acre of it to James Smith . . .

7. The deceased, in his last will, gave all of his possessions to his wife.

Chapter Two, Section B(2)

The Long Wind-Up

1. I should like to state at this moment, unequivocally, and without fear of contradiction that the United States has more lawyers and more litigation than any other country.

2. One cannot possibly ignore the indubitable fact that the defendant's negligence contributed to his injuries.

3. It is highly appropriate to call the attention of the court to the true fact that a person is considered innocent until proven guilty.

4. This is a very important subject that merits the concern of every American citizen.

5. At this point in time I should like to make it perfectly clear that many points remain to be considered before a decision is possible.

6. It is a fairly distinct probability that there may be a conflict of laws in this case.

7. The undeniable fact that this contention by the defendant ignores is his long history of juvenile delinquency.

Answers to Chapter Two, Section B(2)

1. The United States has more lawyers and more litigation than any other country.

2. The defendant's negligence contributed to his injuries.

3. A person is considered innocent until proven guilty.

4. This subject merits the concern of every American citizen.

5. Many points remain to be considered before a decision is possible.

6. This case may involve a conflict of laws.

7. The defendant's contention ignores his long history of juvenile delinquency.

Chapter Two, Sections B(3) and B(4)

Metaphor-osis and Impossible Comparisons

The following sentences contain examples of metaphor-osis and impossible comparisons. Correct these by re-writing the sentences.

1. The Secretary of State rebuked the Ambassador's words in defense talks.

2. SALT negotiators report progress; progress is certainly on the move.

3. They can be bums if they want to, but the city should not support their panhandling. They should work at it just like the rest of us do.

4. The battle must be bridged between the college of liberal arts and the college of business.

5. We are not going to be isolated because our state department is out in left field like a sore thumb.

6. Unlike the above-mentioned cases, California, Texas, and Michigan rely on the rule of foreseeability in defining the duty.

7. Like the court in Amsted v. Rich, the decision here should be based on probable cause.

8. President Nixon's supporters insisted that the liberal press used Watergate as a political football with which to bury him.

9. After years of affluence, the housing market in May tasted its first crunch in real estate transactions because of the excessive interest rate.

10. Unlike inter vivos gifts, the donee does not acquire full title to the property until the death of the donor.

Answers to Chapter Two, Sections B(3) and B(4)
(Metaphor-osis and impossible comparisons)

1. The Secretary of State rebuked the Ambassador for his language in defense talks.

2. SALT negotiators report progress.

3. Persons are privileged to be bums if they wish, but the city should not support them by allowing panhandling.

4. The gulf must be bridged between the College of Liberal Arts and the College of Business.

5. Our state department's blunders must not isolate us.

6. Unlike the above-mentioned holdings, California, Texas, and Michigan holdings rely on the rule of foreseeability in defining the duty.

7. The decision here, like the decision in Amsted v. Rich, should be based on probable cause.

8. President Nixon's supporters insisted that the liberal press used Watergate as a political tool with which to defeat him.

9. The housing market, after years of prosperity, suffered in May its first decrease in real estate transactions, because of the excessive interest rate.

10. In this case, unlike the case of inter vivos gifts, the donee does not acquire full title to the property until the death of the donor.

Chapter Two, Section B(5)

Vague Referents

1. We question the legality of the conviction for illegal possession of imported heroin; does this limit conviction to possession irregardless of the importation issue? Or can we construe this statute on the grounds dealing solely with the knowledge of importation? This might be analogous to *Levy* in which Levy is to display the proper conduct of an officer, but one may well ask what this conduct is and how it is to be applied.

2. The doctor told plaintiff and the insurance agent that he had only superficial cuts and bruises; this was a mutual mistake since neither would have made the contract had they known this is grounds to attack the agreement.

3. There was great disparity in bargaining power between the plaintiff and his insurer. Insurance companies are known to take advantage of potential claimants in this fashion and since this is the kind of form (release form) that an experienced agent uses it should be torn down for unconscionability. This is a contract of adhesion which can be attacked on the grounds I have stated.

4. If one should summon one to court who was not guilty, who pays the court costs, the one who summons that one or the one who was summoned and that one was not guilty? This happened to my husband.

5. Because the defendant spoke harshly to the plaintiff does not mean that it was a gesture.

6. Since the damage to the crop was remote from the theft of the car, it would be a question of fact on which reasonable men could not differ, and defendant should be entitled to summary judgment.

7. The defendants might argue that if they had threatened to beat up plaintiff then and there, it might constitute assault.

8. In order for forced confinement to occur, it must include no consent to the confinement given by the one confined.

9. This tax is indirect, rather than direct, which would not be valid.

10. The examination resulted in a report by a psychiatrist that the accused was insane, which forces the court to hold a competency hearing.

Answers to Chapter Two, Section 5
(Sentence revisions to avoid vague referents)

1. The statute making possession of imported heroin illegal is overly vague because it does not state whether a person found guilty of such possession must have knowledge that the heroin he possesses is imported. The predicament of the heroin possessor is like that of the defendant in *Levy,* who was held to the standard of proper conduct as a police officer but had no knowledge what the standard was.

2. The doctor erroneously told both the plaintiff and the insurance agent that the plaintiff had only superficial cuts and bruises. The release form that the plaintiff then signed can be considered a mutual mistake since neither plaintiff nor agent would have signed it had they realized the doctor's statement was incorrect.

3. Since the plaintiff was at a bargaining disadvantage with relation to the insurance agent, the conduct of the agent was unconscionable when he took advantage of the plaintiff's ignorance to obtain from him a release agreement; and the agreement can be attacked as a contract of adhesion.

4. When a person is summoned to court on charges brought by another person and is subsequently found not guilty of the charges, should court costs be paid by the person who brought the charges?

5. The harsh language of the defendant to the plaintiff does not necessarily constitute a "gesture."

6. Reasonable men could not disagree that the damage to the crop was so remote from the theft of the car that the defendant is entitled to summary judgment.

7. The defendants might argue that a threat by them to beat up the plaintiff then and there would probably constitute assault.

8. One element of the tort of forced confinement is lack of consent to the confinement by the one confined.

9. A direct tax would not be valid; this tax is however, an indirect tax.

10. The court must hold a competency hearing for the accused man because after psychiatric examination the psychiatrist reported that the man was insane.

Chapter Two, Section B(6)

Deleting Unnecessary Expletives

1. As soon as the purse was grabbed, there was battery. There was certainly no consent.[1]

2. When one's personal possessions are being held by another for the purpose of not allowing the person to leave a place, there is false imprisonment.[2]

3. There is a cause of action on behalf of the minor who, the evidence shows, suffered injury from the reckless action of the taxicab driver . . . . It is, in the public conscience, uncommon and outrageous for cab drivers to conduct themselves in the manner shown here.

4. There is a strong suspicion on the part of the police officers that a crime has taken place.

5. There is a presumption that a child born during wedlock is the offspring of the husband and wife.

6. There is almost universal acceptance of the concept of extrinsic parol being admitted as evidence.

7. It was the intention of the defendant to confine the plaintiff against his will.

8. It would seem that the petitioner does not have standing in this matter.

9. It is the parents' duty, according to the 2nd Restatement of Torts, to control his child's behavior under certain circumstances.

10. It is extremely likely that defendant was unaware that he had killed his victim.

11. It is a fact that children who have been abused grow up to abuse their own children.

12. There is a well-established rule in tort theory that a person rendering aid must not place the receiver of that aid in a worse situation than he was in when the person found him.

13. It is highly unlikely that the jury will accept the argument that the murderer acted in self-defense, since the victim was shot in the back.

14. It becomes obvious that relief will be granted to the party who brings suit if that party acted on reliance of the parol agreement.

---

1. Note here also (1) hysteron-proteron and (2) lack of causality indication. (The consent would have had to occur before the grabbing; and because the victim has not consented, battery lies.)

2. In this sentence, note also the shift of viewpoint. In your rewrite, correct both the expletive and the shift of viewpoint.

Answers to Chapter Two, Section B(6)

1. Since the victim had not consented to the act, the grabbing of her purse constituted battery.

2. False imprisonment occurs when the personal possessions of one person are held by another so that the first person is prevented from leaving a place.

3. Action may be brought on behalf of the minor who suffered injury from the taxi driver's behavior, which can be characterized as so reckless and outrageous as to offend the public conscience.

4. Police officers strongly suspect that a crime has taken place.

5. A child born during wedlock is presumed to be the offspring of the husband and wife.

6. Extrinsic parol evidence is almost universally accepted.

7. The defendant intended to confine the plaintiff against his will.

8. The petitioner does not seem to have standing in this matter.

9. According to the 2nd Restatement of Torts, one duty of the parent is to control his child's behavior under certain circumstances.

10. The defendant was probably unaware that he had killed his victim.

11. Children who have been abused often grow up to abuse their own children.

12. A well-established rule in tort theory states that a person rendering aid must not place the receiver of that aid in a worse situation than he was in when the person found him.

13. The argument that the murderer acted in self-defense will doubtless be rejected by the jury since the victim was shot in the back.

14. If the party who brings suit acted in reliance of the parol agreement, he will obviously be granted relief.

Chapter Two, Section B(7)

Problem Words
Choose the proper word within the parentheses

1. Legislation to (affect/effect) the rights of Americans to free legal counsel has had the (affect/effect) of increasing the staffs of public defenders' offices.

2. The (principal/principle) plaintiff in this case said he had brought the case to trial as a matter of (principal/principle).

3. The visitor (lay/laid) his briefcase on the desk and (lay/laid) back in his chair.

4. It is not necessary to look (in/into) lawbooks to find interesting situations (in/into) the law.

5. Come to my house and (bring/take) my books with you; then when you leave you can (bring/take) your books to your apartment.

6. Some authorities say herpes is epidemic in the United States; others respond that it is more accurately described as (widespread/prevalent).

7. To the alumni present, the laying of the cornerstone for the new law complex was a (unique/unusual) and (historic/historical) event.

8. (Further/farther) efforts to aid the injured person proved ineffective.

9. After hearing the (persuasive/convincing) arguments of the defense counsel, I am (persuaded/convinced) of the defendant's innocence.

10. (Economic/economical) conditions being as they are, I looked for more (economic/economical) quarters.

11. The widow of the convicted kidnapper of the (notorious/famous) Lindberg case is now attempting to clear her deceased husband's name.

12. (Healthy/healthful) foods and a (healthy/healthful) lifestyle help keep people (healthy/healthful).

Answers to Chapter Two, Section B(7)

1.	affect . . . effect	7.	unique . . . historic
2.	principal . . . principle	8.	further
3.	laid . . . lay	9.	persuasive . . . convinced
4.	into . . . in	10.	economic . . . economical
5.	bring . . . take	11.	notorious
6.	prevalent	12.	healthful . . . healthful . . . healthy

Chapter Two, Section B(8)

(Shifts in Viewpoint)

1. In *Boring,* the Supreme Court indicated that a court of equity would not substitute its judgment for that of an administrative board when acting within the scope of its authority. [The administrative board's authority.]

2. The Florida supreme court decision in *Bray* established a duty on the part of landowners to keep canals and drains open. The court held that when the municipality undertook to maintain a drainage system it acted in a corporate capacity. It further held that if in the wrong it would be held to the same accountability as an individual. This action was one in tort complaining of injury caused by increased flow of water as a result of the drainage system.

3. The grabbing of the poster from the plaintiff's hand is battery under the rule of *Fisher,* where the grabbing of an object from one's hand was held to be an offensive invasion of one's person, and was intentional.

4. Defendants had a duty to let the inspector inspect the truck; not doing so was a direct violation of the statute.

5. Mr. D's guardian has given Mr. D's will to his doctor, saying it is senseless to postpone the death at the cost of $1000 per day in hospital expenses, arguing that the money could be used better to fund cancer research.

6. A Minnesota case also held that a surgeon, in performing an operation without the consent of the patient, constituted an assault and battery.

7. Possession of the home was not granted until majority.

8. The court decided that suspended public school students were entitled to due process protection by the 14th Amendment and that due process required notice of charges and opportunity to present a defense.

9. Does marking a whale establish ownership when whale escapes and is subsequently trapped?

10. Are an individual's due process rights denied when a contract is not renewed and there is no opportunity to air grievances?

11. A prima facie case of battery occurred when the woman store detective grabbed the customer's purse as she left, because under tort theory the purse is considered part of her body and thus an offensive contact.

Answers to Chapter Two, Section B(8)

1. In *Boring,* the Supreme Court indicated that a court of equity would not substitute its own judgment for that of an administrative board which was acting within the scope of its authority.

2. In this action the plaintiff asserts that he suffered injury due to a defect in a drainage system owned by a municipality. The Florida supreme court held, in *Bray,* that if the municipality was in the wrong it would be held as accountable as if it were an individual landowner. The court further held that landowners have a duty to keep canals and drains open and that when the municipality undertook to maintain a drainage system it acted in a corporate capacity.

3. The intentional grabbing of the poster from the plaintiff's hand constitutes battery since, in *Fisher,* the intentional grabbing of an object from a person's hand was held to be an offensive invasion of that person's body.

4. Defendants violated the statute when they refused to allow the authorized inspection of their truck.

5. Mr. D's guardian has turned Mr. D's will over to Mr. D's doctor because, the guardian argues, the postponement of Mr. D's death at a cost of $1,000 a day in hospital expenses is senseless when that money might better be used for cancer research.

6. In a Minnesota case, the court held that a surgeon had committed assault and battery when he performed an operation without the consent of the patient.

7. The court held that the plaintiff be granted possession of the home only when he reached majority.

8. The court held that suspended public school students were entitled to due process protection by the 14th amendment; this protection requires that they be provided notice of charges brought against them and an opportunity to present a defense. *

9. Does the marking of a whale by its possessor establish his ownership if the whale escapes and is subsequently trapped by another person?

10. Are an individual's due process rights denied when his contract is not renewed and he has no opportunity to air his grievances?

11. A prima facie case of battery occurred when the woman store detective grabbed the customer's purse as the customer left the store, because according to tort theory the purse is considered part of the body and the snatching of the purse is therefore an offensive contact to the woman's body.

Chapter Two, Section B(9)

The Ambiguous Negative

Rewrite the following sentences so that they become clear, by eliminating as many negatives as possible.

1. All portions of your examination not written within the lined writing space will not be considered in evaluating your answer.

2. Appellant's counsel did not advise appellant competently of prospects for a successful defense, which were substantial because he [counsel] was not properly motivated.

3. They reported that people in Cuba do not revolt because of the repressive and powerful rule of Castro.

4. Counsel did not completely investigate the circumstances of the crime, did not request information in the prosecutor's file, and did not question the motives of the prosecutor in reducing the charge.

5. Whether the case of an intrusion by a stranger without title, on a peaceable possession, is not one to meet the exigencies of which the courts will recognize a still further qualification or explanation of the rule requiring the plaintiff to recover only on the strength of his own title, is a question which, I believe, has not as yet been decided by this court.

6. Couples do not elope for fear of parental disapproval.

7. He said the answer was not cutting budgets and hoping the problem will go away.

* Faulty organization, added to shifts in viewpoint, make this sentence difficult to untangle. The restatement is an attempt to convey the intended sense.

Answers to Chapter Two, Section B(9)

1. Only portions of your examination written within the lined writing space will be considered in the evaluation of your answer.

2. Appellant's counsel, lacking proper motivation, failed to advise appellant competently of prospects for a successful defense, which were substantial.

3. They reported that Castro's repressive and powerful rule prevents Cubans from revolting.

4. Counsel failed to (1) completely investigate the circumstances of the crime, (2) request information in the prosecutor's file, and (3) question the motives of the prosecutor in reducing the charge.

5. To my knowledge this court has not yet decided whether the intrusion of a stranger without title upon a peaceable possession will bring about a further qualification of the rule that requires an occupant of property to recover only on the strength of his own title. *

6. Fear of parental disapproval is not what makes couples elope.

7. Cutting budgets and hoping the problem will disappear is not the answer.

Chapter Two, Section B(10)

Elegant Variation and Legerdemain with Two Senses
Re-write the following sentences to eliminate the confusion:

1. Whether the construction material was steel or iron is not material to the decision.

2. The plaintiff in this case has an action against the defendant because the defendant's action was intentional, harmful, and offensive to the plaintiff.

3. Employees can utilize their own retirement system or participate in the program established by their employer; most employees choose the first plan.

4. The appellant's attorney requested a postponement, to which request the appellee's attorney agreed. Later, however, the respondent's attorney protested the delay.

5. Ending the battle in the mideast was only half the battle; the other half of the battle is maintaining the peace.

6 The missing desk was valuable because it was an antique; whether the hand-carved *objet d'art* was stolen or lost is not known.

Answers to Chapter Two, Section B(10)

1. Whether the construction was of steel or iron is not important (crucial, germane) to the decision.

* This re-draft of an excerpt from an actual court decision is only a guess. The negative in the second line of the original quotation seems to have been in error.

2. The plaintiff in this case has an action against the defendant because the defendant's conduct was intentional, harmful, and offensive to the plaintiff.

3. Employees can utilize their own retirement plans or participate in the one established by their employer; most employees choose their own retirement plans.

4. The appellant's attorney requested a postponement, to which request the appellee's attorney agreed. Later, however, the appellee's attorney protested the postponement.

5. Ending the fighting in the mideast solved only half of the problem; to solve the problem completely, we must maintain the peace.

6. The missing desk was valuable because it was an antique; whether the hand-carved desk, an *objet d'art,* was stolen or lost is not known.

Chapter Three, Section B(2)(h)

Instructions: Find in the enthymemes below the unstated premises; then decide whether they are valid and if not, why they are not:

1. Students who do well in law school get the best jobs; therefore, good law students make the best lawyers.

2. Since courts have held that policemen may shoot to stop a fleeing felon, police acted legally in shooting John Smith, a suspect in a recent holdup.

3. Since assault requires an intentional act, a blind man has no ground for an assault action against a person who verbally threatened him with attack.

4. The fact that women dent car fenders more frequently than men proves that more women than men are reckless drivers.

5. John Smith, a teenager, must be a careless driver because his car insurance rates are so high.

6. It is a fact that Supreme Court justices bicker about trivial matters; this is reported in a recent book written by two journalists about Supreme Court justices.

7. Colombian and Iranian students have similar political views; after all, they both held hostage citizens of other nations.

8. Law students learn more readily when their classes are interesting; therefore they learn most in those classes which have the most student discussion.

9. In Fairbanks, Alaska, women drive more safely than men because in 1979 women drivers there had only one-fifth as many motor accidents as men.

10. Since this is a democracy the state cannot force motorcyclists to wear helmets when they ride their motorcycles.

11. Jane Smith is a law student; she must be a supporter of E. R. A.

Answers to Appendix to Chapter Three, Section B(2)(h)

The unstated premises underlying the enthymemes in the Appendix are listed below. You can decide for yourself whether they are valid.

1. Students who get the best jobs make the best lawyers.

2. John Smith was a fleeing felon.

3. A verbal threat is not an intentional act.

4. Reckless driving is the only cause of dented fenders.

5. Auto insurance rates are based on the degree of carelessness of each driver.

6. The information contained in the two journalists' book is accurate.

7. The willingness of students to take hostages of other nations is the sole determinant of their political views.

8. Student discussion is the only factor that makes law classes interesting.

9. The number of motor accidents people have is an accurate indication of how safely they drive.

10. A democratic government cannot pass laws requiring motorcyclists to wear helmets.

11. All female law students support E. R. A.

Chapter Five, Section B

Identify the Logical Fallacies in the Following Sentences:

1. Jane Smith is a capable woman, but this great State needs a man to represent it forcefully.

2. Since radiation is a natural phenomenon, fears about the safety of nuclear energy are obviously unfounded.

3. One can see by the large quantities of land being bought by Middle Eastern Arabs in the U. S. that Arabs are extremely wealthy.

4. Even on one-way streets, all cars should keep to the right because in this country motor vehicles are supposed to drive on the right side of the road.

5. You should not believe any promises that an avowed atheist makes.

6. The professor told the class he did not consider absences in grading, but he gave me a "D" after I cut most of his classes.

7. A man's home is his castle; no City Commission is going to stop me from raising pigs in my front yard!

8. Is there any evidence to suggest that four more years under this President will not merely prolong for four more years the economic chaos under which this nation suffers?

9. A questionnaire distributed to professors of American law schools revealed that American legal education is far superior to that of other nations.

10. Writing for publication takes a lot of time. Therefore, since Professor Smith does not publish much, he must be a great teacher.

11. Dunebuggy riders pay taxes and therefore have as much right to ride their buggies in national parks as other people have to hike in the parks.

12. To prevent more people from becoming addicted to heroin, marijuana must remain illegal, for many heroin users report that they smoked marijuana before starting to use heroin.

13. Any man who can become the president of XYZ corporation at such an early age must know what he is talking about; welcome John Smith, who will speak tonight on nature conservancy.

14. You must decide whether to be a loyal democrat and accept the entire party platform or to renounce your party affiliation.

15. Since some religions oppose blood transfusions, all Red Cross blood banks should be closed.

16. James Smith, noted authority on the sex life of minnows, will speak today on the formula for a successful marriage.

Answers to Chapter Five, Section B
(Logical Fallacies)

1. *Argumentum ad Populum*
2. *Non Sequitur*
3. *Hasty Generalization*
4. *Dicto Simpliciter*
5. *Ad Hominem*
6. *Post hoc*
7. *Dicto Simpliciter*
8. Rhetorical question and *Ad Hominem*
9. Circular reasoning
10. Either/Or and *Non Sequitur*
11. *Tu quoque*
12. *Post hoc*
13. Misplaced Authority
14. Either/Or
15. *Non Sequitur*
16. Misplaced Authority

INDEX

References are to Pages

†